The American Religious Landscape

The American Religious Landscape

Facts, Trends, and the Future

RYAN P. BURGE

OXFORD
UNIVERSITY PRESS

Oxford University Press is a department of the University of Oxford.
It furthers the University's objective of excellence in research, scholarship,
and education by publishing worldwide. Oxford is a registered trade mark of
Oxford University Press in the UK and certain other countries.

Published in the United States of America by Oxford University Press
198 Madison Avenue, New York, NY 10016, United States of America.

© Oxford University Press 2025

All rights reserved. No part of this publication may be reproduced, stored in a retrieval system,
transmitted, used for text and data mining, or used for training artificial intelligence, in any form or
by any means, without the prior permission in writing of Oxford University Press, or as expressly
permitted by law, by license or under terms agreed with the appropriate reprographics rights
organization. Inquiries concerning reproduction outside the scope of the above should be sent
to the Rights Department, Oxford University Press, at the address above.

You must not circulate this work in any other form
and you must impose this same condition on any acquirer

CIP data is on file at the Library of Congress

ISBN 978-0-19-776284-4 (pbk.)
ISBN 978-0-19-776283-7 (hbk.)

DOI: 10.1093/oso/9780197762837.001.0001

Contents

Introduction		1
Chapter 1.	The History of American Religion	3
Chapter 2.	Data	20
Chapter 3.	Evangelicals	28
Chapter 4.	Mainline Protestants	52
Chapter 5.	Black Protestants	72
Chapter 6.	Orthodox Christians	89
Chapter 7.	Catholics	105
Chapter 8.	Jews	124
Chapter 9.	Latter-day Saints	141
Chapter 10.	Muslims	160
Chapter 11.	Buddhists	180
Chapter 12.	Hindus	197
Chapter 13.	Atheists/Agnostics	213
Chapter 14.	Nothing in Particular	232
Chapter 15.	The Future of American Religion	249
Bibliography		265
Index		273

Introduction

There's an inherent problem with living in the modern world: we exist in a bubble. The average American hardly ever ventures away from their small and trusted circle of family and friends. Many vacation to the same places every year, and if they do take an international trip, it is fairly rare. They tend to consume a specific type of media diet that likely confirms their priors, and if they choose to attend a house of worship, they are more often than not surrounded by people who look, believe, and think like they do. No one has the ability, through their own personal experiences, to even begin to understand the rich tapestry that is American life.

That is especially the case when it comes to the American religious landscape. Even today, as our ties to our birthplace and family continue to loosen, the stickiness of religion is still profound. Most Americans, even those born in the last several decades, will die claiming the same religious affiliation of their childhood. Thus, by virtue of our own insularity, it's rare for a Roman Catholic to have intimate knowledge of the contours of Hinduism, or for a Muslim to have a strong grasp of the world surrounding Latter-day Saints. Survey data are obviously imperfect, but they are the only means that we have in the social sciences to try and show readers what American society looks like in broad swaths. That, simply stated, is the aim of this volume.

This book begins by tracing the threads of religious affiliation in the United States all the way back to the colonial period through the modern day. Then it moves on to a series of chapters about many of the larger religious traditions in the United States. There are chapters on various kinds of Protestant Christians, including evangelicals, mainliners, and those who are members of the Black Church, followed by a discussion of American Catholicism. There are sections that deal with numerically smaller religious groups in the United States such as Latter-day Saints, Jews, and Muslims. Then, there are two chapters that focus on the growing number of Americans who claim no religious affiliation; these are individuals who describe their present religion as atheist, agnostic, or nothing in particular. The book ends

---

The American Religious Landscape. Ryan P. Burge, Oxford University Press. © Oxford University Press 2025.
DOI: 10.1093/oso/9780197762837.003.0001

2 THE AMERICAN RELIGIOUS LANDSCAPE

with some educated guesses about a few major trends that could alter the American religious landscape in the future.

I am fully aware that a dozen graphs and a few thousand words cannot do justice to the amazing amount of diversity and nuance that exists in a group like Orthodox Christians or Buddhists. There are scholars who have written volumes in the thousands of pages on Hindus alone. That is not the aim of this book. Instead, its aim is to give the reader a broad view of the American religious landscape without getting too weighed down by the details of any specific faith tradition. It's my hope that this will serve as a great starting place for students who are just starting to become interested in the study of American religion and how survey data can aid them in this pursuit.

When John F. Kennedy was president of the United States, he had a small plaque on his desk that contained the words of an old Breton fisherman's prayer: "O God, thy sea is so great and my boat is so small." I think that's an important reminder for readers as they begin to peruse the pages of this book. There will never be a piece of scholarly work, no matter how detailed, lengthy, and well-researched, that will even begin to scratch the surface of the great ocean of American religion. Also, the tools that we have to even begin to try and understand such a complex aspect of society are woefully inadequate, but we must try. The desire to explain and understand the world around us with the imperfect and faulty tools that are in our repertoire is one that dates back for centuries.

My hope is that once you finish reading these words and studying these graphs and maps, you will have an appreciation for the beauty and mystery of American religion.

1

The History of American Religion

There is no other country on Earth that has the religious composition of the United States. In almost every way it defies expectations. The economic prosperity and educational attainment of its citizens easily put it in the same class as countries like Finland, Spain, and Australia. It is, in every sense of the word, an advanced democracy. In terms of gross domestic product (GDP), which is a measure of a country's economic output, one of the closest comparison cases to the United States is Norway—with GDPs varying by less than 5% (2024 USD).[1] However, while less than 20% of all Norwegians say that religion is very important to them, the same figure in the United States is 52%. The religiosity of the United States rivals countries like Paraguay and Armenia, with GDPs that are $6,153 and $7,018, respectively (2024 USD), while the United States GDP per capita was $76,330.[2] It's empirically accurate to say that the United States is, in almost every conceivable way, a religious outlier. It is both incredibly religious and incredibly prosperous.

But has that always been the case in the history of the United States? That's not an easy question to answer. Gathering up records of religious membership from the country's past is no easy exercise. In fact, very little empirical work has tried to piece together the religious composition of the United States during its Revolutionary period. For decades most American historians relied on piecemeal accounts of religious statistics gathered from biographies and personal letters that were in no way systematic in their assessment of the religious landscape around the time that the Declaration of Independence was signed.[3] However, in the last several decades scholars have turned their attention to compiling statistics about American religion in the most rigorous way possible, given the constraints of centuries-old recordkeeping.

The most well-known of these efforts was undertaken by Roger Finke and Rodney Stark in their seminal work *The Churching of America, 1776–2005*. This volume contains the most concerted and comprehensive effort to trace the changing religious landscape of the United States since the late 1700s. The authors pull together a variety of data sources to paint a portrait of American

The American Religious Landscape. Ryan P. Burge, Oxford University Press. © Oxford University Press 2025.
DOI: 10.1093/oso/9780197762837.003.0002

4   THE AMERICAN RELIGIOUS LANDSCAPE

religion that will form the backbone of this chapter. Their data sources are myriad, but several are worth noting. The first comes from the fact that the U.S. Census Bureau surveyed denominational religious bodies for their data collection efforts, beginning in 1850 and running through the mid-1930s.[4]

However, acquiring data prior to 1850 is an even more herculean task. Recordkeeping was scant in those early days of the republic and was certainly not done in systematic ways. However, Finke and Stark looked toward one of the most comprehensive cartography projects in American history— *The Atlas of Historical Geography of the United States* by Charles Paullian. It was first published in 1932 and contained a series of maps of every church in the United States in 1776. These data were collected under the supervision of M. W. Jernegan, and they represent the most exhaustive effort to comb through newspapers, documents, and other primary source material to locate every house of worship in the colonies. In some cases, the numbers were cross-referenced against clergy records from the time period to arrive at the estimates that Finke and Stark use in their volume, which was published in 2005.[5]

The estimates generated by this data collection effort result in a portrait of the American colonies where the vast majority of Americans were not attached to a house of worship, as can be seen in Figure 1.1. The colony of New Jersey had the highest concentration of religious adherents at 26%, followed closely by Pennsylvania at 24% and Massachusetts at 22%. There were a number of colonies in the Northeast that were around the 20% threshold for religious adherents. However, as one moved south through Virginia and down into the Carolinas and Georgia, the overall level of religious adherence continued to drop. According to these estimates, less than one in ten Georgians and North Carolinians was part of a church or religious congregation.

This is a point that Finke and Stark drive home by comparing other statistics that are available for the time period. For instance, they report statistics collected by D. S. Smith which indicate that in the late 1700s, about one-third of all first births to women in New England occurred less than nine months after they had married their partner.[6] At the same time, the share of colonists in that region who went to church on a regular basis was probably closer to one in five.[7] Thus, any belief that the early settlers of the United States were paragons of colonial piety and puritanical ethics needs to be reassessed based on empirical data related to American religious history. That's not to say that many of the earliest Americans were devoid of religious beliefs, but

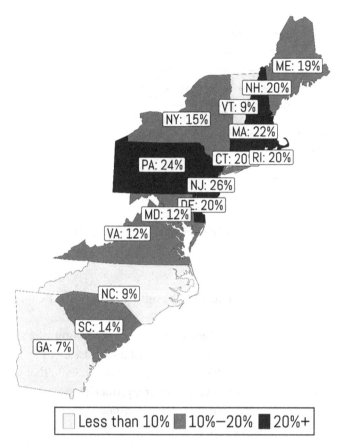

Figure 1.1 Percent of the population who belonged to church/congregation in 1776
Data: Finke and Stark, 2005

that only a small portion of citizens could be classified as highly religious based on metrics that are available to social science.

It's also helpful to note the overall denominational composition of those early church adherents during the period of the signing of the Declaration of Independence, as can be seen in Figure 1.2. The plurality of these members were from the Congregational tradition—a denomination that is relatively unknown to modern Americans. However, this significant number of Congregationalists in the early part of American history is the direct result of a group that is probably more well-known: Puritans. They were some of the first settlers to arrive on the Eastern shores and set out to create a "pure"

6 THE AMERICAN RELIGIOUS LANDSCAPE

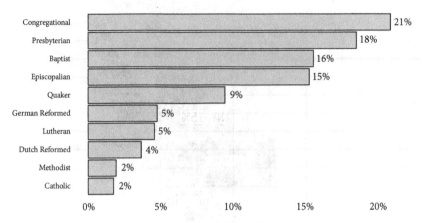

Figure 1.2 The composition of church membership in 1776
Data: Finke and Stark, 2005

church in the United States free from the sinful practices of the churches they left behind in England.

Other groups that had a significant presence in the colonies are still significant parts of the twenty-first-century Protestant landscape: Presbyterians, Baptists, and Episcopalians. It's instructive to note, though, that several of the largest religious traditions in contemporary America were small fractions of believers in early American history. For instance, the data from Finke and Starke indicate that there were just about 4,700 total Methodists in the United States around 1776; what may be even more startling is the fact that only 4,300 Catholics were counted during this same time period.[8] In comparison, the best estimates are that there are nearly 62 million Catholics in the United States today. This means that for every Roman Catholic in 1776, there were 14,526 in 2020.

By 1850, data gathering had become much more robust, and many more states had joined the Union. The statistics reported from this area demonstrate an explosion in religiosity across almost the entirety of the United States—this becomes clear when looking at Figure 1.3. While no state had managed to get above 26% in the figures collected in 1776, many reported that at least a third of their populations were members of a religious community by the midpoint of the nineteenth century. In fact, there were several states in which religious adherents rates moved above 40%, including Ohio, Indiana, and Maryland, with many more in the upper thirties. The South had begun to emerge as a hotbed of religion by this point, but the

THE HISTORY OF AMERICAN RELIGION 7

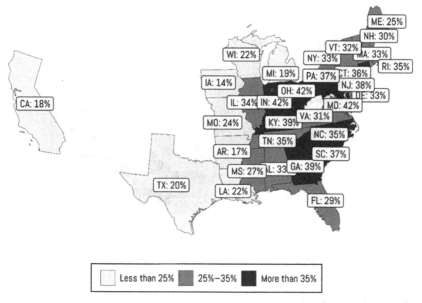

Figure 1.3 Percent religious adherents in 1850
Data: Finke and Stark, 2005

modern understanding of the Bible Belt had not come into full bloom by 1850.

Religiosity levels were still lower on the western edge of the fast-growing United States, however. Just 24% of Missourians were part of a religious congregation, which was lower than other states out East but was still significantly higher than Iowa (14%), Arkansas (17%), and Louisiana (22%). Just one in five Texans was part of a religious congregation in 1850, and it was even lower in California at 18%. However, the overall impression that emerges from this map is that religiosity had made big gains from the Revolutionary period. Religion had really taken hold in significant swaths of the country and was rapidly spreading with westward expansion.

By 1926, the current version of the United States had come into full focus, save for Hawaii and Alaska—both of which were admitted into the Union in 1959. Now, a vision of a very religious country becomes readily apparent in Figure 1.4. Long gone are the days in which the most devout states had 25% of residents aligned with a religious congregation. Now, nearly every state in the eastern half of the country was at least majority religious. The South reported the most significant upticks in religiosity. In the Carolinas, about four

8   THE AMERICAN RELIGIOUS LANDSCAPE

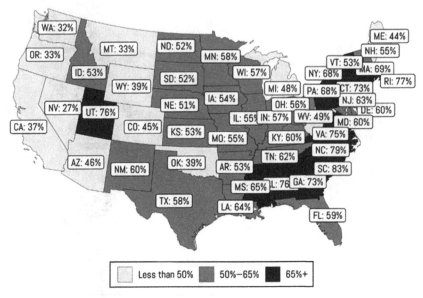

Figure 1.4 Percent religious adherents in 1926

in five residents were part of a house of worship. Both Georgia and Alabama had rates of religious adherence that were about 75%. There was also a significant amount of religiosity in the Northeast. Two-thirds of New York, Pennsylvania, and Massachusetts were aligned with a house of worship.

In comparison, the middle part of the United States was not quite as devout as the South and Northeast. The share that was part of a congregation was just north of 50% in many states across the middle part of the country. That was certainly the case in Indiana, Illinois, Missouri, Iowa, and through most of the upper Midwest. Religion was the weakest out west, though. Just 37% of Californians were part of a religious group, and it was only about a third of residents of Oregon and Washington. But at this stage, the modern understanding of American religion begins to come into sharper focus with a strong base of religion in the South and significant numbers of religious adherents across the middle of the country.

But it is helpful to compare how much religiosity grew in the United States from 1890 through 1926 to give a sense of where things were changing the most rapidly—that's what appears in Figure 1.5. It's important to note that in almost every state in the Union, the share that was attached to a religious congregation was higher in 1926 compared to 1890. In some cases, it was

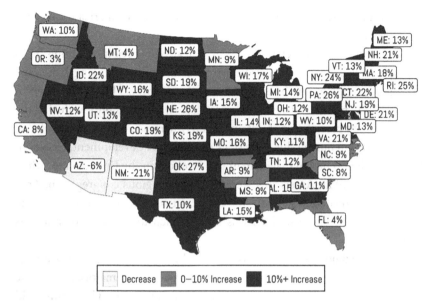

Figure 1.5 Change in religious adherents percent, 1890 to 1926
Data: Finke and Stark, 2005

significantly higher. There were only two states that reported a drop in religious adherents: Arizona and New Mexico.

In comparison, many states evince an increase in religious adherence that is north of 10%. That's certainly the case across nearly every region in the United States. There were big jumps in adherents in New England in states like Rhode Island (+25%) and Connecticut (+22%). There were other states that saw big jumps as well. For instance, Pennsylvania reported an increase of twenty-six percentage points, and so did Nebraska. Several states in the South saw big gains, but others were modest. For instance, the Carolinas only saw growth of 8%–9% compared to 15% in Alabama and Louisiana.

But what clearly comes through is that religion flourished all across the United States during the late nineteenth and early twentieth centuries. During this time period, the number of Americans who were attached to a religious congregation increased by millions. Churches were being built at a rapid pace to keep up with the rate of growth they were experiencing and to serve new towns and cities that were sprouting up all over the Midwest and West. Denominations were building out significant organizational structures that would come to dominate American religious culture and political life throughout the middle part of the twentieth century. Religion, by any measure, was on the march in the United States of America during this time period.

The ascendance of religion within a 150-year period spanning 1776 through 1926 paints a dramatic portrait of a rapidly changing landscape during a formative time in the history of the country. This is visualized in Figure 1.6. As previously described, religiosity was incredibly low during the Revolutionary period. Just about one in ten American adults was part of a religious tradition during this early stage of American development. However, by 1850, religion had managed to grab a foothold in the United States when about a third of all Americans were part of a religious congregation. That figure stayed relatively stagnant for the next two decades. But even as late as 1870, the average American was not attached to a church or religious congregation.

By 1890, religiosity began to rise again when 45% of Americans were religious adherents. That increased again in 1906 when a majority of people living in the United States were part of a religious body. This figure held steady for the next decade, but between 1916 and 1926 the share of religious Americans increased to nearly 60%. Just one in ten Americans was a member of a church in 1776, but it was six times higher 150 years later. It's hard to

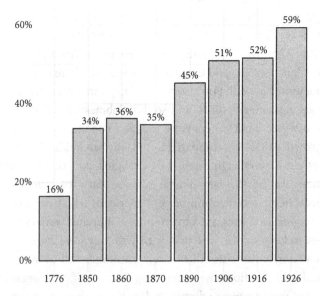

Figure 1.6 The share of the United States who were religious adherents
Data: Finke and Stark, 2005

put into words how dramatically the religious landscape of the United States changed during its first century and a half of existence.

However, while the share of Americans who were aligned with a religious group was increasing significantly during this time period, the overall composition of those Christian groups was also shifting just as quickly. While there were significant numbers of Congregationalists and Quakers in the United States around the founding, they were almost completely gone from the Protestant landscape by the middle of the 1850s, while Baptists, Methodists, and Catholics were ascendant. This comes through when looking at Figure 1.7.

Recall that just 2% of all religious adherents were Catholics in 1776, but by 1850 that had jumped to just over 12% and continued to rise from that point forward. By 1916, nearly one in three Christians in the United States was part of a Roman Catholic Church. Meanwhile, the Methodists went from 2% of Christians in 1776 to nearly 35% by 1850. But that was the high watermark for Methodism. By 1870, they had slipped to just 27% and were only 17% of

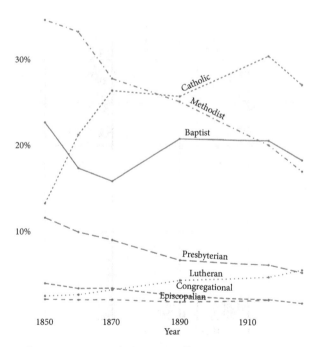

Figure 1.7 The composition of Christian adherents over time
Data: Finke and Stark, 2005

all Christians by 1926. This was quite the roller-coaster ride. Baptists, however, were relatively steady. They were 15% of Christians in 1776 and rose to 22% by 1850. Their share vacillated a bit over time but always stayed close to 20% of all Christians.

The story of Presbyterianism is one of significant decline. They were 18% of Christians during the Revolution but had dipped to just 11% by 1850. From that point forward, their share continued to decline. They were below 10% by 1870, and by 1926 it was just 5%. Meanwhile, Congregationalists went from the plurality of all Christians to little more than a rounding error by 1926—less than 2%. Episcopalians were in a similar situation, becoming so small by 1926 that Finke and Stark stopped counting their numbers in a systematic way.

Figure 1.8 reports the share of all Christians who were part of six different denominations in both the 1776 estimate as well as the figures collected in 1926, to simplify the comparison of the size of each of these groups during

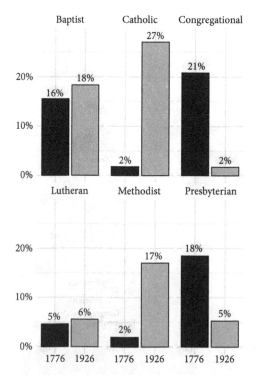

Figure 1.8 Comparing religious adherents in 1776 versus 1926
Data: Finke and Stark, 2005

both time periods. As previously mentioned, the Baptist story is one of relative stability over time. They played a significant part in Protestantism in both 1776 as well as 1926. Besides the Lutherans, who are much smaller in size, the Baptists are the only group that existed in nearly equal shares across this time period. For most other groups, the shifts are dramatic.

For instance, the share of Christians who were Catholic rose from just 2% in 1776 to 27% 150 years later. It's one of the most significant movements in American religious history. In the early nineteenth century, American Catholicism was nothing more than a minor player in the culture and society of the United States. By the early part of the twentieth century, the Church was a significant player in all aspects of American life. However, the Congregationalists and Presbyterians experienced a dramatic free fall during this same 150-year period. Nearly 40% of all Christians were in one of those two denominations in 1776. In 1926, it had dropped to just 7%.

These data allow us to peer into the first 150 years of the United States, but is it possible to see what American religion was like in the early part of the twentieth century? The first significant longitudinal study of American religion began with the advent of the General Social Survey (GSS), which was launched in 1972. But one can use data from GSS to look into the religiosity of the United States during the middle part of the 1900s. This is made possible by the fact that the survey has been asking people about the religion in which they were raised since it began. What that means is that if a sixty-year-old was asked in a survey conducted in the early 1970s about their childhood religion, those answers can be used to reconstruct what American religion looked like before World War II. Obviously, memories are not perfect, but it stands to reason that many people can accurately recollect the basic religious composition of their household.

Figure 1.9 then represents the overall religious composition of the United States from 1900 through 1990 by analyzing the childhood religion of respondents who took the GSS between 1972 and 2021. What is striking is just how dominant Protestantism has been for the last hundred years. In 1910, two-thirds of households in the United States were Protestant. In comparison, just 18% of households were Catholic during this time period, while 12% were from another faith tradition and almost no American was raised in a household without religion around the turn of the last century.

However, over time those proportions began to change. Protestantism slowly declined between 1900 and 1950, but then the trend line turned downward more sharply. By 1970, less than half of households were Protestant.

14 THE AMERICAN RELIGIOUS LANDSCAPE

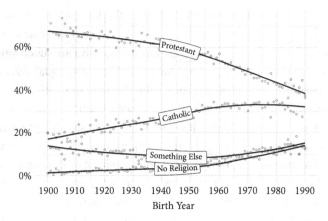

Figure 1.9 In what religion were you raised?
Data: General Social Survey

By 1990, that percentage had dipped to just below 40%. At the same time, Catholics were gaining ground. Somewhere in the mid-1930s, a quarter of all households were Catholic. That reached 30% by 1950 and settled around one-third of all families by the mid-1960s, and it has stayed there ever since.

Meanwhile, the share of households that were nonreligious stayed relatively low for a long period of time. In fact, less than one in twenty households was nonreligious all the way through the mid-1950s. However, from that point forward, there has been a slow and steady rise. Around 1970, the share of nonreligious households reached double digits and continued to inch upward with each subsequent year. By 1990, that percentage was just about 15%—the highest on record.

However, breaking the Protestant category into three families in Figure 1.10—evangelical, mainline, and Black Protestant—helps to bring the picture into clearer focus. (These three types of Protestants will be described in depth in later chapters.) What jumps out from this graph is the dramatic decline in the share of Americans who were raised in a mainline Protestant household. Around 1900, over 40% of people reported being raised as a mainline Protestant. That's double the rate that was raised in an evangelical tradition. But the mainline trend line has been in terminal decline over the last century. Among those who were raised in the 1990s, just 10% report being raised as a mainline Protestant.

In comparison, evangelicalism has been incredibly steady. Slightly more than one in five households was evangelical around 1900. In the most recent

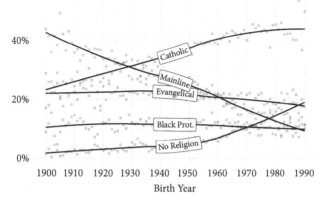

Figure 1.10 In what religion were you raised?
Data: General Social Survey

data that number had dropped to about 19%—a total decline of three percentage points over nearly a century. In comparison, the mainline share has dropped thirty points. Black Protestantism has also been steady as well. About 10% of households were Black Protestants in 1900, and it's almost exactly the same share today.

The other two big movements in American religion are those previously discussed but worth reiterating. American Catholicism has continued to increase its market share over time—rising from just 23% of households in 1900 to about 43% in 1990. That's a healthy sign for the future of the Catholic Church. The other noteworthy shift is the rise of the nones—almost all of which happened in the last fifty years. According to this data, people raised in the 1990s were just as likely to be in an evangelical household as a nonreligious one.

The GSS also asks about the current religious tradition of respondents, and that affords us the opportunity to sketch out the American religious landscape over the last fifty years with a greater degree of accuracy. Scholars who study religion in the United States often debate over the proper way to categorize and classify the various expressions of faith in America. This volume will use the RELTRAD categorization scheme that essentially creates six categories: evangelicals, mainline Protestants, Black Protestants, Catholics, other faith groups, and those who claim no religious affiliation. The justification for these six types of religion will be discussed in much greater detail in the chapters to come.

16   THE AMERICAN RELIGIOUS LANDSCAPE

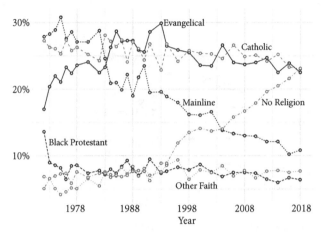

Figure 1.11 Religious composition of the United States
Data: General Social Survey

For now, let's get a high-level view of American religion between 1972 and 2018; displayed in Figure 1.11. When the first questionnaire for the GSS was constructed in the early 1970s, the faith landscape looked much different than it does today. Mainline Protestants and Catholics both made up around 27% of the total population. Evangelicals were significantly smaller at just 17%. Black Protestants were about 12% of the sample, while all other faith groups combined for about 7% of Americans. Those who claimed no religious affiliation were just a small portion of the sample (just 82 respondents in all) or 5%. Things have changed dramatically since those early data collection efforts.

Mainline Protestants have seen a precipitous decline—dropping to below 20% by the mid-1990s and continuing to shed members throughout the subsequent decades. They are currently just about 10% of the population. The causes and consequences of that substantial drop will be described in a chapter devoted to that religious tradition. Meanwhile, evangelicals grew substantially through the early 1990s—reaching nearly 30% of the population. But from that point forward they have begun to lose market share. Today they are just about 22% of the adult population.

The American Catholic Church has seen relative stability in comparison. The percentage of Catholics in the United States has bounced around a bit but stayed close to the 25% figure for the better part of four decades. It's just been in recent years that their numbers have slipped a bit to just about 22%

of the country. Black Protestants have seen a fairly slow decline as well. For decades they clocked in around 8%–9% of the adult population, but that has now dropped to about 6% of the United States in more recent surveys.

As far as those from other faith groups, there has been remarkably little change since 1972. They were around 5% of the sample in those early years and have slowly crept up just slightly to around 8% of the population in data collected in the last decade or so. While this graph lumps all kinds of faith groups (Muslims, Latter-day Saints, Jews, Hindus, Muslims, and Buddhists) into one category, there will be chapters dedicated to each individual group in this volume. Each group presents its own interesting puzzle of growth or decline as well as significant compositional changes that could have long-ranging impacts on American society.

Finally, the nonreligious may represent the most compelling and con-sequential shift in American religious society over the last five decades. In 1968, the sociologist Glenn Vernon described the nones as "the neglected category" in a paper that was published in the *Journal for the Scientific Study of Religion*.[9] They were overlooked for good reason—they were just a small fraction of the population and only very large surveys (which were virtually nonexistent at the time) managed to report them in any significant numbers. That was the case all the way through the early 1990s when the nones had barely risen.

However, the last three decades have witnessed the unbelievable rise of nonreligious Americans. They broke double digits by 1996 and have never looked back. By 2014, they had climbed to over 20% of the sample. In the most recent survey data collected from a variety of sources, there is evidence that points to them being closer to 30% of American adults today—which makes them easily larger than any other religious group in the country. This work will devote two chapters to the rise of the nones and will try to tease out some significant differences between those who claim to be atheist/agnostic compared to those who describe their religion as "nothing in particular."

Conclusion

Nothing in American life is static, and that is especially the case with American religion. Just fifty years ago, nearly 90% of all adults identified with a Christian tradition. Today, that share has dropped to just over 60%. Many religious groups have seen their membership swell to more than a million in

18 THE AMERICAN RELIGIOUS LANDSCAPE

just the last few decades, including Muslims, Hindus, and Buddhists. At the same time, there is an increasing number of Americans who have decided to eschew any religious labels, swelling the percentage of nones in the United States. Anyone who endeavors to understand the current state of American culture would be wise to understand the basic contours of religious demography in the United States.

The purpose of this volume is to do just that—give readers a high-level view of several religious traditions that exist in significant numbers in the United States. Each chapter will contain a little bit of religious history but also do a deep dive into the size and composition of religious groups that run the gamut from Black Protestants to Buddhists. Each group has its own set of advantages and obstacles it must face going forward. There are some chapters that focus on the incredible growth of a specific movement, while others focus on the tremendous decline of a tradition.

There's no doubt that if this book were to be written twenty or thirty years from now, the facts and figures reported in this volume would not accurately represent the current state of American religion in 2045. That's the beauty of studying social science—nothing is ever permanent. These charts, graphs, and maps of the American religious landscape cover nothing more than a single snapshot in time. But where these religious groups go from here will have unmistakable implications for the future of culture, politics, and American society in general.

Notes

1. The World Bank. 2024. *World Development Indicators*. Washington, DC: The World Bank (producer and distributor). Data are for 2022, in 2024 USD. https://data.worldbank.org/indicator/NY.GDP.PCAP.CD.
2. The World Bank, *World Development Indicators*.
3. Roger Finke and Rodney Stark. 2005. *The Churching of America, 1776–2005: Winners and Losers in Our Religious Economy*. 2nd ed. New Brunswick, NJ: Rutgers University Press, 2.
4. Finke and Stark, *The Churching of America*, 13.
5. Charles Oscar Paullin and John Kirtland Wright. 1932. *Atlas of the Historical Geography of the United States*. Washington, DC: published jointly by Carnegie Institution of Washington and the American Geographical Society of New York. Cited in Finke and Stark, *The Churching of America*, 19–27.
6. Daniel Scott Smith. "Child-Naming Practices, Kinship Ties, and Change in Family Attitudes in Hingham, Massachusetts, 1641 to 1880." *Journal of Social History* 18, no. 4 (1985): 541–566. Cited in Finke and Stark, *The Churching of America*, 25.
7. Smith, "Child-Naming Practices." Cited in Finke and Stark, *The Churching of America*, 25.
8. Finke and Stark, *The Churching of America*, 157.
9. Glenn M. Vernon. "The Religious 'Nones': A Neglected Category." *Journal for the Scientific Study of Religion* 7, no. 2 (1968): 219–229.

Data References

Davern, Michael, Rene Bautista, Jeremy Freese, Pamela Herd, and Stephen L. Morgan. 2023. General Social Survey 1972–2022. Principal investigator, Michael Davern; Co-principal investigators, Rene Bautista, Jeremy Freese, Pamela Herd, and Stephen L. Morgan. Sponsored by National Science Foundation. NORC ed. Chicago: NORC at the University of Chicago. https://gssdataexplorer.norc.org/.

Finke, Roger, and Rodney Stark. 2005. *The Churching of America, 1776–2005: Winners and Losers in Our Religious Economy*. 2nd ed. New Brunswick, NJ: Rutgers University Press.

2
Data

In 2006, the mathematician Clive Humby first uttered, "Data is the new oil."[1] A few years later, Michael Palmer added to that maxim by stating, "(Data) is valuable, but if unrefined it cannot be really used."[2] This has become the guiding principle for the empirical backbone of this book. Data are incredibly valuable on their own, but when refined and presented in a clear and accurate way, they're priceless. They help us to understand the world in a way that would be impossible with rigorous empirics. They help us to get out of our own political, theological, and regional bubbles to see the big picture regarding the changes in American society. Yet this kind of work would be nearly impossible even a decade ago.

When I first started graduate school in 2005, there were very few large-scale datasets that were available for quantitative scholars to use. The vast majority of the data-driven work in the study of American religion really used the same source: the General Social Survey. It began to feel like that single data source had been squeezed of all its empirical power as hundreds of scholars sliced and diced the same spreadsheet in search of new ways to understand and explain American religion.

Then, in the last decade or so, things began to change. The number of research organizations that began to fund and produce high-quality survey data began to increase fairly rapidly. This was likely a confluence of a number of factors. One was that the American public became much more aware of the power of data to help them understand what was happening around them. There was a proliferation of "data journalism" at a number of high-profile outlets. No story was more compelling than Nate Silver, who went from a relatively obscure graduate student in economics to running one of the most popular websites—FiveThirtyEight—when he was able to predict (with stunning accuracy) the outcome of several presidential elections.[3]

But at the same time, another revolution was happening—data became much cheaper to acquire. For decades, surveys have been collected through either in-person interviews or through random-digit dialing of phone numbers across the United States. Both techniques can produce high-quality

The American Religious Landscape. Ryan P. Burge, Oxford University Press. © Oxford University Press 2025.
DOI: 10.1093/oso/9780197762837.003.0003

results, but they are incredibly labor-intensive and therefore very costly. This made it economically prohibitive for all but the most well-resourced organizations to conduct a scientifically valid survey. That began to change as the Internet became more ubiquitous. A number of reputable companies began to advertise their ability to collect a statistically representative sample by administering their survey through a Web browser. This led to a significant decrease in the cost of data collection without sacrificing data quality.

The upshot of those factors is that lots of surveys have been conducted in the last several years, and oftentimes their sample sizes are so large that it allows social scientists to answer more granular questions than they would have been able to just a few short years ago. This book is built on the foundation of the tireless efforts of research teams at a variety of universities and organizations across the United States. The purpose of this chapter is to give readers a brief tour of several of the data sources that were utilized to generate the charts, graphs, maps, and analyses that will appear throughout the pages of this volume.

The General Social Survey

The General Social Survey (GSS) is one of the most important sources of social science data in the United States. The GSS is administered by the National Opinion Research Council (NORC), which is housed at the University of Chicago. The survey was first administered in 1972 and has been conducted every year or every other year for the last five decades.[4] The GSS holds tremendous value for scholars who study American religion because it has an extensive battery of questions that tap into the behaviors, beliefs, and belonging of respondents. What enhances its utility is that the GSS has asked the same questions for the same response options since its inception—this provides a high level of replicability.

For decades, the GSS was administered through an in-person survey method with respondents. These surveys lasted approximately ninety minutes.[5] This is obviously a time-intensive process when the team at NORC is trying to gather information from a large number of respondents (the average sample size is about 2,100 respondents). The COVID-19 pandemic made it impossible to collect data in this manner in 2020, and the team pivoted to a 2021 collection that switched to a mixture of face-to-face and phone interviews, which was carried forward into their 2022 survey as well.[6]

22 THE AMERICAN RELIGIOUS LANDSCAPE

The GSS is one of the few tools that social science has which affords the ability to track long-term changes in the American population. Using the same method with the same questions is the primary means through which scholars can track the rise of the nones or the trajectory of Catholicism over a period that spans five decades. The value of this is incalculable for those who want to understand American religious history over the last fifty years. It also allows quantitative scholars to track some birth cohorts over the course of their lives. For those who were born in the mid-1950s, the GSS began asking questions of their cohort when they were still in their teenage years. Now, other people born around the same time period are being polled as they move into retirement.

However, there are limitations to the GSS. The biggest one is simply explained: sample size. This is a common theme throughout the substantive chapters of this volume—it's hard to track the size of small religious groups when the overall sample size is just 2,000–3,000. For instance, Latter-day Saints are often thought to be about 1% of the total population. It would not be out of the realm of possibility for a survey collected by the GSS to have just a dozen members of the Church of Jesus Christ of Latter-day Saints. Thus, the GSS is very good at tracing the trend lines for a group like Protestants or Catholics, but it has quite a bit less utility for analyzing most other religious traditions in the United States.

The Cooperative Election Study

Beginning in 2006, a research team based out of Harvard University began a data collection effort that is now called the Cooperative Election Study (CES).[7] The CES team has created a common core of questions that are asked of every respondent to the survey. These typically focus on political issues and voting behavior; however, the CES also includes a small number of questions about religious belonging and behavior. Many of the questions that they employ are modeled after the efforts of the Pew Research Center to assess religiosity in the American population. What makes the CES stand out is the funding model. The team at the CES sends out a call to research teams to provide funding for the survey. In 2022, if a team provided $13,000 of funding for the CES, they were allowed to ask a short battery of questions to 1,000 respondents from the survey pool.[8] This increases the number of respondents that are part of the Common Content but also affords the research team room to ask more specialized questions in their area of exploration.

The end result of this has been a widely successful research endeavor that has increased the size of the CES far beyond that which is available through the GSS. The first survey from the CES was conducted in 2006 and had a sample size of 36,421 respondents. Over time, this sample size has only increased. In 2010 it jumped to 55,400 respondents. The largest-ever survey took place in 2016 when the CES team received surveys from 64,600 respondents. The total number of survey respondents throughout the sixteen waves of the CES is over 607,000. For comparison, the entirety of the GSS (which dates back to 1972) has 72,390 respondents.

There are many instances in this book when the analysis will include the last three years of available CES data (2020, 2021, and 2022). This yields a total sample of 146,700 respondents and because religion does not shift dramatically across a twenty-four-month period, this has the benefit of creating a much larger sample without sacrificing data quality. This becomes a valuable tool when an analyst is interested in looking at religion at the state level. For instance, the state with the median sample in the 2022 CES was Kentucky with 946 respondents. If the last three years are combined, that sample increases to 2,377. As the sample size increases, so does our confidence in the estimates the data provide.

However, the CES is not without its drawbacks. The CES was designed by a team of political scientists, and thus most of the questions in the instrument focus on topics like voting behavior and public opinion. In fact, there are just a handful of questions about religion. The CES asks about religious attendance and religious belonging, but it has no questions about religious belief, beyond "How important is religion to you?" There are no queries about childhood religion or views of the Bible to be found in the CES. However, because it offers a full battery of demographic questions, the CES allows social scientists to answer questions such as "Which denomination has the highest average age?" or "What share of Muslims have a four-year college degree?"

The Religion Census

The prior two instruments mentioned—the GSS and the CES—are traditional social science surveys. They gather a random sample of the American population and ask them a series of questions. This is an

24   THE AMERICAN RELIGIOUS LANDSCAPE

incredibly effective way to gather all kinds of information about a specific group of people. However, it's not without its flaws. For instance, lots of Americans are not able to recall the denomination of the church that they attend. They may just know that they are Baptist, but they are not aware if that's a Southern Baptist Church (which is evangelical) or an American Baptist Church (which is part of the mainline). Thus, using survey data to understand the overall composition of American religion provides a limited understanding.

The Religion Census takes an entirely different approach.[9] Every ten years a group of scholars who are members of the Association of Statistics of American Religion Bodies (ASARB) takes on the herculean task of counting the number of Americans who are attached to a house of worship across the United States.[10] They do this by contacting these religious groups directly, not by using self-reports from surveys. The research team asks for several key pieces of information—how many congregations that group has in each county across the United States as well as the number of people on the membership rolls.

Collecting data on some religious groups in this manner is incredibly difficult. For instance, some sects of Judaism reject the concept of a census entirely, based on religious principles.[11] Other religious groups are not as centralized as some Protestant denominations. The task of estimating the share of American Muslims proved difficult for the research team.[12] Researchers gathered a list of 2,948 mosques across the United States using Internet searches. Each mosque was sent a first-class letter asking for basic information, but this yielded just 164 responses (5.5%). To try and gather more data about Muslims, the team then followed up with a phone interview with a random sample of the remaining mosques. This entire process took nearly a year.

The end result of these sustained efforts was one of the richest datasets that is available to scholars of American religion. The true utility of such work is that analysts can track religion at the county level. This is a level of aggregation that is essentially impossible to obtain through traditional surveys. If one were to wish to do a survey that would have a large enough sample size to have three hundred respondents from each country, the total survey would need nearly a million responses. This would be logistically difficult and financially unfeasible for even the most well-resourced think tanks and research centers. And, again, it would still rely on people's self-reports about their own religious affiliation.

What enhances the value of the Religion Census is that the data are collected every ten years. This means that scholars can now track the changing size of American religion at the county level over the period of several decades. This affords analysts to answer questions like: "What is the largest religious tradition in a specific county in Iowa?" or, "How many counties have an Amish community?" The maps that appear in this volume are almost always the result of analyzing the data provided through the Religion Census.

But this approach to data collection is not without criticism. Anyone who has spent time in a religious congregation knows that membership rolls are often filled with names of people who have not darkened the door of the church for years. And it's entirely possible that an individual could appear on multiple membership rolls as they shifted allegiance without asking for their name to be removed from membership at their previous house of worship. Thus, it's almost certainly true that the Religion Census reports overly inflated numbers for many religious bodies. However, there is no simple solution to this problem as every religious organization has its own set of rules about how it cleans up its membership rolls.

The other significant drawback of the Religion Census is that the type of data that it collects is incredibly narrow. In fact, just a handful of data points are collected: number of members and number of congregations. The Religion Census does not ask for data related to the average weekly attendance or the amount of donations that each house of worship receives. It's not possible to use Religion Census data to understand the theological positions of each house of worship or the age distribution of the congregation. The data that the research team collects are incredibly specific for good reason— if they tried to collect more information, there is a good chance that their response rates would go down and this would hurt the overall accuracy of the data that they do collect.

The Nationscape Survey

The Democracy Fund and UCLA collaborated on the Nationscape Survey. Beginning in July 2019, the team at Nationscape surveyed an average of 6,250 people per week. That collection effort continued throughout all of 2020 and ended in January of 2021. The total sample size for this instrument was over 477,000 respondents.[13] Recall that the GSS typically collects 2,000–3,000

26 THE AMERICAN RELIGIOUS LANDSCAPE

surveys every other year and has a total sample of nearly 73,000. The sheer size of Nationscape is what provides tremendous utility for scholars who are studying American society.

However, the main drawback for those who focus on religious demography is that the Nationscape asked just two questions about religion—the present religion of the respondent and whether they self-identified as an evangelical. This survey doesn't touch on religious behaviors like attendance or prayer nor does it ask about the importance of religion. However, that does not mean that the work cannot be useful. Because of its sheer sample size, scholars can conduct state-level analysis with Nationscape. For instance, even a small state like Wyoming has over 700 respondents in Nationscape, while large states like California have over 47,000.

Conclusion

One point that needs to be stressed when working with data is that no single survey or census is well-suited to answer every question. Every dataset has its own set of strengths and weaknesses, and relying too much on just a single source to conduct analysis is inadvisable, especially when one's goal is to provide the most accurate portrait possible of American religion. A nice feature of the data that are included in this work is that it is publicly available for download and analysis to anyone with an Internet connection and a bit of data analysis skill. Replicability is a cornerstone of good social science, and that is a through line in this work.

Another key thing to note is that quantitative data are not the only way to understand American religion. There are hundreds of scholars who study religion by using qualitative methods. They include interviews, focus groups, and ethnographers. These efforts are invaluable when it comes to understanding the nuances of American religion at the individual level. Oftentimes survey questions emerge through the work of qualitative scholars who unearth an interesting aspect of American religion that had been overlooked in previous questionnaires. The purpose of good social science is simply to explain the world using a variety of methodological tools, and qualitative research has undeniable utility in meeting this goal.

For those of us who devote our lives to the deep study of a topic like American religion, we are often left with a sense of feeling overwhelmed with all the nuance and wonder that can be found in humans experiencing the Divine. Some religious traditions use a term to describe this: *ineffable.* In short, it means an experience that is beyond words. There's an inherent limitation to any type of work in this area. Words fail us, and so do charts, graphs, and maps. Understanding how religion works in a society is a lifetime of effort. It's my hope that this volume helps to describe the ineffable in some small way.

Notes

1. Charles Arthur. 2013. "Tech Giants May Be Huge, but Nothing Matches Big Data." *The Guardian.* https://www.theguardian.com/technology/2013/aug/23/tech-giants-data.
2. Michael Palmer. 2006. "Data Is the New Oil." *ANA Marketing Maestros* [blog]. https://ana.blogs.com/maestros/2006/11/data_is_the_new.html.
3. Samuel Popkin. 2012. "Nate Silver: Poll Prophet." *Salon.* https://www.salon.com/2012/10/29/nate_silver_poll_prophet/.
4. "GSS General Social Survey FAQ: NORC." *The General Social Survey.* https://gss.norc.org/us/en/gss/faq.html.
5. "GSS General Social Survey FAQ: NORC." *The General Social Survey.* https://gss.norc.org/faq.
6. Michael Davern, Rene Bautista, Jeremy Freese, Stephen L. Morgan, and Tom W. Smith. 2021. General Social Survey 2021 Cross-section. [Machine-readable data file]. Principal investigator, Michael Davern; Co-principal investigators, Rene Bautista, Jeremy Freese, Stephen L. Morgan, and Tom W. Smith. NORC ed. Chicago. 1 datafile (68,846 cases) and 1 codebook (506 pages), 1. https://www.google.com/url?q=https://gss.norc.org/Documents/codebook/GSS%25202021%2520Codebook%2520R1.pdf&sa=D&source=docs&ust=1705792597898904&usg=AOvVaw3Ba_EG74avzjI_GqrNCJsI.
7. "Cooperative Election Study." *Harvard University.* https://cces.gov.harvard.edu/home.
8. "Call for Teams for the 2022 CES." *Harvard University.* https://cces.gov.harvard.edu/news/call-teams-2022-ces.
9. "Home: U.S. Religion Census: Religious Statistics & Demographics." *US Religion Census.* https://usreligioncensus.org/.
10. "Association of Statisticians of American Religious Bodies." 2023. *Association of Statisticians of American Religious Bodies.* http://www.asarb.org/.
11. Kaminker, Mendy. 2011. "Why Do We Not Count Jews?" *Chabad.org.* https://www.chabad.org/library/article_cdo/aid/1635539/jewish/Why-Do-We-Not-Count-Jews.htm.
12. Ihsan Bagby. 2023. "Appendix K: Muslim Estimate." In *2020 U.S. Religion Census: Religious Congregations & Membership Study.* Association of Statisticians of American Religious Bodies. https://www.usreligioncensus.org/sites/default/files/2023-03/Appendix_K--Muslim_Estimate.pdf.
13. Derek Holliday, Tyler Reny, Alex Rossell, Aaron Rudkin, Chris Tausanotich, and Lynn Vavreck. 2021. "Democracy Fund + UCLA Nationscape Methodology and Representativeness Assessment." *Democracy Fund Voter Study Group.* https://www.voterstudygroup.org/data/nationscape

3

Evangelicals

There may be no more discussed religious movement in the United States today than evangelical Christianity. It's hard to discount the influence that evangelicals have had on every aspect of American culture, society, and politics. In almost every urban, suburban, and rural area of the United States, people will pass by an evangelical house of worship, whether it is the historic Southern Baptist church on the town square, a storefront church in the Pentecostal tradition, or the hip new nondenominational gathering in a growing exurb—evangelicals are everywhere. At one point in the not-too-distant past, evangelicalism was a cloistered, rather insular religious tradition, but that's no longer the case.

Yet evangelicalism has faced a number of challenges over the last several decades. The rise of nonreligious Americans, the backlash to evangelicals' outspoken position on politics and social issues, and the changing demographics of the United States have all made it more difficult for evangelicals to convert new members or retain those who were raised as young people in the faith tradition. However, despite these obstacles, evangelical Christianity has still managed to maintain its position as one of the largest religious denominations in the United States, while other forms of Protestantism have undergone a significant decline in their numbers. Evangelicalism serves as a prime example of how religious groups can adapt in some areas, while also maintaining unchanged in others, all while the cultural landscape is rapidly evolving.

A Brief History of Evangelicalism in the United States

In the early part of the colonial period of American history, evangelicalism did not play a dominant role. Many of the people who came to the New World in the eighteenth and early nineteenth centuries were members of religious traditions that would be more accurately described as moderate Protestant Christianity (Congregationalists, Episcopalians, and Presbyterians). These

The American Religious Landscape. Ryan P. Burge, Oxford University Press. © Oxford University Press 2025.
DOI: 10.1093/oso/9780197762837.003.0004

denominations were strongly hierarchical and required that clergy obtain a significant level of education in order to be ordained into the pastorate. In the United States, several denominations established prestigious institutions of higher education, including Harvard University and Yale University, with the primary aim of training young men to become ministers.

However, these denominations began to lose their grip on the exploding population in the New World in the 1730s and 1740s, as the religious landscape was significantly reshaped by the First Great Awakening. Fiery and charismatic preachers like John Wesley and George Whitefield extolled crowds of colonists to repent of their sins and be reconciled to God. For most Americans, religion to that point had been understood to be a communal exercise that focused on corporate worship without a strong emphasis on personal piety. However, these preachers pushed for personal conversion and a rebirth in Jesus Christ that would lead to a life of piety and devotion.

This type of theology and style of preaching would form the foundation of evangelicalism in the United States and lead to a dramatic rise in a number of upstart religious traditions like the Baptists and the Methodists. In Finke and Stark's *The Churching of America*, their data indicate that just 2.5% of all colonists were Methodists during the signing of the Declaration of Independence.[1] By 1850, that number had risen to an astonishing 34%, fueled by a Second Great Awakening in the early part of the nineteenth century.[2] At the same time, the share of Americans who were Congregationalists dropped from 20% to 4%, Episcopalians fell from 16% to 4%, and the Presbyterians declined from 19% to 12%.[3] Evangelicalism's focus on personal salvation fit nicely into the American ethos of rugged individualism, and this led to explosive growth throughout the United States.

During the latter half of the nineteenth century, American evangelicalism struggled with how to deal with a number of denominational schisms that occurred over the issue of slavery. One of the most consequential examples of this conflict was among the Baptist faith, which was founded in the United States in 1638 by Roger Williams. During the Revolutionary period, regional differences were prevalent within the Baptist tradition. Nonetheless, by the early 1800s, the Baptists had successfully achieved unification through the establishment of the Triennial Convention. However, this unity was challenged by escalating discontent toward slavery among the Northern Baptists, deepening the regional divides.

The issue came to a head in the 1840s over the question of whether a missionary supported by the Baptist denomination could own slaves.

30   THE AMERICAN RELIGIOUS LANDSCAPE

Recognizing that these issues were not going to be easily or quickly resolved, the Baptists living in the South broke away from the Triennial Convention and formed their own denomination—the Southern Baptist Convention.[4] Those churches that did not join the Southern Baptist Convention would eventually form the Northern Baptist Convention in 1907, which eventually changed its name to the American Baptist Church in the 1960s.[5] The Southern Baptist Convention would go on to become the epitome of evangelical Christianity and rise to over 16 million members, while the more moderate American Baptists would be just a fraction of that size.

In the last hundred years, American evangelicals have had to significantly rethink how they interact with the larger society. They were deeply stung by the events of the Scopes Monkey Trial in Tennessee in 1925. The Tennessee legislature had passed a bill making it illegal to teach evolution in public schools. John Scopes openly defied that legislation and was charged with a crime. The state of Tennessee brought in William Jennings Bryan, likely the most famous evangelical in the United States, to be the prosecutor for the case, while Clarence Darrow, an avowed atheist, defended Scopes in the courtroom.

The Scopes trial was a media sensation, and the courtroom drama was recounted in every major newspaper of the day. The climax came when Darrow called Bryan to the stand to interrogate him about his beliefs in a literal Bible. When Bryan stated that he believed that Jonah was actually swallowed by a whale and that the Earth stood still as described in the Bible, his testimony was lambasted across the country.[6] Evangelicals watched in horror as they were portrayed as uneducated, backwater hillbillies by the likes of the famed journalist H. L. Mencken.[7]

In the wake of Scopes, evangelicals retreated from public life. According to Karen Armstrong, they "created an enclave of Godliness in a world that seemed hostile to religion, forming their own churches, broadcasting stations, publishing houses, schools, universities, and Bible colleges."[8] Instead of trying to bring new converts into the fold, evangelicals were content with living in their own bubbles of fidelity and homogeneity. However, those bubbles started to burst in the late 1970s when a number of evangelical leaders such as Jerry Falwell and Pat Robertson began to exhort evangelicals to get off the political sidelines and make their voices heard on issues like abortion and homosexuality.

Over the past fifty years, the substantial size and intense conviction of evangelical Christianity have significantly shaped the direction of the United

States across all conceivable areas of influence. This chapter will trace the contours of evangelicalism in the late twentieth and early twenty-first century while paying special attention to some of the challenges that this religious movement will face in the decades to come as it tries to navigate the best way to impact the culture and politics of the United States.

The Size of American Evangelicalism

The General Social Survey is the most helpful instrument in tracking the size of American evangelicalism over time. Its primary utility comes from the fact that it uses an incredibly detailed scheme to sort people not just into larger religious traditions (Protestant, Muslim, Mormon) but also into specific denominations (Southern Baptist, United Methodist). This means that scholars can use those categories to place individuals into the evangelical tradition not based on self-identification, but instead based on what type of church they attend. The most popular way to do this was proposed by Steensland et al. (2000) and is called RELTRAD.[9] The research team constructed a list of evangelical denominations along with the necessary computer code to recreate their calculations in the General Social Survey.

In 1972, Figure 3.1 shows that 17% of American adults indicated that they were part of an evangelical denomination. Their number rose quickly in the years to come with nearly 24% being evangelical by 1980. Over the next few years, American evangelicalism continued to gain more market share. By 1993, about three in ten American adults were in the evangelical tradition—the high watermark for evangelicals in the last five decades. From this point, the percentage began to return to those levels seen in 1980. By 2000, the evangelical share was 24%, and it continued to slowly trickle down to about 23% of Americans in the 2018 data. If the period from 1983 to 2000 is excluded as an aberration, the share of Americans who are evangelical has been relatively steady around 23%–24% over the last four decades.

However, there are other approaches to measuring evangelicalism in the United States. While the prior approach relied on denominations to sort people into categories, some survey questions ask individuals directly if they have had a born-again experience or see themselves as an evangelical Christian. The General Social Survey asks, "Would you say you have been 'born again' or have you had a 'born again' experience—that is, a turning

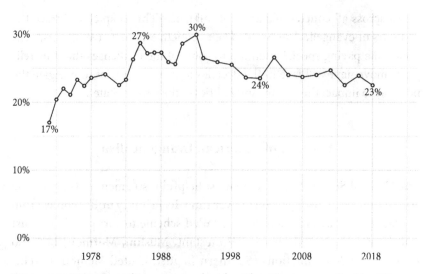

Figure 3.1 The share of Americans who identify with an evangelical tradition
Data: General Social Survey

point in your life when you committed yourself to Christ?" Note that this question is not gauging a current evangelical affiliation, but whether the respondent has ever had a born-again experience, or if they have changed their view of religion after that moment in time.

In 1988, 37% of respondents said that they had experienced a born-again moment in their lives, as can be seen in Figure 3.2. That number remained relatively steady over the next twenty years—with somewhere between 34% and 38% of adults answering that question affirmatively. But around 2012, there was a consistent and notable uptick in those who had a born-again experience. In more recent survey waves, at least 40% of Americans have reported this type of religious moment in their lives. Thus, from this angle, two in five Americans have had some type of evangelical experience.

The Cooperative Election Study asks all respondents, "Would you describe yourself as a 'born-again' or evangelical Christian, or not?" and the results are fairly stable over time, as can be seen in Figure 3.3. In 2008, about one-third of respondents said that they were born-again or evangelical. That percentage has slowly eroded over time. The percentage of evangelicals in the population was 30% around 2016 and has continued to slide very slowly since that point. In 2022, about 27% of American adults self-identify as evangelical. Over 40% of people have had a born-again experience, and over a quarter still call themselves an evangelical in recently collected data.

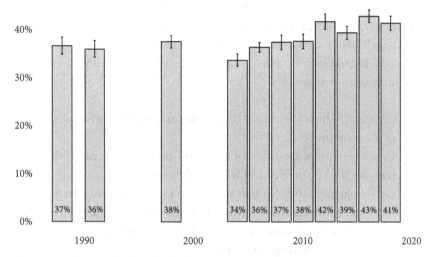

Figure 3.2 Share who have had a born-again experience
Data: General Social Survey

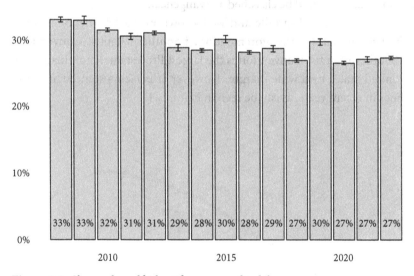

Figure 3.3 Share who self-identify as evangelical/born-again
Data: General Social Survey

Evangelicals and Denominations

When scholars try to create categories like evangelical, what traditions are included in their classification scheme? This isn't an easy question to answer, and there can be a significant amount of disagreement among academics who take on this task. The criteria that are used to guide this inquiry vary, but one typology that is used frequently in the classification of evangelicals is called the Bebbington Quadrilateral. First described by David Bebbington in 1989,[10] the author believes that there are four hallmarks of an evangelical:

1. Biblicism: a high view of the Bible (often referred to as a literalist belief in the scriptures)
2. Crucicentrism: a great deal of emphasis on the atonement of sins that was provided by the death of Jesus on the cross
3. Conversionism: the idea that nonbelievers need to have a born-again experience with Jesus and have their hearts opened to the Holy Spirit
4. Activism: an understanding that beliefs must be coupled with behaviors to bring about the Kingdom of God

Using these four points as a guide, there is some consensus about what types of denominations could be classified as evangelical.

Easily the most high-profile and well-known evangelical denomination in the United States is the aforementioned Southern Baptist Convention. The Southern Baptist Convention is the largest Protestant denomination in the United States by a wide margin. However, it is facing some significant declines in recent years, as can be seen in Figure 3.4.

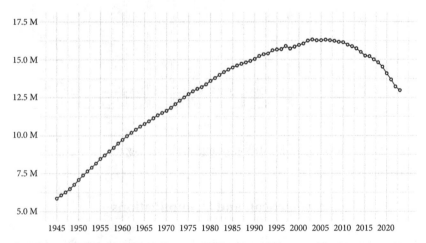

Figure 3.4 Reported membership of the Southern Baptist Convention
Data: Denominational records

During the postwar period, the Southern Baptists reported enormous growth. In many years, they added a quarter million new people to their membership rolls. Between 1946 and 1972, the Southern Baptist Convention doubled in total membership from 6 million to more than 12 million. In the next fifteen years, they would add another 2 million. Then growth would slow, with total membership cresting at 16.2 million in 2006. From that point forward, the declines began to accelerate. Membership dropped below 15 million by 2018 and then less than 14 million by 2021. In 2022, the Southern Baptists were down to 13.2 million, the same size they were in 1978.

Despite that decline, the Southern Baptist Convention maintains a tremendous amount of influence in large swaths of the United States. According to the 2020 Religion Census, and visualized in Figure 3.5, the Southern Baptist Convention is the largest religious tradition in nearly one-third of all counties. There are a total of 67 counties in Alabama, and the Southern Baptists are the largest tradition in all 67 of them. The Southern Baptist Convention leads in 71 out of 75 counties in the state of Arkansas. In a total of seven states, the Southern Baptist Convention is the largest tradition in at least 70% of counties. There are also concentrated pockets of Southern

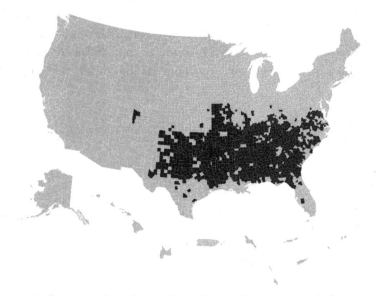

Figure 3.5 Counties where the Southern Baptist Convention is the largest religious group
Data: Religious Census

Baptists in states outside the Bible Belt, such as Illinois, Virginia, Ohio, and Colorado.

However, if the Southern Baptist Convention has seen a loss of approximately 3 million members in the last fifteen years, then why has the overall share of Americans who are affiliated with an evangelical tradition not dropped significantly? The answer is the incredible rise in the number of Americans who align with a nondenominational church.

According to data from the 2020 Religion Census, displayed in Figure 3.6, there were over 21 million nondenominational Christians in the United States. Given the diffuse nature of this expression of evangelicalism, it's obviously enormously difficult to get an accurate head count of such a disorganized group. If anything, this estimate provided by the Association of Statisticians of American Religious Bodies is an undercount of all the nondenominational Christians in the United States. Even with this estimate, it's clear just how dominant they have become in American religion and evangelicalism specifically. If the two largest evangelical denominations are combined (Southern Baptists and Assemblies of God), they still do not equal the total number of nondenominational Christians in the United States.

Figure 3.7 shows this stunning increase also appears in the data from the General Social Survey, as well. In 1972, less than 3% of Americans identified as nondenominational. That's fewer nondenominational Christians than religious nones. Between the early 1970s and the mid-1990s, the percentage of Americans who were nondenominational doubled to about 5%. By 2010,

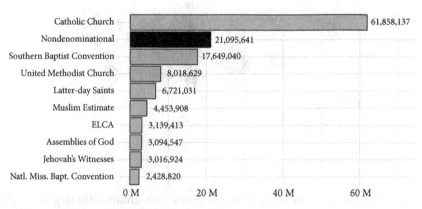

Figure 3.6 The ten largest religious traditions in the United States
Data: Religious Census

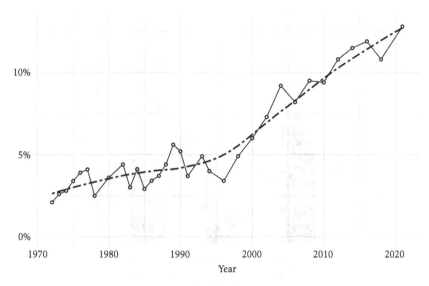

Figure 3.7 Share of all Americans who identify as nondenominational
Data: General Social Survey

the share had doubled again to 10%. In the 2021 survey, nearly 13% of all Americans said that they were nondenominational.

These shifts are having a real impact on the overall denominational composition of evangelicals. For instance, in 1988, about one in three evangelicals was aligned with the Southern Baptists while less than one in ten was from a nondenominational church, as can be seen in Figure 3.8. In 2018, the percentage of evangelicals who were Southern Baptists dropped by nearly half to just 17%. At the same time, the nondenominational percentage rose from 9% to 28%. With the current trajectory of both the Southern Baptist Convention and nondenominational evangelicals, the importance of the Southern Baptist Convention in the larger discourse of American evangelicalism will be significantly diminished.

This compositional shift portends an interesting future for evangelical Christianity. Even with its overall decline, no religious tradition enjoys a fraction of the media coverage that is afforded to the Southern Baptist Convention. It's very likely that the Southern Baptist Convention will continue to decline numerically, as well as in cultural and political influence over the next several decades. It's much more difficult for scholars and media observers to conceptualize and understand evangelicals when they become primarily nondenominational. Without a central denominational structure,

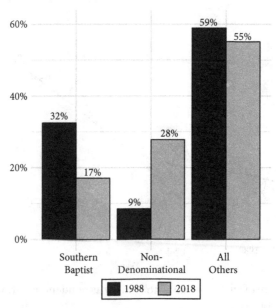

Figure 3.8 The denominational composition of evangelicals
Data: General Social Survey

it will be made up of islands of informal church networks that rarely communicate and are reluctant to coordinate with one another. This will likely lead to a disjointed and, at times, chaotic future of evangelicalism.

Where Are Evangelicals and What Are Their Demographics?

When speaking about geography, it should come as little surprise, and a quick look at Figure 3.9 will confirm, that the highest concentrations of evangelicalism can be found in the South. As previously mentioned, the Southern Baptist Convention has a tremendous amount of influence in states like Arkansas, Mississippi, and Louisiana. However, the state with the highest concentration of evangelical Christians is Kentucky at 42%. It's interesting that its neighbor to the east, Virginia, is only 24% evangelical. That same juxtaposition holds in the South, too. Alabama is 36% evangelical, while Florida to its south is only 19% evangelical.

EVANGELICALS 39

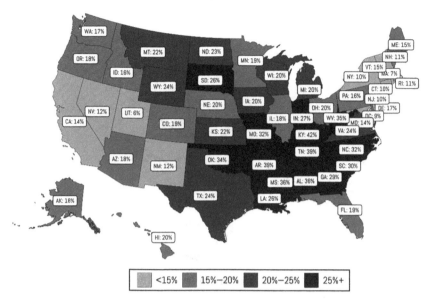

Figure 3.9 Share of the population that is evangelical
Data: Cooperative Election Study

But evangelicals can be found all over the United States. One in five Iowans identifies as evangelical, and it's the same share in the state of Hawaii. There are some regions where they are less pervasive, though. Evangelicalism is fairly rare in the Northeast. Only 7% of those living in Massachusetts and 10% of New York residents are evangelical Christians. It's also worth pointing out that the state of Utah has the lowest share of evangelicals at just 6%, which is likely due to the high concentration of Latter-day Saints in that area.

One thing worth watching when considering the place of evangelicals in the twenty-first century is their overall age. When a tradition's mean age is increasing rapidly, it points toward the possibility of decline in the future. If there are fewer young adults in a congregation, then the likelihood of maintaining membership through retaining young children is lower. Also, it means that funerals will be a common occurrence, exacerbating the need for a church to bring in more new converts to offset those losses. For evangelicals, there are warning signs on the horizon (see Figure 3.10).

In the 1970s, the average adult evangelical Christian was just slightly older than the average adult in the general population. For instance, in 1975, the average adult was forty-three and a half years old, and the average evangelical

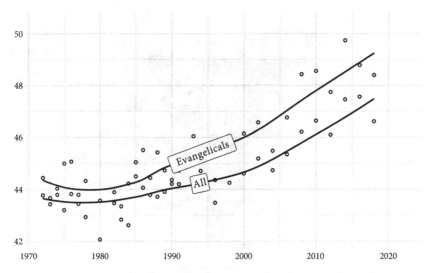

Figure 3.10 Average age of evangelicals compared to the general population
Data: General Social Survey

was forty-four years old. Not a statistically meaningful difference. But over time the gap between those two lines has widened. By 2000, the gap had increased to about one and a half years. By 2010, it was two years. Just from observing these trend lines, it's clear that this age gap will only continue to increase each year. It's very likely that the average evangelical adult in 2035 will be fifty years old.

But part of this discussion about age and evangelicals is wrapped up in a larger trend in American society when it comes to race. According to data from the United States Census Bureau in 2019, the median white age was 43.7, compared to 29.8 for Hispanics, 34.6 for Black residents, and 37.5 for Asian Americans.[11] Thus, any tradition that has a larger concentration of white Americans will inevitably see an increase in their median age that is beyond the average.

That is undoubtedly the case when it comes to evangelicals in the United States. According to the Cooperative Election Study, 80% of all evangelicals identified as white in 2008, while 9% were Black and 5% were Hispanic, as seen in Figure 3.11. The overall sample was 74% white, 12% Black, and 9% Hispanic. Over time, the racial composition of evangelicalism has barely changed. In 2022, 78% of evangelicals were white, and none of the other racial groups shifted by more than a single percentage point.

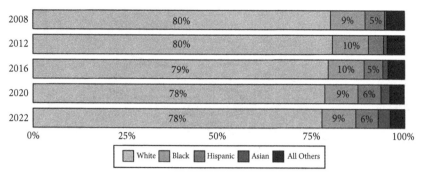

Figure 3.11 Racial composition of evangelicals
Data: Cooperative Election Study

That is striking when considering how much change was evident in the overall racial composition of the sample. In 2022, the sample was 69% white, 13% Black, 9% Hispanic, and 5% Asian. As the white share dropped five percentage points in the general population, it only slipped by 2% among white evangelicals. Thus, from this angle, it's fairly easy to see why evangelicalism has seen a steady increase in median age. A concerted effort to become more racially diverse would likely yield some positive outcomes for the future trajectory of evangelicals in the United States.

Another interesting facet of evangelicalism in the United States is their overall level of education. As previously mentioned, one of the stereotypes is that evangelicals are often people who barely finished high school and that churches are full of people at the bottom end of the socioeconomic spectrum. The data in Figure 3.12 don't point toward that overall conclusion. In the 1970s, about one in ten evangelicals had a four-year college degree. That was just three or four percentage points behind the overall average. That gap has widened a bit over time. By the early 2000s, about 20% of evangelicals held a bachelor's degree, compared to 26% of the overall population. In the most recent data, 26% of evangelicals held a four-year college degree compared to nearly a third of the general public.

Thus, evangelicals exhibit a lower overall level of education than the public at large, but that gap is not a chasm. Consider this: the mean level of education among evangelicals today is about the same level as the general public around the year 2000. However, in the last decade or so, the trend lines seem to have begun converging just a bit. It's unlikely that this education gap will move much past the five to six percentage points that existed in

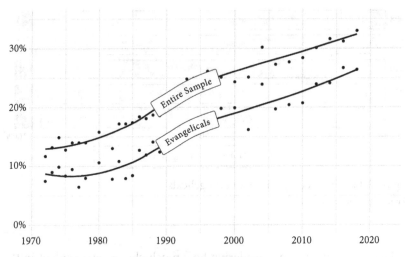

Figure 3.12 Share with a four-year college degree
Data: General Social Survey

the early 2000s. Evangelicals do have lower levels of education than the general public, but this divide is not that large.

Religious Beliefs and Religious Practice among Evangelicals

If there is one hallmark of evangelicals, it is that they are incredibly devoted to their religious tradition. As previously mentioned, evangelicals place a tremendous premium on a personal relationship with Jesus Christ. When an individual has a born-again experience, they are expected to avoid behaviors that evangelicals believe to be sinful. This understanding of religion is one that becomes all encompassing, with evangelical leaders constantly exhorting congregants to stay away from the "the world" and pursue a life of religious devotion and personal piety.

A prominent sociologist, Christian Smith, once conducted in-depth interviews of hundreds of evangelical Christians to understand how they thought about their place in the world and the large state of American society. His conclusion was that evangelicalism was "embattled and thriving."[12] It was embattled because they were constantly being cautioned about all the ways that the larger society was persecuting and marginalizing evangelicals.

But it was thriving because that sense of always being under attack helped evangelicals build stronger bonds with each other, making it less likely that they would leave the religious tradition.

A key factor that plays a role in generating feelings of group cohesion is regular religious attendance. It's hard for a congregation to feel a sense of togetherness when a majority of members only show up for services a few times a year. That's not the case when it comes to evangelicals. In a time when religious attendance has declined exponentially across American society, evangelicals indicate a level of religious activity that is incredibly robust.

Figure 3.13 shows that in the 1970s, about 45% of evangelicals said that they attended religious services nearly every week or more. That share stayed relatively stable over the next several decades. But at some point in the late 1990s, that trend line began to slowly move upward. By 2005, over half of evangelicals reported that they were attending religious services nearly every week. In some of the most recent data, almost three in five evangelicals are weekly attenders. The perception that evangelicals are always at church is very much confirmed in these results from the General Social Survey.

But their religious devotion goes far beyond religious attendance. Evangelicals also push for doctrines that rest on a certain belief in God and a literal reading of the Bible. That is clear when looking at survey data. The General Social Survey asks respondents to choose from a number of options

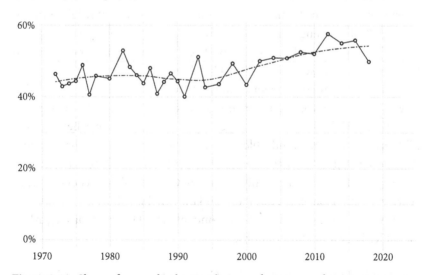

Figure 3.13 Share of evangelicals attending nearly every week or more
Data: General Social Survey

44 THE AMERICAN RELIGIOUS LANDSCAPE

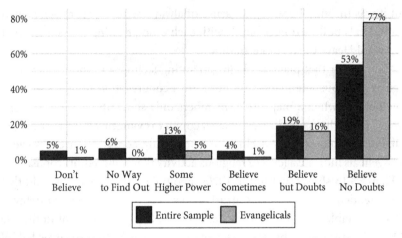

Figure 3.14 Belief in God among evangelicals and the general population
Data: General Social Survey

when it comes to belief in a higher power ranging from no belief in God to a certain belief in God. Evangelicals clearly stand apart from the general population on this metric, as can be seen in Figure 3.14.

For instance, while 5% of the general population says that they don't believe in God and another 6% say that they cannot know if God actually exists—those same views are only shared by 1% of all evangelicals. In fact, 28% of the general public can be found in the bottom four categories of religious belief; it's just 7% of all evangelicals. In data from 2018, 77% of evangelicals say that they believe in God without any doubt. The share among the general population who share that sentiment is just a bit above half (53%).

Another critical component of understanding evangelicals is their high view of the Bible. As previously mentioned, one key aspect of the Bebbington Quadrilateral is biblicism. For many evangelicals, they do not believe that the Bible is full of allegories and fables about people of faith, but real happenings. For them, belief in the actual resurrection of Jesus of Nazareth is a central part of their faith tradition. This unique view of the Bible sets evangelicals apart from other Christian traditions and the general public.

The General Social Survey asks respondents about their feelings regarding the Bible. They have three options:

- The Bible is the actual word of God and is to be taken literally, word for word.

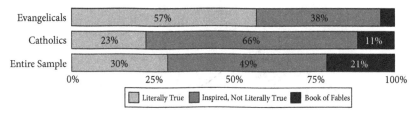

Figure 3.15 Views of the Bible
Data: General Social Survey

- The Bible is the inspired word of God, but not everything in it should be taken literally, word for word.
- The Bible is an ancient book of fables, legends, history, and moral precepts recorded by men.

Figure 3.15 displays the data from 2018 which indicate that 57% of evangelicals agreed with the statement that the Bible is literally God's word. That compares to only 23% of Catholics who agree and 30% of the entire sample. At the same time, 38% of evangelicals said that the Bible was inspired by God but should not be taken literally. This is easily the most popular response option among Catholics (66%) and the general public (49%). Less than 5% of evangelicals say that the Bible is a book of fables, which is about half the rate of Catholics. One in five adults believes that the Bible is nothing more than a storybook.

The Future of Evangelicalism

With the overall decline of religion in the United States, it would be easy to assume that evangelicalism would be pulled down by the larger forces of secularization. However, the real future of the evangelical church in the United States is much cloudier than that. There are some data points that would lead one to believe that the future of evangelicalism is fairly robust and may only suffer minor losses in membership compared to other Christian traditions. However, there are other trend lines that indicate a bleak future for this religious movement.

One such example, displayed in Figure 3.16, is the share of Americans who self-identify as evangelicals by year of birth. Among older adults, a significant

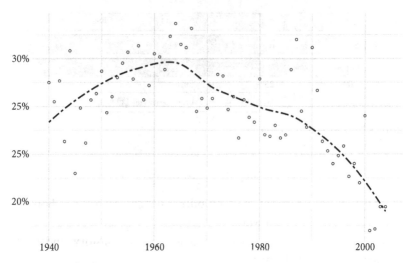

Figure 3.16 Share who self-identify as evangelical/born-again
Data: General Social Survey

portion still indicates that they are evangelical/born-again. That's the case for nearly 30% of people born around 1960. However, from that point, the percentage drops off precipitously. Among those born in 1980, the evangelical share drops to 25%. Among the youngest adults (those born around the year 2000), less than 20% say that they are evangelical. Recall that in the overall sample, about 27% of Americans self-identify as evangelical. It seems very likely that this percentage will begin to decline as older Americans die off and are replaced by younger ones who are much less likely to say that they are evangelical.

This downward trajectory is compounded by the trends related to retention rates among evangelicals. The General Social Survey asks respondents in what religion they were raised and then their current religion. Because the General Social Survey began in 1972, there were hundreds of people who were born in the early 1900s in the sample, allowing researchers to look back into American religious history before modern surveys began. That makes it possible to trace evangelicalism over one hundred years in Figure 3.17.

For decades, evangelicalism had a tremendous number of converts in their ranks. That's evident by looking at the share of Americans who were raised evangelical compared to the percentage who were currently evangelical. Among those who were born around 1925, 22% were raised evangelical, but about 27% were currently evangelical. That means that about one in five

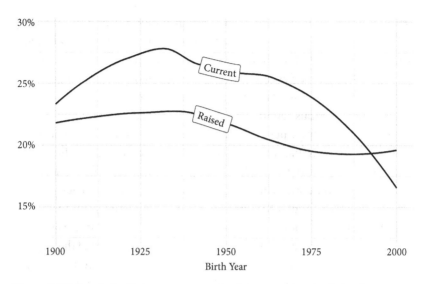

Figure 3.17 In what religion were you raised versus current religion?
Data: General Social Survey

evangelicals born during that time period was converted to the faith. That's a very positive development for any religious tradition.

But clearly, things have changed over time. The percentage of people who were raised evangelical has slowly crept downward in the last several decades. Among those born in the year 2000, less than 20% were raised in an evangelical household. At the same time the percentage of people who were evangelicals as adults took a nosedive. The end result is that for people born after 1990, evangelicalism is a leaky boat—the share of Americans who were raised evangelical exceeded the percentage that is currently evangelical.

This suggests a rather bleak future for American evangelicalism. The name itself, "evangelicalism," is centered on the term "good news" and the spreading of that message of salvation. Yet it's become increasingly the case that evangelicals have been unable to keep their own young people inside the faith tradition. But it also means that they have been unable to convert others in such numbers to backfill the losses that are sustained through defection among young people readied in the faith. In other words, all the indicators of religious vitality are flashing warning signs for evangelicalism. However, there are some data points that seem to soften this blow just a bit.

Undoubtedly, metrics like conversions and retention matter when it comes to the future of evangelicalism, but the number of children that are being born into evangelical churches also plays an important role in predicting the future. The General Social Survey has been asking respondents about how many children that they have ever had—including all children that were born alive at any time (even during previous marriages). This provides a good understanding of total fertility rate over the last five decades.

In 1972, evangelicals reported a robust level of fertility, as can be seen in Figure 3.18. The average person in the survey indicated that they had about 2.5 children in their lifetime. That was about .2 higher than the overall sample. Over the next twenty-five years, fertility would plunge for both evangelicals and the entire sample. By the mid-1990s, the overall fertility rate in the sample was about 1.85 children per person. Evangelicals were a bit higher than that at about 2 children person. From that point forward, fertility looks a bit different for evangelicals compared to the rest of the population. In 2021, evangelical fertility was about 2.1 children per respondent; in the general population it dropped to a bit less than 1.8 children. This paints a slightly rosier picture, if evangelicals can retain many of these children born in their churches in the decades to come.

For instance, if one looks at religious attendance among evangelicals but breaks it down into age categories, as in Figure 3.19, a surprising finding comes through: young evangelicals are becoming even more religiously

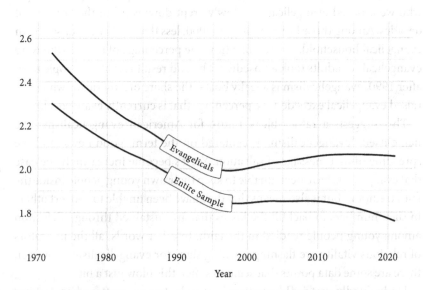

Figure 3.18 How many children have you ever had?
Data: General Social Survey

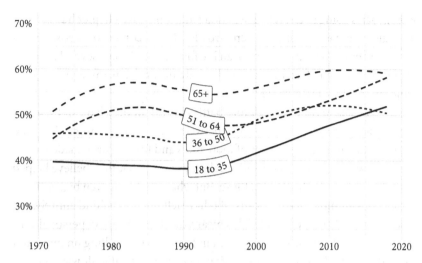

Figure 3.19 Share of evangelicals attending nearly every week or more by age
Data: General Social Survey

active. In the 1980s, about 40% of evangelicals between the ages of eighteen and thirty-five reported attending church nearly every week. That share began to increase in the early 1990s. Now, over half of evangelical young people are weekly attenders, which is a higher rate than evangelicals between the ages of thirty-six and fifty.

These data lead to the conclusion that while a smaller share of young people is aligning with the evangelical tradition, they are becoming even more fully enmeshed in their religious faith. This makes sense when thinking about the prior discussion about how evangelicals feel embattled but are still thriving. For a young person to embrace an evangelical identity when their friends and classmates are increasingly rejecting religion means that they must have a significant sense of attachment to their religious beliefs, far more than just a cultural connection. Thus, evangelicalism may get smaller in the future, but it may become even more fervent in belief and behavior.

Conclusion

Evangelicals have played a central role in American society, religion, and politics for the last hundred years. It seems likely that when outsiders think about the average American when it comes to religion, they conjure up images of

50 THE AMERICAN RELIGIOUS LANDSCAPE

evangelicals going to church on a Sunday morning. This chapter has detailed a religious movement at a true crossroads when it comes to its past and its future. After riding high in American life for most of the last several decades, evangelicalism has faced a slow and steady decline that threatens its relevance in the decades to come.

Evangelicals may be facing more battles now than they have in their history. With the increasing linkage between American conservatism and evangelical Christianity, scores of moderates and liberals have made it clear that they want nothing to do with a religious group that they believe helped Donald Trump win the White House. But what may be an even bigger threat is the rising number of Americans who have left religion behind entirely, not just evangelicalism specifically. This means that the message of personal conversion and redemption through faith in Jesus Christ is falling on more and more deaf ears. This makes conversion an even more difficult way to move forward in an era of rampant secularization.

That's not to say that evangelicals won't survive these latest trials. As mentioned previously, they went into their own self-directed exile one hundred years ago when they felt like the larger culture was not taking them seriously. That may be the case in the decades to come as evangelicalism feels marginalized in politics, media, and academia. But it seems appropriate to believe that evangelicalism will never truly vacate the American religious stage. If anything, evangelicals will wait in the wings for a more appropriate time to stake their claim in American life.

Notes

1. Roger Finke and Rodney Stark. 2005. *The Churching of America, 1776–2005: Winners and Losers in Our Religious Economy*. 2nd ed. New Brunswick, NJ: Rutgers University Press, 56, 156.
2. Finke and Stark, *The Churching of America*, 56, 156.
3. Finke and Stark, *The Churching of America*, 56.
4. Dalia Fahmy. 2019. "7 Facts about Southern Baptists." *Pew Research Center*. https://www.pewr esearch.org/short-reads/2019/06/07/7-facts-about-southern-baptists/; Andrew J. W. Smith. 2018. "Report Discloses History of Slavery and Racism at Southern Seminary." *The Southern Baptist Theological Seminary*. https://news.sbts.edu/2018/12/12/report-discloses-history-slav ery-racism-southern-seminary/.
5. "Our History." 2019. *American Baptist Churches USA*. https://www.abc-usa.org/what-we-beli eve/our-history/.
6. John Thomas Scopes. 1997. *The World's Most Famous Court Trial: Tennessee Evolution Case: A Complete Stenographic Report of the Famous Court Test of the Tennessee Anti-Evolution Act, at Dayton, July 10 to 21, 1925, Including Speeches and Arguments of Attorneys*. Union, NJ: The Lawbook Exchange, 284–291; Douglas Linder. 2008. "Day 7." Scopes Trial—Day 7—UMKC School of Law. http://law2.umkc.edu/faculty/projects/ftrials/scopes/day7.htm.

7. Douglas Linder. n.d. "H. L. Mencken (1880–1956)." UMKC School of Law. Famous Trials. https://famous-trials.com/scopesmonkey/2094-mencken.
8. Karen Armstrong. 2009. *The Case for God*. 1st ed. New York: Alfred A. Knopf, 274.
9. Brian Steensland, Lynn D. Robinson, W. Bradford Wilcox, Jerry Z. Park, Mark D. Regnerus, and Robert D. Woodberry. 2000. "The Measure of American Religion: Toward Improving the State of the Art." *Social Forces* 79, no. 1: 291–318.
10. D. W. Bebbington. 1989. *Evangelicalism in Modern Britain: A History from the 1730s to the 1980s*. London: Unwin Hyman, 2–17.
11. William H. Frey. 2020. "The Nation Is Diversifying Even Faster Than Predicted, According to New Census Data." *Brookings*. https://www.brookings.edu/articles/new-census-data-shows-the-nation-is-diversifying-even-faster-than-predicted/.
12. Christian Smith. 1998. *American Evangelicalism: Embattled and Thriving*. Chicago: University of Chicago Press.

Data References

Davern, Michael, Rene Bautista, Jeremy Freese, Pamela Herd, and Stephen L. Morgan. 2023. General Social Survey 1972–2022. Principal investigator, Michael Davern; Co-principal investigators, Rene Bautista, Jeremy Freese, Pamela Herd, and Stephen L. Morgan. Sponsored by National Science Foundation. NORC ed. Chicago: NORC at the University of Chicago. https://gssdataexplorer.norc.org/.

Grammich, Clifford, Kirk Hadaway, Richard Houseal, Dale E. Jones, Alexei Krindatch, Richie Stanley, and Richard H. Taylor. 2023. 2020 U.S. Religion Census: Religious Congregations & Membership Study. Association of Statisticians of American Religious Bodies. https://www.usreligioncensus.org/node/1639.

Schaffner, Brian, Stephen Ansolabehere, Sam Luks, Shiro Kuriwaki, and Marissa Shih. 2006–2023. Cooperative Election Study Common Content, 2006–2022. Harvard Dataverse. https://cces.gov.harvard.edu/.

4

Mainline Protestants

If there is one word to describe the current American religious landscape, it's "fractured." There are a significant number of Catholics and many evangelicals, but there are also pockets of Muslims, Jews, Latter-day Saints, and other faith groups across the United States. No religious tradition is clearly dominant in any sphere of American life, and this is likely to be the case for the foreseeable future, as defined faith communities continue to give way to those who eschew religion entirely or seek to practice their own spirituality in more fragmented and atomized ways.

However, American religion has not always been that way. Just a few decades ago, there was a religious tradition that dominated American society in virtually every sphere: mainline Protestant Christianity. According to religious historian James Hudnut-Beumler, 52% of all Americans aligned with a mainline denomination in 1958.[1] Now, very few Americans have even heard of the term "mainline Protestant." It's a stunning collapse for what was easily the most popular expression of organized religion for the better part of the twentieth century.

The continued existence of mainline Protestant Christianity is very much in doubt. The denominations that provide the foundation for this faith tradition are shedding members at a rapid rate, and the number of young families in mainline churches is shrinking with each year that passes. This means that the only viable path forward relies on conversion rather than retention—a challenging pursuit in an American climate that is becoming increasingly secular with each year. For decades, the mainline has offered a theological and cultural counterbalance to the conservatism espoused by their evangelical cousins. But the scales of American Christianity are continuing to tip to the right as the membership of the mainline continues to vanish, while evangelicalism is holding steady.

This chapter outlines the trajectory and contours of what was once the dominant expression of Christianity in the United States. Mainline Protestants represented a largely white, educated, middle-class form of religion that reflected the overall composition of the population. However, in

The American Religious Landscape. Ryan P. Burge, Oxford University Press. © Oxford University Press 2025.
DOI: 10.1093/oso/9780197762837.003.0005

the face of changing demographics and religiosity, the mainline now seems like a relic of a bygone era. Its ability to appeal to younger Americans, who are more racially, theologically, and politically diverse, will be the determining factor for its survival in the next century.

A Brief Introduction to Mainline Protestantism

While most Americans have an implicit understanding of the theological and cultural contours of American evangelicalism, the term "mainline Protestant" is less well-known among the general population. In simple terms, the mainline represents a collection of denominational traditions that are generally less conservative than their evangelical counterparts. This doesn't mean that all mainline Protestants are liberals, but they tend to adopt less rigid positions on social issues compared to evangelical Christianity. Many of the mainline denominations emerged from a series of splits within some of the largest denominational families in the United States.

For instance, Baptists in the United States were largely unified in the early 1800s. However, the issue of slavery began to create a divide between those in the North, who were predominantly abolitionists, and those in the South, who did not strongly oppose slavery. In 1845, these disagreements culminated over the question of whether Baptist missionaries could be slaveholders. Two factions emerged from this debate: the Southern Baptist Convention, which became the largest evangelical denomination in the United States, and the Northern Baptist Convention (which would eventually become the American Baptist Churches USA).[2] The American Baptists are considered one of the core members of the mainline tradition.

On theological matters, evangelical Christians often adopt a more literal interpretation of the Bible, whereas mainline Protestants are less likely to believe that the Bible should be taken word for word. Instead, they advocate for interpreting it in the context of historical developments and societal changes. The difference between evangelicals and mainline Protestants regarding biblical interpretation has been pronounced for the last fifty years, as can be seen in Figure 4.1. Data indicate that between 55% and 60% of evangelicals support a literal view of the Bible. In contrast, only about a quarter of mainline Protestant members today hold a literalist stance.

This divergence manifests itself in a number of visible ways. One of the most easily identifiable is over the issue of female pastors. Evangelicals, by

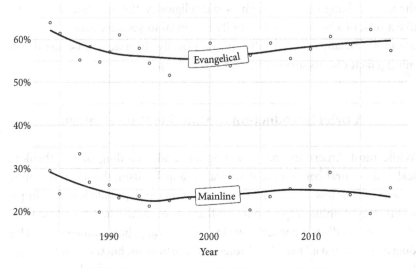

Figure 4.1 Share saying the Bible is literally true
Data: General Social Survey

and large, take 1 Timothy 2:12 to be literally true when the author writes, "I do not permit a woman to teach or exercise authority over a man; rather, she is to remain quiet."[3] Thus, women in leadership are not permitted. The Southern Baptist Convention reaffirmed their belief in this interpretation of scripture at their 2023 Annual Meeting when they chose to not reinstate two formerly Southern Baptist churches that had ordained women.[4] Conversely, every major mainline denomination has allowed women to assume leadership roles in churches for several decades. Mainline Protestants argue that other biblical passages suggest that some of the earliest and most significant Christian figures were women, indicating a more inclusive approach to gender roles within the church.

The doctrinal divide between evangelicals and mainline Protestants is also starkly evident on issues such as homosexuality. Evangelicals often interpret various passages from both the Old and New Testaments as clear indications that sexual relationships between individuals of the same sex are sinful. In contrast, mainline Protestants generally adopt a less literalist approach to these scriptures and are more inclusive, affirming same-sex couples both as members and leaders within their churches. This difference highlights the broader theological and interpretative disparities between these two segments of Christianity.

MAINLINE PROTESTANTS 55

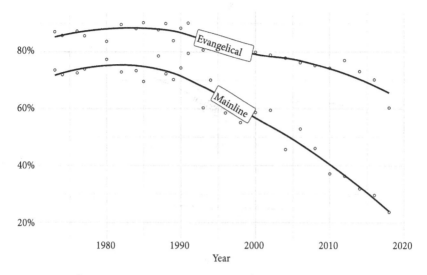

Figure 4.2 Share saying same-sex marriage is always wrong
Data: General Social Survey

In the 1970s, the difference in views between these two Christian traditions regarding the morality of homosexual relations was relatively modest—about twelve percentage points, as indicated in Figure 4.2. This gap persisted into the mid-1980s. However, from that point onward, the divide between the two groups became more pronounced. By 2000, less than 60% of mainline Protestants believed that homosexual relations were always wrong, compared to 80% among evangelicals. This gap further widened over the next decade; by 2010, 75% of evangelicals still viewed homosexuality as wrong, in contrast to only 40% of mainline Protestants. The most recent data show that two-thirds of evangelicals continue to believe that homosexuality is immoral, whereas only about a quarter of mainline Protestants share this view.

Another significant difference between mainline and evangelical Protestants lies in religious practices, particularly in terms of church attendance. The General Social Survey highlights a substantial gap in frequent attendance between the two groups, as depicted in Figure 4.3. During the 1980s, approximately 45% of evangelicals attended church nearly every week, compared to just 28% of mainline Protestants. This gap has widened in recent years; in 2018, nearly 55% of evangelicals were attending weekly services, while the figure for mainline Protestants was only about 30%.

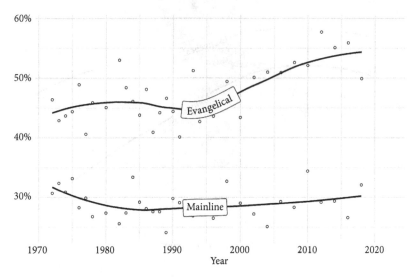

Figure 4.3 Share attending church nearly every week or more
Data: General Social Survey

Occasionally, members of the mainline community will toss criticisms toward their evangelical brethren, or evangelicals will call out what they believe to be heretical teachings coming from mainline churches. Evangelicals believe that the mainline has capitulated to the larger culture and has lost fidelity to the truth of Christianity on issues like homosexuality. Members of the mainline often see evangelicals as intolerant and bigoted to women and people from the LGBTQ+ community, which they believe violates the teachings of Jesus regarding inclusion.

Despite these differences, the mainline tradition is increasingly becoming a marginalized community within the American cultural landscape. This shift suggests that the evangelical tradition may become the predominant expression of Protestant Christianity familiar to the average American. The implications of this shift for American culture and religion are yet to be fully understood.

The Size and Trajectory of Mainline Christianity

As previously mentioned, denominational statistics from the 1950s point toward a mainline that was ascendant in American life. In the bustling centers of America's metropolises, pastors of prominent Methodist and Episcopal churches played a pivotal role, not only as religious figures but also as influential leaders in the realms of politics and culture. The historian George Marsden writes of the period, "Mainline Protestant leaders were part of the liberal-moderate cultural mainstream, and their leading spokespersons were respected participants in the national conversation."[5] As will be illustrated in the coming pages, the pews of the mainline were full of the most well-educated, wealthiest, and well-connected members of American society. Now, many of the mainline largest denominations are thinking about ways to close or consolidate hundreds of churches.

According to data from the General Social Survey, depicted in Figure 4.4, 28% of Americans identified as mainline Protestants in the early 1970s. This percentage rose slightly over the next few years, reaching its zenith in 1975 when nearly 31% of respondents indicated alignment with the mainline tradition. To put that in context, in the five decades of the General Social Survey, no religious tradition has claimed a higher percentage of the population than the mainline did in 1975. Their numbers held relatively steady for the next few years, as well. Even into the early 1980s, nearly three in ten Americans were aligned with the mainline.

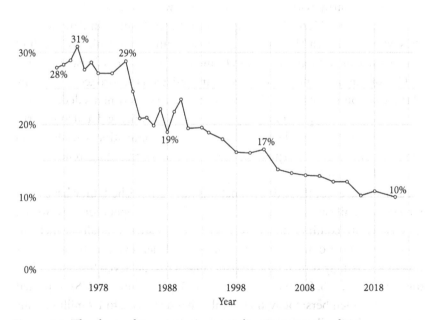

Figure 4.4 The share of Americans in a mainline Protestant tradition

58   THE AMERICAN RELIGIOUS LANDSCAPE

Then, the situation drastically changed. Between 1982 and 1988, the proportion of Americans identifying as mainline Protestants fell by a full ten percentage points. In the field of religious demography, changes typically occur at a very slow pace; a religious group might see a decline of 2% over a period of three or four years. Over a span of ten to fifteen years, such gradual losses can accumulate, resulting in a significant change in size. However, for a group to lose one-third of its membership within just seven years is extraordinary and unprecedented.

From that significant decline in the late 1980s, the trajectory of the mainline tradition shifted to a slow and steady decrease. Between 1988 and 2000, the membership fell by just two percentage points. Following this period, the decline settled into the more typical demographic trend of a gradual decrease—about half a percentage point each year over a decade. This pattern persisted through the 2010s, leading to mainline Protestants comprising just 10% of the U.S. population by 2021. Looking at the broader picture, it's almost astounding to reflect on the fact that the mainline tradition once encompassed half of the U.S. population in the 1950s, only to dwindle to a mere 10% in 2021.

The decline of the mainline tradition is also evident through denominational statistics. Many experts on American religion identify the mainline primarily with the "Seven Sisters," which include the American Baptist Churches USA, the Evangelical Lutheran Church in America, the Presbyterian Church (USA), the Episcopal Church, the United Church of Christ, the United Methodist Church, and the Disciples of Christ. A notable feature of the mainline tradition is their meticulous recordkeeping. Many of these denominations once had robust research departments dedicated to carefully maintaining membership records and producing detailed reports. These documents have been invaluable for denominational leaders and scholars of religion for purposes of analysis and understanding trends within the mainline tradition.

As the budgets of these denominations have diminished, they have been forced to significantly reduce their recordkeeping operations. However, they generally continue to publish top-line statistics annually, which include the number of members and churches. A brief review of these records reveals a strikingly similar pattern of decline across all Seven Sisters, as illustrated in Figure 4.5. In 1987, the American Baptist Churches USA reported 1.57 million members; today, that number has decreased to 1.2 million. This represents the smallest decline among these denominations.

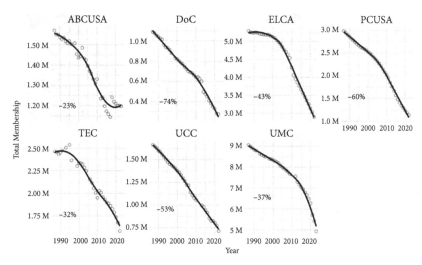

Figure 4.5 The decline in membership of the Seven Sisters of the mainline. ABCUSA, American Baptist Churches USA; DoC, Disciples of Christ; ELCA, Evangelical Lutheran Church of America; PCUSA, Presbyterian Church (USA); TEC, the Episcopal Church; UCC, United Church of Christ; UMC, United Methodist Church
Data: Denominational Records

The decline in membership is not limited to the American Baptist Churches USA but extends across all mainline denominations, often with even more dramatic reductions. The Evangelical Lutheran Church in America saw its membership decrease from 5.2 million in 1987 to just over 3 million. The Presbyterian Church (USA) experienced a particularly steep decline, dropping from 3.1 million members in 1987 to 1.1 million in 2021, which represents a loss of over 60%. The Episcopal Church's membership fell by nearly 40%, and the United Church of Christ saw its numbers halved. The Disciples of Christ, which reported about 1.1 million members in the late 1980s, has dwindled to 282,000 in the most recent data. Cumulatively, these seven denominations reported a total membership of 24 million in 1987, which had decreased to 13.7 million by 2021.

An intriguing consequence of the decline in the overall number of mainline Protestants is that overall religious attendance, as shown in Figure 4.6, has remained relatively stable over the last five decades. Despite the broader trend of secularization in the United States and decreased attendance among Catholics, mainline attendance patterns have stayed consistent

60 THE AMERICAN RELIGIOUS LANDSCAPE

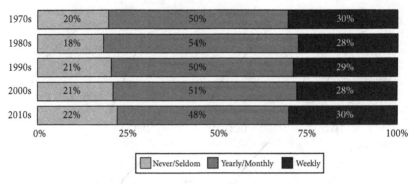

Figure 4.6 Church attendance among mainline Protestants over time
Data: General Social Survey

since the 1970s. This stability is a classic example of a compositional effect: as the mainline denominations began to shrink, those who remained were often the most devout and connected to their religious communities. Consequently, as the number of adherents diminished, the group that remained was more intensely devoted on average.

However, there's substantial reason to believe that the size of the mainline will significantly decrease from its current level in the coming years. The United Methodist Church is notably the largest of the Seven Sisters and its influence on American culture throughout the twentieth century has been profound. At its peak in the 1960s, the United Methodist Church boasted over 11 million members, surpassing even the Southern Baptist Convention, its evangelical counterpart.

To illustrate the extensive reach of the United Methodist Church, consider that there are 3,143 counties in the United States. According to the 2020 Religion Census, a United Methodist congregation exists in 2,989 of these counties, as indicated in Figure 4.7. This means that only 5% of all counties lack a United Methodist Church place of worship, surpassing the presence of any other religious tradition, including the Catholic Church, which is found in 2,961 counties, and the Southern Baptists, located in 2,677 counties. However, given the ongoing trends, it's highly probable that the United Methodists will no longer be the most geographically widespread tradition when the next Religion Census is conducted in 2030.

The reason for this is that the United Methodist Church is going through what will likely be the largest denominational split in American religious history. While it's impossible to quickly summarize all the causes for the

MAINLINE PROTESTANTS   61

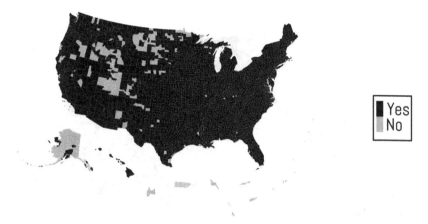

Figure 4.7 Counties that have a United Methodist Church

fracturing of the United Methodist Church, the most important underlying factor is that the United Methodist Church's membership has grown significantly outside the United States. Those international United Methodists tend to be more culturally conservative than the typical mainline American Methodist. This faction has joined forces with the more conservative wing of American Methodism to form the Global Methodist Church. At the end of 2023, 7,659 United Methodist congregations voted to leave the denomination - representing about 25% of all the churches in the United States.[6]

While it's uncertain how many members the United Methodist Church will retain after the full effects of the schism are realized, the denomination reported a loss of over 550,000 members between 2020 and 2021. This decrease amounted to an 8.8% decline, marking the most significant year-over-year drop for any major American denomination in the past half-century. There's good reason to anticipate that the percentage decline will be even more substantial when the figures for 2022 are released. To put this into perspective, remember that there were 13.7 million mainline Protestants in 2021. Given the ongoing schism within the United Methodists, it's highly probable that this number could decrease by another million in just a single year.

Mainline Christianity, as has been illustrated, does not have a specific regional affiliation within the United States. Rather, mainline churches can be found in both small towns and large cities throughout the country. In this respect, mainline Protestantism may remain the most geographically widespread form of American Christianity, even if its cultural influence

62 THE AMERICAN RELIGIOUS LANDSCAPE

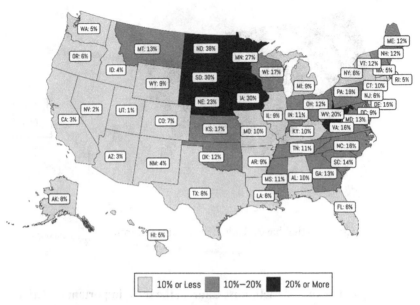

Figure 4.8 Share of all adherents who are mainline Protestant
Data: Religion Census

has waned. Figure 4.8 depicts the proportion of all religious individuals in each state who are affiliated with one of the "Seven Sisters" of mainline Protestantism, highlighting the broad yet diminishing footprint of mainline churches across the nation.

The epicenter of the mainline Protestant tradition is notably in the upper Midwest, where a significant portion of adherents are aligned with mainline denominations. In the Dakotas and Iowa, at least three in ten adherents belong to a mainline denomination. Additionally, 27% of those in Minnesota and 23% in Nebraska are part of the mainline tradition. A major contributor to this concentration is the Evangelical Lutheran Church of America, headquartered in Chicago, Illinois. The Evangelical Lutheran Church of America's denominational heritage is deeply connected to the waves of Scandinavian and German immigrants who arrived in the United States in the late nineteenth and early twentieth centuries, bringing their strong Lutheran affiliations and establishing communities, particularly in places like Minneapolis, Minnesota, and its surrounding areas.

Mainline Protestants are also notably present east of the Mississippi River, especially along the Atlantic coast. For example, 16% of religious adherents in North Carolina are mainline Protestants, with significant numbers in

Georgia and South Carolina as well. Additionally, there's a discernible presence of mainline Protestants running through the Rust Belt, in states like Indiana, Ohio, and Pennsylvania. In contrast, the mainline presence is much sparser in the western United States, with only about 3% in California and Arizona, highlighting the regional disparities in the distribution of mainline Protestantism across the country.

Key Characteristics of Mainline Protestants

In Ron Chernow's biography of John D. Rockefeller, he highlights the significant role that faith played in the life of the oil magnate. Despite his immense wealth, Rockefeller remained a lifelong member of a Baptist congregation, where the average congregant was of modest means. This was in contrast to the advice of many of his friends, who suggested he join Saint Paul's Episcopal Church, known for its affluent congregation "where elegant couples stepped from tony carriages each Sunday morning."[7] This anecdote reflects a broader perception of the mainline Protestant tradition as being associated with upper-middle-class, educated whites. The tradition is often viewed as attracting individuals who are drawn as much, if not more, by the social status and networking opportunities the church offers as by the theological teachings and spiritual guidance it provides.

This viewpoint does find factual support when looking at the halls of power in Washington, DC. Many recent presidents were members of the mainline when they won the highest office in the land. George W. Bush was a United Methodist and his father, President George H. W. Bush was an Episcopalian. Barack Obama was baptized in the United Church of Christ in Chicago, and Donald Trump was on the membership roll of a Presbyterian Church (USA) in New York City when he took the oath of office. Additionally, a number of Supreme Court Justices were part of the mainline. At one point in the early 1990s, four of the nine justices were from one of the Seven Sisters. Thus, the mainline has always been seen as the appropriate landing place for educated professionals who are trying to network with other members of similar social standing.

The survey data support this understanding of the mainline, as well. For instance, in the 2022 Cooperative Election Study, just less than 70% of the sample identified as white. Compare that in Figure 4.9 to those who aligned with the Evangelical Lutheran Church of America, where 92% identified as

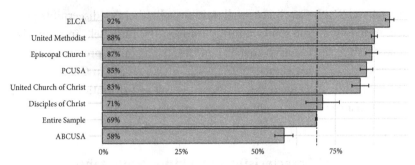

Figure 4.9 Share of the mainline who are white. ELCA, Evangelical Lutheran Church of America; PCUSA, Presbyterian Church (USA); ABCUSA, American Baptist Churches USA
Data: Cooperative Election Study

white. This is likely due in no small part to the fact that Lutheranism found its foothold in the United States through significant numbers of immigrants from Western European countries who passed their faith tradition on to the second and third generations when they came to American shores. In fact, the vast majority of the Seven Sisters are overwhelmingly white.

For instance, nearly 90% of United Methodists and Episcopalians identified as white in Figure 4.9. Just 15% of the members of the Presbyterian Church (USA) were people of color. About seven in ten members of the Disciples of Christ were white in 2022, which was right in line with the overall average. The only mainline denomination that can claim any real sense of racial diversity is the American Baptist Church, which was just 58% white. As the United States continues to be a more racially diverse country and younger generations are increasingly coming from a variety of racial and ethnic backgrounds, it will make it more difficult for the mainline to attract young people to join their congregation.

The perception that mainline Protestants are generally well-educated and economically successful is not just a stereotype but is supported by empirical data. When median income and educational attainment across various Protestant denominations are plotted on a scatterplot, as shown in Figure 4.10, the mainline denominations stand out for their high levels of both education and income. Notably, the four denominations with the highest levels of educational attainment and economic prosperity in the United States—namely the Episcopal Church, the Presbyterian Church (USA), the Evangelical Lutheran Church in America, and the Disciples of Christ—all

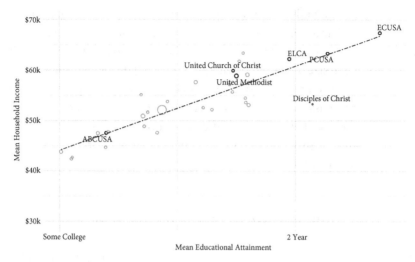

Figure 4.10 The relationship between education and income for denominations. ABCUSA, American Baptist Churches USA; ELCA, Evangelical Lutheran Church of America; PCUSA, Presbyterian Church (USA); ECUSA, Episcopal Church USA
Data: Cooperative Election Study

fall within the mainline tradition. In each of these denominations, the average member has attained at least a two-year college degree.

The United Methodist Church and the United Church of Christ also exhibit educational attainments and incomes that meet or exceed the national average. For example, while the average income for a Southern Baptist is just over $50,000, it approaches $60,000 for members of the United Methodist Church and the United Church of Christ. The only mainline denomination that does not follow this trend is the American Baptist Churches USA, whose members typically earn around $48,000 per year and are less likely to have completed a two-year college degree.

Despite declining membership and attendance, the financial situation of many mainline denominations has remained relatively stable, partly due to the high average incomes of their members, allowing for significant donations to their congregations. Additionally, many mainline denominations benefit from substantial endowments established centuries ago. For instance, the Episcopal Church owns valuable real estate in Manhattan, New York City, contributing significantly to its financial stability, as highlighted by a 2019 *New York Times* article titled "The Church with the $6 Billion Portfolio."[8]

However, the mainline tradition faces significant challenges regarding future viability. The Seven Sisters have all experienced considerable declines in membership over the past three decades. If current trends continue, it's likely that the average size of mainline denominations will decrease by half within the next twenty years. The primary issue is generational replacement: as older members pass away, they are not being replaced by younger individuals at a sufficient rate. This is evidenced by mainline clergy conducting more funerals than baptisms or weddings, signaling a potentially precarious future for these denominations.

Indicators of Decline in the Mainline

Almost all publicly available surveys are conducted only among adult respondents. That means that the youngest respondent is at least eighteen years old. Thus, it's impossible to calculate the average age of a specific denomination based on traditional survey data. However, it can provide a fairly accurate portrait of the overall generational composition of a religious group. When the mean age of the Seven Sisters is calculated, it becomes exceedingly clear that the graying of those in the pews is a serious area of concern for mainline Protestant Christianity.

In the 2022 Cooperative Election Study, the average age of a respondent is just over forty-eight years old. One can see in Figure 4.11 that the oldest mainline tradition is the United Methodist Church, where the average member is nearly fifty-nine years old. In the Episcopal Church, it's fifty-eight and the Evangelical Lutheran Church in America follows closely behind at

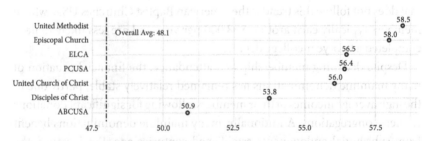

Figure 4.11 Average age of adults in the seven mainline traditions. ELCA, Evangelical Lutheran Church of America; PCUSA, Presbyterian Church (USA); ABCUSA, American Baptist Churches USA

Data: Cooperative Election Study

nearly fifty-seven years old. In fact, five of the Seven Sisters are at least eight years older than the average adult in the general population.

The Disciples of Christ and the American Baptist Church look young in comparison at fifty-four and fifty-one years old, respectively. But even in both of these cases, that age is notably older than the general population. This means that the average mainline church is teeming with gray-haired retirees. While this group is vital to providing most of the financial support and volunteer hours to make a religious organization run, they cannot carry their local church that far into the future. Many will be physically unable to carry on in the next few decades, leaving the younger generation in charge of governance and community outreach.

What compounds that fact is that religious communities thrive by passing their faith tradition to the next generation. When the average age of a congregant in a local mainline church is nearly sixty years old, that means that not only have they moved far beyond their childbearing years, but they have also likely seen their children grow up and possibly leave their home church behind. Passing the leadership baton from one generation to the next ensures both institutional memory but also organizational vitality. For many in the mainline congregations, there are members that are getting close to the end of the race, and there is no one to pick up the baton and lead the church in the decades to come.

This failed generational handoff comes into sharper focus when looking at the number of children per person in the major mainline denominations in Figure 4.12. In the overall sample, the average person has 0.42 children

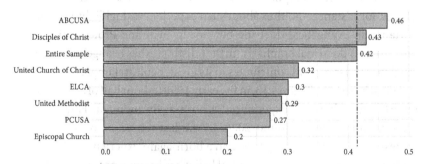

Figure 4.12 Average number of children per person in the mainline. ABCUSA, American Baptist Churches USA; ELCA, Evangelical Lutheran Church of America; PCUSA, Presbyterian Church (USA)
Data: Cooperative Election Study

68 THE AMERICAN RELIGIOUS LANDSCAPE

who are under the age of eighteen. Again, the American Baptists and the Disciples of Christ are the outliers, with a higher fertility rate than the overall sample. However, the largest denominations in this tradition are far below this baseline.

The fertility rates within mainline Protestant denominations highlight a significant challenge for their future growth and sustainability. For example, the average Episcopalian today has just 0.2 children, meaning a hypothetical Episcopal church with 100 adult members would only have about 20 children in its congregation. The situation is slightly better in the United Methodist Church, with an average of 0.29 children per adult member, but even this rate is insufficient to sustain the denomination's population. Even if all these children remained within their parents' denomination as they reached adulthood, the denominations would still experience a net loss in membership due to generational replacement alone.

Another challenge for mainline Protestantism is its relatively low cultural visibility compared to evangelicalism. The average American is likely more familiar with the beliefs and political leanings of evangelicals and may not even be aware of the term "mainline Protestant." Mainline denominations often embody political diversity and moderate stances on social issues, which may lead to less media coverage compared to more homogenous or politically vocal groups. This lack of visibility contributes to a lower cultural relevance for mainline Christianity in the United States.

Evangelicalism, however, has gained cultural prominence across the country over recent decades. This is partly due to practices such as the emphasis on born-again experiences, which are a hallmark of evangelical faith but are not typically emphasized in mainline traditions. The General Social Survey, for instance, inquires about such experiences, highlighting their importance in evangelical doctrine but not in mainline Protestantism. This difference in doctrinal emphasis further distinguishes evangelicalism in the religious landscape and contributes to its greater cultural impact.

As can be seen in Figure 4.13, in the early 1990s, about half of all Protestants reported that they had experienced a born-again moment. However, that share began to climb around 2006. In the last ten years, over 60% of all Protestants believe that they have had a born-again experience. This is clear evidence that mainstream evangelical belief has become pervasive not just in evangelical circles but also among mainline Protestants, as well. In 1998, just 27% of mainliners reported a born-again experience. In 2021, that had risen to about 40%.

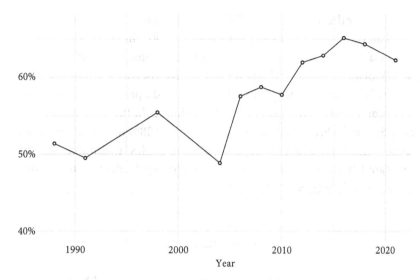

Figure 4.13 Share of Protestants who have had a born-again experience
Data: General Social Survey

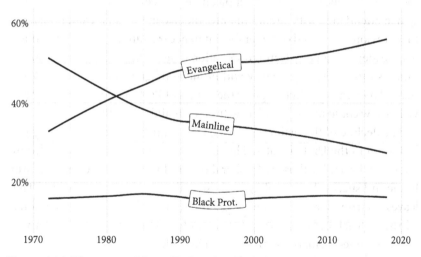

Figure 4.14 The composition of Protestant Christianity

The other way this expresses itself in the data is the overall composition of Protestant Christianity, displayed in Figure 4.14. In the early 1970s, about half of all Protestants were aligned with the mainline, one-third was evangelicals, and about 17% were Black Protestants. But significant changes

70 THE AMERICAN RELIGIOUS LANDSCAPE

occurred over the next ten years. The mainline declined rapidly, while evangelicalism was gaining more market share. By 1982, the two traditions were about equal in size. But another ten years later, the mainline had dropped to just 35% of all Protestants while evangelicals had risen to nearly 50%.

From that point forward, evangelicalism gained a percentage point or two every year, largely at the expense of the mainline. In the most recent data, nearly 55% of all Protestants were evangelical and 28% were mainline. Black Protestants stayed steady at approximately 17%. It's a stunning shift for Protestant Christianity with the mainline and evangelicalism switching sizes almost perfectly between 1972 and 2018.

Conclusion

Over the last fifty years, American religion has been shaped by two significant trends: the dramatic increase in the nonreligious population and the notable decline of mainline Protestant Christianity. Once the bastion for the affluent, educated, and influential, mainline churches now often feature sparse attendance with predominantly older congregants. Denominations that previously wielded considerable influence on public opinion and policy, with leaders frequently featured in national news, have seen their visibility diminish to coverage primarily within niche religious news outlets. While many Americans might recognize the names of Protestant pastors from television, few could identify leaders within the mainline tradition.

The decline of the mainline may be partly attributed to the growing polarization in the United States. The nonreligious segment has expanded by offering a haven for those with liberal political views, while evangelicalism has found success by appealing to those with conservative ideologies. This leaves a narrow space for mainline denominations that maintain traditional Christian teachings on Jesus and salvation but are more open to modern issues like same-sex marriage and women in leadership roles.

For atheists and agnostics, mainline Protestantism is still too steeped in religious tradition; for evangelicals, it lacks sufficient orthodoxy. This "middle way" appeals to a dwindling number of adherents who identify with mainline Protestant values but are increasingly out of sync with a culture that often demands clear stances in debates. Faced with an aging demographic and declining birth rates, the "Seven Sisters" of mainline Protestantism must confront tough decisions about their future viability and the responsible management of their assets in accordance with their faith. These challenging discussions could ultimately define a lasting legacy for mainline Protestantism that endures beyond the era of its institutional prominence.

Notes

1. James David Hudnut-Beumler and Mark Silk, eds. 2018. *The Future of Mainline Protestantism in America*. New York: Columbia University Press, 1.
2. Dalia Fahmy. 2019. "7 Facts about Southern Baptists." *Pew Research Center*. https://www.pewresearch.org/short-reads/2019/06/07/7-facts-about-southern-baptists/; Andrew J. W. Smith. 2018. "Report Discloses History of Slavery and Racism at Southern Seminary." *The Southern Baptist Theological Seminary*. https://news.sbts.edu/2018/12/12/report-discloses-history-slavery-racism-southern-seminary/; "Our History." 2019. *American Baptist Churches USA*. https://www.abc-usa.org/what-we-believe/our-history/.
3. 1 Tim. 2:12 NRSV.
4. Brendan O'Brien. 2023. "Southern Baptists Finalize Expulsion of Two Churches with Female Pastors." *Reuters*. https://www.reuters.com/world/us/southern-baptists-finalize-expulsion-two-churches-with-female-pastors-2023-06-14/.; Jason DeRose. 2023. "Southern Baptists Say No to Women Pastors, Uphold Expulsion of Saddleback Megachurch." *NPR*. https://www.npr.org/2023/06/14/1182141691/southern-baptist-convention-sbc-women-pastors-saddleback-megachurch.
5. George M. Marsden. 2014. *The Twilight of the American Enlightenment: the 1950s and the Crisis of Liberal Belief*. New York: Basic Books, 98–99.
6. Kate Shellnutt and Daniel Silliman. 2023. "United Methodists Down 7,659 Churches as Exit Window Ends." *News & Reporting*. https://www.christianitytoday.com/news/2023/december/united-methodist-church-split-total-umc-disaffiliation-lgbt.html.
7. Ron Chernow. 2010. *Titan: The Life of John D. Rockefeller, Sr.* New York: Vintage Books, 189.
8. Jane Margolies. 2019. "The Church with the $6 Billion Portfolio." *The New York Times*. https://www.nytimes.com/2019/02/08/nyregion/trinity-church-manhattan-real-estate.html.

Data References

Davern, Michael, Rene Bautista, Jeremy Freese, Pamela Herd, and Stephen L. Morgan. 2023. General Social Survey 1972–2022. Principal investigator, Michael Davern; Co-principal investigators, Rene Bautista, Jeremy Freese, Pamela Herd, and Stephen L. Morgan. Sponsored by National Science Foundation. NORC ed. Chicago: NORC at the University of Chicago. https://gssdataexplorer.norc.org/.

Grammich, Clifford, Kirk Hadaway, Richard Houseal, Dale E. Jones, Alexei Krindatch, Richie Stanley, and Richard H. Taylor. 2023. 2020 U.S. Religion Census: Religious Congregations & Membership Study. Association of Statisticians of American Religious Bodies. https://www.usreligioncensus.org/node/1639.

Schaffner, Brian, Stephen Ansolabehere, Sam Luks, Shiro Kuriwaki, and Marissa Shih. 2006–2023. Cooperative Election Study Common Content, 2006–2022. Harvard Dataverse. https://cces.gov.harvard.edu/.

Tausanovitch, C., and L. Vavreck. 2023. Democracy Fund + UCLA Nationscape Project (version 20211215). Harvard Dataverse. https://doi.org/10.7910/DVN/CQFP3Z.

5

Black Protestants

One of the most difficult aspects of classifying and measuring religion in the United States is sorting Protestants into coherent categories. The previous two chapters have addressed two Protestant families: evangelical and mainline. However, there is a third group that scholars tend to see as a separate entity in the American religious landscape: Black Protestants. For anyone who has ever worshiped in a Protestant congregation that is mostly African American, it's readily apparent that the style of worship is distinct from the evangelical or mainline tradition. The Black Church experience is one like no other—integrating music into nearly every aspect of the service, and with expansive and emotional sermons that often elicit verbal and physical reactions from the congregation. For mainline Protestants, it's not unusual for the entire worship service to be wrapped up in less than sixty minutes; for many Black Protestant congregations, the Sunday morning gathering can stretch into a third hour.

But beyond the stylistic differences during congregational worship, Black Protestants and other types of Protestant Christians differ in several other significant ways. The Black Church evolved as a distinct institution due to significant societal factors. Even after the Civil War abolished slavery, African Americans were still denied full societal access. As the history books attest, there were segregated water fountains, bathrooms, and restaurants across the United States, especially in the South. Simultaneously, many Protestant traditions implicitly excluded African Americans from worship. Thus, the Black community began establishing their own denominations that would serve African Americans who wished to find a welcoming place to gather.

But, because of the deep segregation that was endemic throughout the United States, the Black Church developed into a key institution in the social, political, and spiritual lives of African Americans. While whites could worship with the Presbyterians on Sunday, socialize at the Elks Club on Tuesday, and listen to a politician deliver a stump speech in the all-white high school in their neighborhood on Friday night—these opportunities were denied to many African Americans. Because of this, the Black Church consolidated

The American Religious Landscape. Ryan P. Burge, Oxford University Press. © Oxford University Press 2025.
DOI: 10.1093/oso/9780197762837.003.0006

worship, socialization, and political engagement under a single roof. The local church became the social, economic, religious, and political gathering place for African Americans in their community.

Thus, because of that historical context and the way that the Black Church adapted to meet the unmet needs of their constituency, Black Protestantism is an entirely different institution than evangelical or mainline Christianity. What cements this divide even more is an aspect of American life this volume has largely avoided to this point—politics. As this chapter will explain, Black Protestants look very similar to evangelicals in several aspects of theology and religious practice. However, where they could not differ more is in the area of their voting behavior. Evangelicals, particularly white evangelicals, are overwhelmingly Republican, while the vast majority of Black Protestants tend to cast a ballot for the Democrats when they enter the voting booth. This fact cannot be ignored by scholars who study the role of politics in every aspect of American life.

This chapter tries to describe the contours of Black Protestantism, examining the position of Black Church members relative to other religious traditions in terms of theology, religious practice, socioeconomic factors, and politics. The Black Protestant tradition in the United States defies convention. It serves as a reminder to scholars and observers of American politics and religion that while race may not always be the key variable of interest, it always looms in the background of any analysis. Black Protestants play a vibrant and vital role in many U.S. communities, yet they often receive less media attention than their evangelical counterparts. Hopefully, this chapter will lead more readers to consider how history has contributed to the evolution of religion in the United States.

How Large Is Black Protestant Christianity?
What Denominations Are the Largest?

In 2000, a significant breakthrough in the field of religious studies occurred when a team of academics, well-versed in the intricacies of religion, developed a comprehensive typology of Protestant denominations. This typology introduced a novel classification system, categorizing Protestants into three distinct groups: evangelical, mainline, and Black.[1] This typology, known as RELTRAD, rapidly gained traction within academic circles. Its widespread adoption can be attributed to several factors.

74 THE AMERICAN RELIGIOUS LANDSCAPE

First, the team of academics behind RELTRAD published a detailed appendix containing computer code, which made it easier to replicate their results. In addition, RELTRAD offered an objective and widely agreed-upon lens through which to examine the size and growth of the Black Protestant tradition over the past five decades. Thus, those denominations listed by the authors of the RELTRAD scheme have become the de facto measuring stick for analysts who engage in the study of American religious demography.

In the 1970s, several yearly estimates of the Black Protestant church put it between 8% and 9% of the general population, as can be seen in Figure 5.1. By the 1980s, that percentage began to fluctuate a bit but was clearly declining slightly—averaging between 7% and 8%. Even into 2000, some yearly estimates of Black Protestant Christianity were as high as 9%. However, estimates from that point forward are undoubtedly lower. In 2008, the share was back to 7.5%, and in 2014, the percentage dropped to its lowest figure—just above 6%.

Speaking broadly about the portion of Americans who were Black Protestant since the 1970s, it appears that there was a great deal of stability in the data for decades. The share that was Black Protestant may have dipped just a single percentage point between 1972 and 1998. However, it is fair to conclude that in the last twenty years or so, there has been a more noticeable

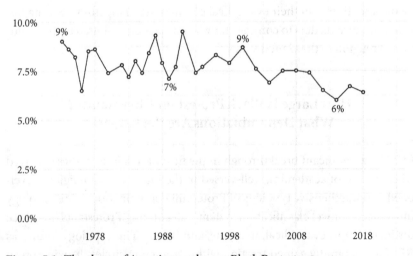

Figure 5.1 The share of Americans who are Black Protestants
Data: General Social Survey

drop. It's empirically defensible to contend that the share is probably 6% now and likely headed downward in the next decade or so.

The aforementioned RELTRAD classification scheme includes nearly two dozen denominations that are to be classified as Black Protestant, but among that list, there are several that stand apart due to their size and influence in the Black Church tradition. What is often considered to be the oldest denomination in this category is the African Methodist Episcopal Church (AME). The denomination was founded in 1816 by Richard Allen in Philadelphia, Pennsylvania.[2] While it grew slowly in the first few decades of its existence, reporting fewer than 20,000 members in 1846, it experienced a tenfold increase in membership over the next three decades.[3]

While the aforementioned AME Church finds its theological roots in the Wesleyan tradition, which is the foundational doctrine of Methodism, there are other theological traditions in Black Protestantism. For instance, there are several Baptist denominations in the Black Church, including National Missionary Baptists, National Baptists, Progressive National Baptists, and members of the National Baptist Convention of America. The other prominent theological tradition in Black Protestantism is Holiness/Pentecostalism, as seen through a denomination such as the Church of God in Christ (COGIC).

In congregation and membership numbers, the National Missionary Baptist Convention (NMBCA) is the largest denomination within Black Protestantism. As shown in Figure 5.2, based on data from the Religion Census, the NMBCA had over 7,500 congregations and 2.4 million members in 2020. For context, the Southern Baptist Convention boasts over 50,000 congregations, and there are over 30,000 United Methodist churches. Although the NMBCA is numerically much smaller than those two denominations, it still ranks among the top-ten largest Protestant denominations in the United States by congregation and membership count.

The next largest denomination in the Black Church is the African Methodist Episcopalians with nearly 3,700 churches and just over 1 million members. The only other denomination in this tradition that reports at least 1 million members is the National Baptist Convention with 1.56 million members spread across 2,530 churches in the United States. In total, these eight denominations represent about 7 million members of the Black Protestant tradition and include just over 21,000 congregations. Of course, those listed in Figure 5.2 do not encompass every Black Church across the

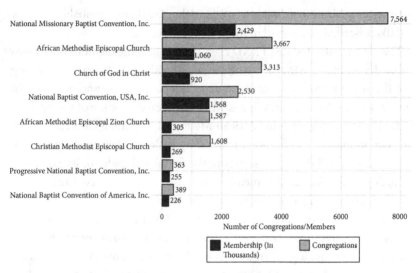

Figure 5.2 The largest denominations in the Black Church
Data: Religion Census

United States, but the majority of Black Protestants have their membership in one of these denominations.

Figure 5.3 is a state-level map that visualizes which states have the highest concentration of members of one of these eight denominations that are the largest in the Black Protestant tradition. It quickly becomes apparent that the locus of power for Black Protestant Christianity is in the states that make up the Deep South. Eight percent of residents of the state of Mississippi are members of the aforementioned denominations—that's followed closely by Alabama at 7%. But there are also significant concentrations of Black Protestants in neighboring states, as well. About 5% of the population of Louisiana, South Carolina, Georgia, and Tennessee are Black Protestants in these eight denominations. It's 6% of the state of Arkansas.

But beyond these states, Black Protestantism is a fairly small share of the population in the rest of the country. There are some pockets of the Black Church to be found around Chicago and the surrounding suburbs and also some large churches in this tradition around St. Louis, but many states in the Midwest and Northeast report just 1%–2% membership in these Black Church denominations. Once one moves into the Western Plains into states such as Utah, Colorado, and Nevada, Black Protestants make up less than 1% of the state's population. Clearly, Black Protestantism has a strong core

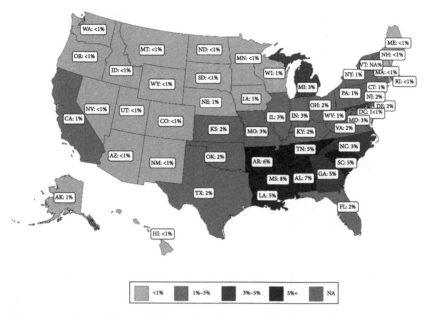

Figure 5.3 Share of the population that is a part of the largest denominations in the Black Protestant tradition
Data: Religion Census

of support in the South with some ripples into neighboring states, but Black Protestantism is much less pervasive in the rest of the United States.

However, what clouds this picture is that the Black Protestant tradition does not have clear boundaries. As previously mentioned, there are several denominations that are understood to typify the Black Church, and those are noted in Figure 5.2. That doesn't mean that there are not African Americans who are members of denominations that are traditionally understood to be not part of the Black Church tradition.

Figure 5.4 shows that about a third of American Baptist Church (ABCUSA) members are African American. However, scholars classify ABCUSA as mainline due to its split from the Southern Baptist Convention over slavery in the 1840s. Undoubtedly, some American Baptist churches share characteristics with denominations in the Black Church tradition, such as the National Missionary Baptist Convention. Despite advancements in survey techniques and sample sizes, these methods remain blunt instruments. They typically do not capture the nuances of a respondent's local congregation, focusing instead on broader denominational affiliation.

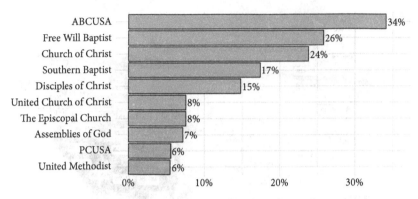

Figure 5.4 Share of other denominations who identify as African American
Data: Cooperative Election Study

Note that there are also significant contingents of African Americans in other denominations, as well. For instance, the largest evangelical denomination in the United States is the Southern Baptist Convention, yet 17% of members are African American. Given that the Southern Baptist Convention has over 13 million members, this would mean that there are over 2 million Black Southern Baptists in the United States. The data from the Religion Census visualized in Figure 5.2 indicate that there is only one denomination in the Black Church with a larger membership—National Missionary Baptists. There are also hundreds of thousands of Black members of mainline traditions like the Episcopal Church, the United Church of Christ, and the United Methodist Church.

Black Protestants versus Evangelicals— Theology and Politics

Up to this point, the interplay between religion and politics has not been the focus of this volume. However, when it comes to the justification for classifying Black Protestants into their own category instead of combining them with evangelicals or the mainline, one must concede that politics is what provides the justification for creating a third category. A well-understood facet of the American political landscape is that African Americans are one of the most important voting blocs to Democratic politicians running for elected office. That clearly comes through when looking at the vote choice

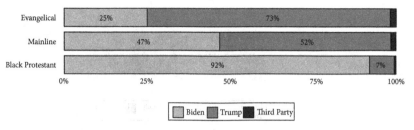

Figure 5.5 Vote choice among Protestants in 2020
Data: Cooperative Election Study

of the three types of Protestants in the 2020 presidential election—which is visualized in Figure 5.5.

Just a quarter of evangelical Christians cast a ballot for Joe Biden when they went to the polls in November of 2020, while about three-quarters were supporters of the Republican Donald Trump. If this is restricted to just white evangelicals (which is often the case when the media writes about this topic), Trump garnered about 80% of the vote. Mainline Protestants are clearly divided on Election Day. In the 2020 election, the GOP got a slim majority of the mainline vote at 52%, while Biden got 47%. However, among Black Protestants the results are unambiguous—nearly all of them voted for Joe Biden in 2020. For every Black Protestant who cast a ballot for Donald Trump, there were thirteen Black Protestants who supported Joe Biden.

Numerous factors contribute to the significant divergence in voting patterns between evangelicals and Black Protestants. A key factor was President Lyndon Johnson, a Texas Democrat and strong advocate for civil rights, who signed the Civil Rights Act in 1964 and the Voting Rights Act in 1965, both of which significantly protected minorities across American society. In response, Republicans like Richard Nixon adopted the "Southern Strategy," aimed at winning over conservative white voters in the South. This approach subtly opposed desegregation and critiqued welfare policies, suggesting they benefited the undeserving.[4]

Consequently, white evangelicals emerged as a crucial bloc for the Republican Party, while Democrats depended on Black voters' support for electoral victories. In districts with significant African American populations, Democratic politicians often deliver stump speeches in local Black Churches. Historically, due to widespread segregation, churches were central in the Black community, offering a unique platform for politicians to reach African American voters. Republicans courting white evangelicals

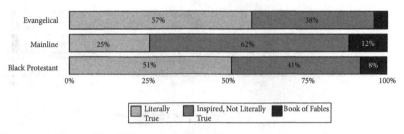

Figure 5.6 View of the Bible among Protestants
Data: General Social Survey

did not need to utilize the pulpit in these churches because they had other venues to deliver their message to potential supporters.

What is noteworthy, though, about the comparison between Black Protestants and evangelicals is that on matters of theology, the differences between the two groups are much smaller. This is a fact that is often lost when religion gets reduced to nothing more than political coalitions. Many Black Protestant pastors preach Sunday sermons that would align well with traditional evangelical orthodoxy. Capturing differences in theology can be difficult through survey data, but the General Social Survey has been asking respondents about their view of the Bible for decades. One response option is that it should be taken as the literal word of God, another indicates that it's inspired by God but should not be taken as literally true, and a final choice is that the Bible is a book of fables written by men.

Figure 5.6 visualizes the results of this analysis in a survey conducted in 2018. As previously mentioned, mainline Protestants tend toward a more moderate view of the Christian scriptures, with a strong majority (62%) indicating that the Bible was inspired by God, but should not be taken as literally true. Evangelicals and Black Protestants differ significantly from the mainline on this metric. Among evangelicals, 57% believe that the Bible should be taken as literally true, and it's nearly the same share of Black Protestants—51%. When speaking of which groups tend to be theologically conservative, many Americans would point to evangelicals as the standard bearer, but Black Protestants are not substantively different in their view of the Bible from their evangelical cousins.

Exploring theological differences further, questions about human sexuality provide insight. Since 2004, the General Social Survey has asked respondents about the rights of homosexual couples to marry. Figure 5.7 visualizes the results. Crucially, support for gay marriage in the general

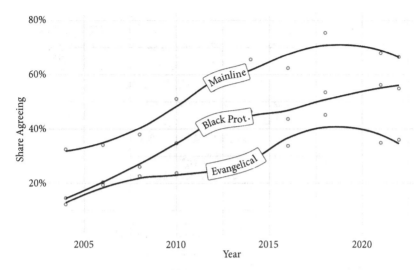

Figure 5.7 Homosexual couples should have the right to marry one another
Data: General Social Survey

population has surged from 37% in 2004 to 67% in 2022. However, this trend varies among Protestant groups.

In 2004, the share of evangelicals and Black Protestants who supported same-sex marriage was statistically the same—about 17%. Mainline Protestants were quite a bit higher at just about a third. Over time, there has been an increase in support among all Protestant groups but not at the same rate. Mainline approval of same-sex marriage is easily the highest at 68% in 2022. Evangelical support is about half that share—35%. Black Protestants fall in between those two estimates at 58%. But notice that as late as 2018, the trend line between evangelicals and Black Protestants was less than ten percentage points, while the division between mainline and Black Protestants was twice as large. It's clear from this that Black Protestants aren't quite as conservative on this issue as evangelicals, but they certainly are not as progressive as the mainline, either.

Beyond views of the Bible and same-sex marriage, there are other approaches to measuring the centrality of religion in a population. The Cooperative Election Study asks about religious importance but also the frequency of prayer. These two metrics are valuable because religious importance provides an insight into a general orientation toward religion, while prayer is more focused on individual religious behavior.

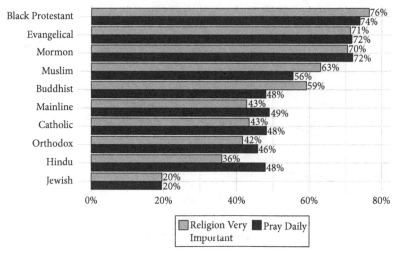

Figure 5.8 Religious activity among religious groups
Data: Cooperative Election Study

In Figure 5.8, the groups are sorted into those who are most active at the top and those who are least religiously engaged at the bottom. For instance, just one in five Jews says that religion is very important to them, and the same share report praying at least once per day. Other groups near the bottom on both these metrics include Hindus, Orthodox Christians, and Catholics. It is noteworthy how members of most religious groups fall below the 50% threshold when it comes to daily prayer. Only four traditions have a majority of members who pray at least once a day: Muslims, Latter-day Saints, evangelicals, and Black Protestants.

On both these metrics, though, Black Protestants are clearly the most religiously devout. Seventy-four percent report praying every day—that's two points higher than evangelicals and twenty-five points higher than mainline Protestants. Also, 76% of Black Protestants say that religion is very important; again, this is higher than any other religious group. Evangelicals and Latter-day Saints are further behind at 71% and 70% respectively. It's evident from these two metrics that Black Protestants are some of the most religiously engaged individuals in American society—far outpacing other groups that tend to be more left-leaning in their politics like Jews and Muslims.

Black Protestants also score relatively well on the most widely used measure of religious activity—weekly attendance. Figure 5.9 visualizes the share who attended nearly every week or more from the General Social

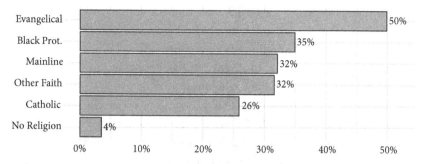

Figure 5.9 Share attending nearly every week or more
Data: General Social Survey

Survey conducted in 2018. It should come as no surprise that just 4% of those with no religion are weekly attenders. Catholics are in second position with just 26% attending weekly Mass (a topic that will be explored in Chapter 7. About one-third of mainline Protestants are attending church services weekly. Black Protestants have a slightly higher level of weekly attendance, with 35% reporting near weekly attendance. The only group that is ahead of them is evangelicals at 50%.

Looking at this data in its entirety, it becomes clear that Black Protestants have a very similar religious profile as their evangelical counterparts. Black Protestants have a fairly high view of the Bible—in the same neighborhood as evangelicals. On the issue of same-sex marriage, they tend to be slightly more permissive than evangelicals but are clearly not in the same category as mainline Protestants. When it comes to religious behavior, they score near the top on a variety of categories, including religious importance, frequency of prayer, and level of religious attendance. Thus, it seems empirically accurate to say that Black Protestants represent some of the most religiously engaged people in the United States.

Issues Facing the Future of Black Protestantism

As can be previously observed in the long-term data from the General Social Survey visualized in Figure 5.1, the overall share of Americans who identify as Black Protestants is slowly declining over time. It was as high as 9% in the early 1970s, but that figure in more recent surveys has declined to likely around 6% of the total population. The preponderance of the data seems to point to further drops in the decades to come for a variety of reasons. One likely reason is that Black Protestants tend to have some of the lowest levels of educational attainment and household income in the United States. Recent data have suggested those on the higher end of the socioeconomic spectrum are more likely to be engaged in a religious tradition.[5]

In Figure 5.10, the mean household income of each religious group is plotted along the x-axis, while the share of each group with a four-year college degree is plotted along the y-axis. Obviously, there's a positive relationship between these two variables—those with a higher level of education tend to report a greater annual household income and vice versa. Hindus and Jews are outliers here in the top right corner, representing very high incomes and education levels. Those findings will be discussed in more depth in subsequent chapters. A significant number of groups are clustered in the middle of the graph, representing about 40% with a college degree and a mean household income that ranges from $52K to $60K. This list includes both evangelical and mainline Protestants, along with Buddhists, Latter-day Saints, Orthodox Christians, Catholics, and Agnostics.

The far left of the graph only includes two groups—those who claim their religion is "nothing in particular" and Black Protestants. In this analysis, just about a quarter of Black Protestants have a four-year college degree, which is not empirically different from evangelicals. However, there is a large

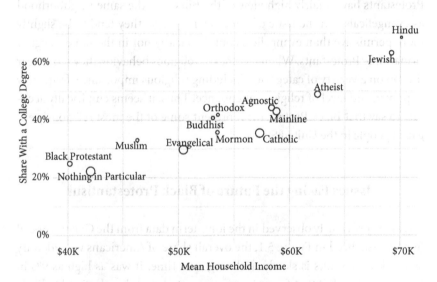

Figure 5.10 Income and education among religious groups
Data: Cooperative Election Study

disparity between Black Protestants and evangelicals when it comes to income. Black Protestants report just about $40,000 of income per year; for evangelicals it's nearly $11,000 higher.

There is growing empirical evidence that there is a strong positive relationship between education, income, and religious attendance. Some studies have found that the group that is the most likely to attend religious services weekly are those with a four-year college degree who have incomes between $60,000 and $100,000 per year. Other factors that contribute to a high level of religious attachment are being married and being the parents to children under the age of eighteen.[6] These factors are not working in favor of Black Protestants. As previously mentioned, Black Protestants tend to have relatively high levels of religious participation, but that is despite their socioeconomic status. Their low levels of education and income could lead to a significant drop in Black Protestantism in the future.

When using data from the General Social Survey that just focused on Black respondents this comes into clearer view—as can be seen in Figure 5.11. In early waves of the General Social Survey, nearly 90% of all Black respondents said that they were Protestants. But that began to decline slowly around the mid-1980s. By 2000, the share of Black respondents who were Protestant dropped to just about 75%. By 2014, it had declined another ten

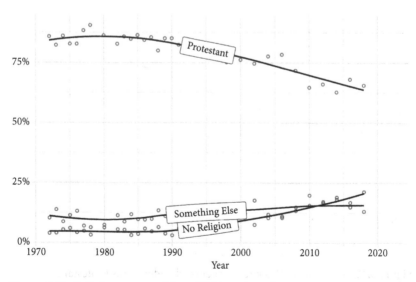

Figure 5.11 Religious composition of African Americans
Data: General Social Survey

percentage points. Currently, just three in five Black Americans identify as Protestant.

While the Protestant line was curving downward, the "no religion" and the "something else" lines began to creep up. From the 1970s through the late 2000s, the share of Black respondents who were Catholic, Muslim, or some other religious tradition hung around 10% and slowly crept above 15%. The share of Black Americans who indicated no religious tradition was very low—less than 5% in many samples. It didn't start to edge up until the early 1990s, reaching around 12% around 2006. By 2010, the lines for "something else" and "no religion" finally crossed. In the most recent data, about 23% of Black respondents reported no religion, clearly more than the share who were in the "something else" category.

There are even more warning signs for the future of Black Protestantism when looking at data from the Cooperative Election Study. Again, restricting the sample to just Black respondents, Figure 5.12 visualizes the share who identify as Protestant based on their age when they took part in the survey. This trend line may prove to be the strongest piece of evidence that Black Protestantism is in serious trouble in the near future.

Protestantism dominates among the oldest Black respondents, with nearly three-quarters of those in their seventies reporting being Protestant.

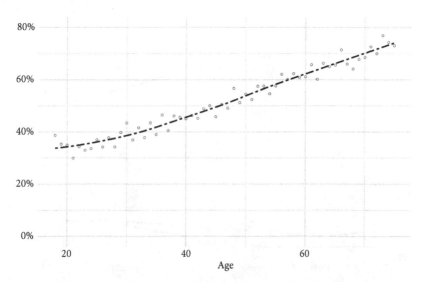

Figure 5.12 The share of Black respondents who identify as Protestant
Data: Cooperative Election Study

However, this share decreases among younger groups. Only 62% of African Americans aged sixty identify as Protestant, and the trend drops below 50% for those in their early forties. Among those aged thirty, only 38% identify as Protestant, and for the youngest adults, it's about a third. The over forty percentage point drop from the oldest to the youngest is staggering, signaling a significant future decline in Black Protestant affiliation.

Conclusion

The Black Protestant tradition is one of the most unique religious groups in the United States. In some ways, they hold views that are closely aligned with some of the most religiously engaged and politically active traditions in the United States. Their view of the Bible, high frequency of prayer, and responses to questions about religious importance make that clear. But while they look like evangelicals on those metrics, their history makes them much more likely to be politically aligned with the Democrats on election day. In each presidential election, it's hard to find a religious group that is more unified than Black Protestants behind the Democratic candidate.

Black Protestants exemplify the limitations of viewing religious groups solely through a theological lens. This book will explore how religion intertwines with race, age, gender, region, immigrant status, and political orientation. Black Protestantism in the United States has evolved through significant historical events, including the Emancipation Proclamation, Reconstruction, Jim Crow laws, the civil rights movement, and the election of the first Black president. Throughout these periods, the Black Church adapted to changing realities, maintaining religious convictions, serving their communities, and welcoming new members.

In an American religious landscape that is quickly polarizing with very conservative, highly religious people on the right side of the spectrum and very liberal, typically nonreligious voters on the other side—Black Protestants find themselves firmly in neither camp. While they are highly religious, they are also active participants in Democratic causes. With increasing political polarization and a dramatic uptick in secularization, the pressure on the Black Church to choose a side only increases with each passing year.

Notes

1. Brian Steensland, Lynn D. Robinson, W. Bradford Wilcox, Jerry Z. Park, Mark D. Regnerus, and Robert D. Woodberry. 2000. "The Measure of American Religion: Toward Improving the State of the Art." *Social Forces* 79, no. 1: 291–318.
2. James T. Campbell. 1995. *Songs of Zion: The African Methodist Episcopal Church in the United States and South Africa.* New York: Oxford University Press, 65, 104.
3. James T. Campbell. 1995. *Songs of Zion: The African Methodist Episcopal Church in the United States and South Africa.* New York: Oxford University Press, 32.
4. Rick Perlstein. 2012. "Exclusive: Lee Atwater's Infamous 1981 Interview on the Southern Strategy." *The Nation.* https://www.thenation.com/article/archive/exclusive-lee-atwaters-infamous-1981-interview-southern-strategy/.
5. Ryan Burge. 2023. "Let's Have a Talk about Education and Religious Attendance." *Graphs about Religion.* https://www.graphsaboutreligion.com/p/lets-have-a-talk-about-education.
6. Ryan Burge. 2023. "Religion Has Become a Luxury Good." *Graphs about Religion.* https://www.graphsaboutreligion.com/p/religion-has-become-a-luxury-good.

Data References

Davern, Michael, Rene Bautista, Jeremy Freese, Pamela Herd, and Stephen L. Morgan. 2023. General Social Survey 1972–2022. Principal investigator, Michael Davern; Co-principal investigators, Rene Bautista, Jeremy Freese, Pamela Herd, and Stephen L. Morgan. Sponsored by National Science Foundation. NORC ed. Chicago: NORC at the University of Chicago. https://gssdataexplorer.norc.org/.

Grammich, Clifford, Kirk Hadaway, Richard Houseal, Dale E. Jones, Alexei Krindatch, Richie Stanley, and Richard H. Taylor. 2023. 2020 U.S. Religion Census: Religious Congregations & Membership Study. Association of Statisticians of American Religious Bodies. https://www.usreligioncensus.org/node/1639.

Schaffner, Brian, Stephen Ansolabehere, Sam Luks, Shiro Kuriwaki, and Marissa Shih. 2006-2023. Cooperative Election Study Common Content, 2006–2022. Harvard Dataverse. https://cces.gov.harvard.edu/.

6

Orthodox Christians

Many Americans have a general sense that there are two predominant forms of Christianity in the United States: Protestantism and Catholicism. In fact, about half of all Americans identify with one of those two religious families. However, beyond those forms of Christianity, there is another tradition that is much smaller and less understood, the Orthodox Church. While the Catholic Church boasts tens of millions of members across the United States and many Protestant denominations have thousands of churches, the Orthodox Church reports several hundred thousand members and a few hundred churches. Yet a deeper dive into the data surrounding this tradition reveals some indicators that point toward a possibly growing faith, while other flavors of Christianity are on the decline.

The Orthodox Church traces its history back to the earliest Christians who are described in the pages of the New Testament, specifically in the Acts of the Apostles. However, over the next several centuries, a number of divisions began to emerge in the rapidly growing Christianity community. As early Church leaders wrestled with what beliefs would be considered orthodox and which ones would be seen as heretical, there were also divisions emerging among Christians based on culture and language.

Throughout the first thousand years of Christianity, several councils were convened to decide the official canon of the Christian scriptures and hash out the core theological beliefs of their rapidly growing faith tradition. However, these councils were not successful in truly uniting the disparate forms of Christianity that were appearing throughout the Western world. These conflicts came to a head in 1054 with the East-West Schism over the issue of papal supremacy. Many churches in the East grew wary of how the papal office had consolidated power, and there was growing discontent in the selection of popes who had largely ignored potential church leaders in the East.

Indeed, the Great Schism was influenced by a complex web of factors beyond just leadership disputes, with cultural differences playing a significant role. Language was a particularly contentious issue that highlighted

The American Religious Landscape. Ryan P. Burge, Oxford University Press. © Oxford University Press 2025.
DOI: 10.1093/oso/9780197762837.003.0007

90 THE AMERICAN RELIGIOUS LANDSCAPE

and exacerbated the divide between the Eastern and Western Churches. Churches in the West had moved primarily to Latin as the language of religious worship, while churches in the East were largely using Greek. After trying to hold together disparate traditions for centuries, the Great Schism allowed those churches in the East to establish their own leadership structure without a pope and unite around a shared culture.[1] It is notable that even today, the official name of this tradition is the Orthodox Catholic Church.

If one were to participate in a worship service in a Catholic Church followed by a visit to an Orthodox Church, there would be many similarities between the two gatherings. Those leading the event wear special vestments like robes and stoles, and the congregation sings hymns, recites a creed, and engages in corporate prayer. There is a short sermon (called a homily) and then Communion is received. There are differences, however. The Orthodox worship space is typically adorned with iconography of religious events and individuals, while the Catholic space focuses more on statues and stained glass to convey these stories. Additionally, while Catholic priests cannot marry, there is no such prohibition in the Orthodox tradition. Catholics cannot fully participate in communion in an Orthodox Church and the reciprocal is true during Catholic Mass.

Today, the Orthodox Church reports a worldwide membership of over 250 million in dozens of countries all over the globe.[2] There are large contingents of Orthodox Christians in countries like Greece and Russia, along with many former Soviet bloc countries like Belarus, Serbia, Bulgaria, and Moldova. Additionally, there are pockets of Orthodox Christians in other parts of Europe, such as Germany and Spain. The Coptic Orthodox Church is based in Egypt but also has a significant membership in Africa and throughout the Middle East. And, as this chapter will describe, there is also a vibrant community of Orthodox Christians in the United States.

How Many Americans Are Orthodox Christians?

A common theme throughout this volume is the difficulty in measuring religion. There's no "gold standard" that will allow a researcher total accuracy in this endeavor. Instead, we have several avenues to arrive at a census of a religious tradition, none of which are ideal. When considered in concert, they can provide a general sense of the size and scope of a group. That's most certainly the case when it comes to the Orthodox Church. One primary issue when studying a group like this is its relatively small size. That means that it's a group that doesn't show up in large numbers on surveys. There are also several branches inside orthodoxy (Greek, Russian, Coptic, etc.) that make data collection about membership rolls problematic, as well. Thus, the numbers here are the best guesses available, given the aforementioned methodological hurdles.

One of the best estimates of the size of the Orthodox Church in the United States comes from Alexei Krindatch, who served as the national coordinator for the Census of Orthodox Churches in 2020.[3] In this research, twenty-three branches of Orthodox Christianity are identified, and each reached a request for information about the number of churches, members, and regular attendees in their tradition. This process was also employed in 2010, which means that researchers can track the growth or decline of the Orthodox tradition in the United States over the prior decade.

This Religion Census indicates in Figure 6.1 that American Orthodox Christianity has experienced a significant decline in recent years. There were about 817,000 Orthodox Christians in the United States in 2010. However, in the most recent census, those numbers have declined to 676,000. That's a percentage drop of just slightly more than 17% in the prior decade. The largest type of Orthodox Christianity is easily the Greek Orthodox Church with about 376,000 members or 56% of all Orthodox Christians. For comparison, the Orthodox Church in the United States is just a bit smaller than

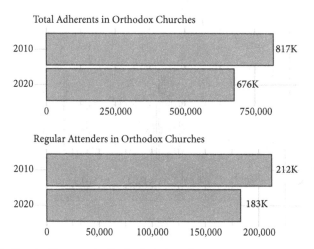

Figure 6.1 Total adherents in Orthodox churches
Regular attendees in Orthodox churches

the United Church of Christ Protestant denomination, which reported about 773,000 members in 2021.

The Religion Census also asked clergy to respond to the following question: "Approximately how many persons—including both adults and children—attend liturgy in our parish on a typical (not festive) Sunday?" The total number of regular attendees in Orthodox Christianity was just a bit over 212,000 in 2010. In 2020, the number declined to 183,000. In percentage terms that decline is 13.7%, about three percentage points less than the overall membership decline. That means on an average weekend in the United States about 1 in 2,000 Americans attend an Orthodox worship service.

Does the survey data corroborate the membership census? As can be seen in Figure 6.2, not really. In 2008, about 0.4% of the sample of the Cooperative Election Study were Orthodox Christians. The overall trend for the next fourteen years is one of small, but noticeable increases. By 2016, it's clear that Orthodox Christianity began a slight upward trend. In the last few years of the Cooperative Election Study, the Orthodox share has settled around 0.7%. It seems reasonable to assume that there's been a very slight increase in self-identified Orthodox Americans, maybe a jump of one-quarter of a percentage point.

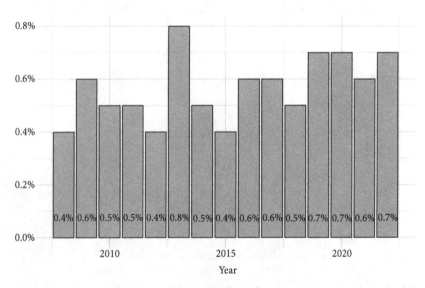

Figure 6.2 Share of the respondents who identify as Eastern or Greek Orthodox
Data: Cooperative Election Study

Why the disconnect between the data from the Religion Census and what appears in random sample surveys? It's hard to know for certain. One possibility is that the Orthodox Church has made a meaningful effort to purge its membership rolls of those who haven't attended in a long period of time. However, that wouldn't explain why the survey data indicate an increase. It's possible that a number of new converts to Orthodoxy, or just younger members of the church, are appearing on surveys now. There's some reason to think that's the case, as will be described later on in this chapter.

It's hard to look at these data points and come to a firm conclusion about the trajectory of Orthodox Christianity. It may be growing, or it may have suffered some pretty consequential declines in the last ten years. However, what's undoubtedly true is that it is a fairly small tradition in the American religious landscape. The number of active Orthodox Christians can be counted in the hundreds of thousands, certainly not the millions. Additionally, it seems highly unlikely that the total number of adherents is much higher than a million nationwide. However, that's not to say that the trajectory and size of the Orthodox tradition will not change in the future.

Where Are Orthodox Christians?

Having established that Orthodox Christianity is a relatively small segment of the American religious landscape, we now turn to where those Orthodox congregations are geographically located in the United States, displayed in Figure 6.3. These data come from the Religion Census and encompasses the twenty-three different types of Orthodox Christianity that were measured as part of that data collection effort. The metric here is simply whether a county has any type of Orthodox congregation.

Figure 6.3 visualizes the fact that seven hundred counties in the United States have an Orthodox congregation. The state with the highest number of counties with an Orthodox church is Pennsylvania with forty-seven out of sixty-seven total counties. Typically, the states with the highest overall populations are also the most likely to have several Orthodox churches: California, Texas, New York, Virginia, and Florida. A quick glance at the map also makes it clear that Orthodox Christianity can best be described as coastal. In fact, Orthodoxy looks similar to other smaller religious traditions like Judaism and Islam.

94   THE AMERICAN RELIGIOUS LANDSCAPE

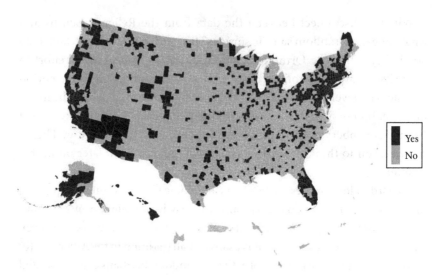

Figure 6.3 Counties that have an Orthodox congregation
Data: Religion Census

That's not to say that there are no Orthodox congregations in other parts of the United States, however. There are pockets to be found in places around Chicago, Detroit, and Denver. But, again, the concentrations of these churches are generally anchored in densely populated areas. It's rare to find an Orthodox church in a truly rural part of the country. For instance, there are only five counties with an Orthodox church in the entire state of Nebraska and just six in Kentucky. Thus, it's fair to say that significant portions of rural Americans do not encounter Orthodox Christianity on a regular basis.

However, there are very few counties in the United States where Orthodox Christians make up a significant share of the local population. In the 2020 Religion Census, there are only forty-nine counties where they make up at least 1% of the total county's population and just ten counties where they are 2% or more. Thus, while Orthodoxy may be found in hundreds of counties across the country, it certainly is not the dominant religion in any of them. In fact, determining which counties have the highest concentrations of Orthodoxy is instructive.

Figure 6.4 shows that eight out of the ten counties with the largest Orthodox Christian populations are located in Alaska. For instance, Lake and Peninsula Borough, which encompasses the archipelago that extends south from the state, is 45% Orthodox Christian, but the total population of this area is less than 1,500 residents. The Dillingham Census area is 24%

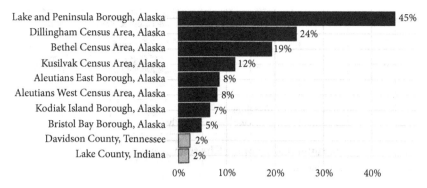

Figure 6.4 Counties with the highest concentration of Orthodox Christians
Data: Religion Census

Orthodox, but its population is slightly less than 5,000. The Orthodox Church has a significant foothold in Russia, and it logically follows that many of those living in Alaska can trace their ancestry back to that country. The only two counties in the top ten that are not in the state of Alaska are Davidson County, Tennessee (Nashville) and Lake County, Indiana (which encompasses the far eastern suburbs of Chicago).

Overall Religiosity of Orthodox Christians

One interesting aspect of Orthodox Christians' religious behavior is the total length of the worship service. While the average Protestant or Catholic gathering lasts about an hour, a typical Divine Liturgy lasts 90–120 minutes, while the gathering on a religious holiday like Easter or Christmas can stretch to three hours in length. Thus, regular attendance for an Orthodox Christian requires a significant time commitment compared to other Christian traditions. However, despite this difference, Orthodox Christians report a relatively high level of church attendance, as can be seen in Figure 6.5.

According to data collected between 2020 and 2022, 44% of Protestants indicate that they attend services each week and another 24% report monthly or yearly attendance. That 68% share is similar to Orthodox Christians. However, it's important to note that only 34% of Orthodox Christians report weekly attendance, a full ten points lower than their Protestant counterparts. It's also worth pointing out that self-reported religious attendance among Orthodox Christians is noticeably higher than Catholics.

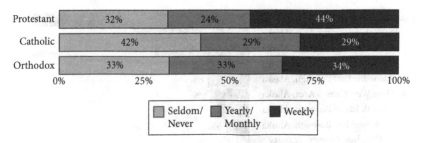

Figure 6.5 Church attendance among Christian groups
Data: Cooperative Election Study

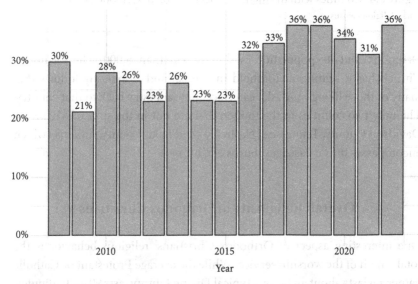

Figure 6.6 Share of Orthodox Christians attending church weekly
Data: Cooperative Election Study

Just 29% of Catholics are weekly attenders, while 42% attend less than once a year. Only a third of Protestants and Orthodox Christians are seldom or never attenders.

Another interesting trend in relation to Orthodox Christians is that their overall level of religious attendance has risen in the last several years. About ten years ago, the overall impression from the data was that about a quarter of Orthodox Christians were attending the Divine Liturgy each week. That has certainly crept up since 2016. In the last six to eight years, the self-reported attendance of Orthodox Christians has ticked up to around 35%, as noted in Figure 6.6. In a time of increasing secularization and the overall emptying of

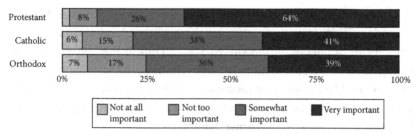

Figure 6.7 How important is religion to you?
Data: Cooperative Election Study

the pews, it's noteworthy that Orthodox Christians are bucking that trend and attending services more often.

As previously mentioned, the Orthodox worship service is quite a bit longer than a gathering in the Catholic or Protestant tradition. While some may see this as an impediment; among those who study religion, there is a sense that some people crave a religious tradition that is difficult to follow. An Easter gathering that lasts three hours and includes extended periods of standing and kneeling is physically and spiritually taxing. The fact that Orthodox Christianity requires such a significant commitment means that it clearly stands in opposition to the larger culture. The distinct separation that some individuals seek may be a factor in the increased frequency of Orthodox attendance. New converts, in particular, may find joy and fulfillment in engaging in extended hours of worship each Sunday.

On the issue of worship attendance, Orthodox Christians are clearly more religiously active than Catholics, but when it comes to religious importance, that gap disappears. In Figure 6.7, Protestants are the most likely to place a great deal of importance on their faith (64%), but that's not the case with Catholics (41%) or Orthodox Christians (39%). It's a seeming contradiction in the data that does not point toward an easy explanation. From this angle, it appears that Orthodox Christians have a more cultural understanding of their faith which is akin to Catholics, while Protestantism seems to be less about an ethnic identity and more about an affirmative commitment to a religious tradition.

Immigration and Race among Orthodox Christians

The Orthodox Church in the United States is obviously one that is based largely on immigration. That becomes clear by merely looking at the names of some of the largest branches of Orthodoxy (Greek, Russian, Coptic). Orthodox Christianity has a stronger tie to geographical areas than most other forms of religion in the United States. Thus, it logically follows that immigration is an essential thread that runs through the American Orthodox community. The Cooperative Election Study asks respondents if they themselves have immigrated to the United States or if their parents or grandparents had been the first to arrive on American shores.

The results in Figure 6.8 make it clear that Orthodox Christians in the United States are much more likely to come from an immigrant background than the general public. In this data, 27% of all Orthodox Christians immigrated to the United States themselves, compared to just 9% of the general public. Additionally, another 27% of Orthodox Christians report that their parents had immigrated to the United States,

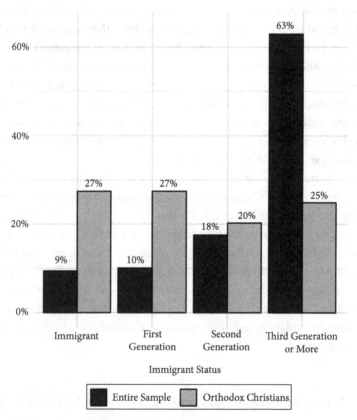

Figure 6.8 Immigrant status of Orthodox Christians
Data: Cooperative Election Study

while they were born in the United States. This is nearly three times higher than the general public. Broadly speaking, over half (54%) of Orthodox Christians are immigrants or are the children of immigrants. Just one-quarter of Orthodox Christians have been in the United States for three generations or more, compared to 63% of all respondents to the Cooperative Election Study.

However, what sets the Orthodox community apart from other religious traditions that have a high level of immigration (Catholics, Hindus, Muslims, Buddhists) is that Orthodox Christians tend to immigrate to the United States from European countries. In this data, displayed in Figure 6.9, 76% of all Orthodox Christians in the United States are white, which is a significantly higher percentage than the country as a whole (69%). It's also

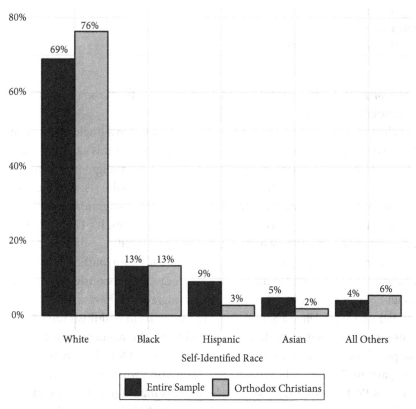

Figure 6.9 Racial composition of Orthodox Christians
Data: Cooperative Election Study

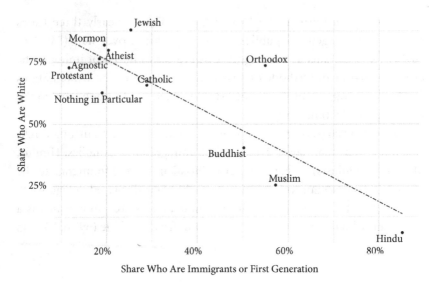

Figure 6.10 Relationship between immigration and race among religious groups
Data: Cooperative Election Study

noteworthy that very few Orthodox Christians identify as Hispanic—just 3% compared to 9% of the total population.

When visualizing both race and immigration status in a single graph, as in Figure 6.10, it becomes easier to see the connections. In this case, the share of each tradition that are immigrants or children of immigrants are on the x-axis, and the share of each tradition that is white is on the y-axis. Note first, how many traditions have very small percentages of immigrants. Just 10% of Protestants are immigrants or are children of immigrants. It's 17% of Latter-day Saints and 16%–18% of nonreligious groups, as well.

This visualization makes it clear how much of an outlier Orthodox Christians are compared to other religious groups. As previously mentioned, about 55% of Orthodox Christians are immigrants or have a parent who immigrated to the United States. That's fairly similar to Buddhists (50%) and Muslims (57%). But in both of those traditions, the majority of members are people of color. Just 40% of Buddhists and 25% of Muslims are white. In comparison, 74% of Orthodox Christians are white, which is nearly the same share as Protestant Christians and slightly less than Agnostics. The immigration patterns of Orthodox Christianity are truly unique in the American religious context.

Future Growth for Orthodox Christianity?

Despite the fact that the Orthodox Church is fairly small in the United States and that its overall membership numbers have diminished fairly significantly over the last decade, there are some signs in the data that the Orthodox Church may be on an upward trajectory in the next several decades. That can clearly be seen in Figure 6.11 by looking through the lens of age. If a religious group has lots of older individuals and very few young members, it's very likely that this will end in a long-term decline.

The overall American adult population has aged about three and a half years between 2008 and 2022. In 2008, the average adult was just about forty-five years old. In 2022, that had risen to forty-eight and a half. The overall aging of the American population is one of the key macro-level trends facing the United States as the Baby Boomers move into retirement and are not being replaced by large numbers of young people moving into adulthood. For Orthodox Christians, the trend line is totally flat. In 2008, the average age was just about forty-two years old, and in 2022 that had increased to forty-two and a half years of age, an increase that is not statistically significant.

That age advantage comes into sharper focus when looking at just the share of each tradition that is between the ages of eighteen and forty-five

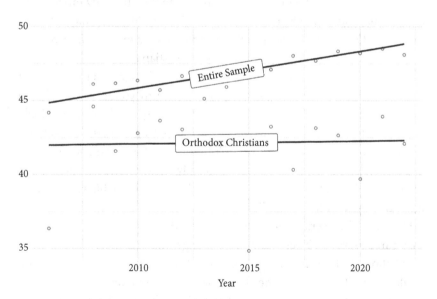

Figure 6.11 Average age of Orthodox Christians
Data: Cooperative Election Study

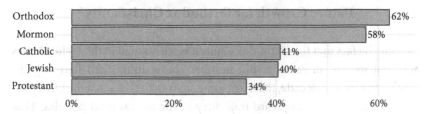

Figure 6.12 Share who are eighteen to forty-five years old
Data: Cooperative Election Study

years old, displayed in Figure 6.12. This age group is in their prime childbearing years, which is crucial when trying to pass a religious tradition down to the next generation. If a religious group is primarily people in their fifties or above, there's little chance of perpetuating the tradition by generational replacement; instead, conversion is the only way to maintain their number or grow. Trying to win people over to your faith tradition is a tough proposition in an increasingly secularizing climate.

Fortunately for Orthodox Christianity, there are large numbers of adherents who are still able to have a child. Sixty-two percent of Orthodox Christians are between eighteen and forty-five—that's easily the highest among other majority-white religious groups. In fact, the only other group where a majority of adults have not seen their forty-fifth birthday is Latter-day Saints. Only about 40% of Catholics and Jews are in peak child-bearing years. It's just about one-third of Protestant Christians.

What's even more encouraging for Orthodox Christians is that the most religiously engaged members also happen to be fairly young, as can be seen in Figure 6.13. For Protestant Christians, the average age is obviously high, as previously discussed. The average never-attending Protestant is fifty-six years old, compared to a mean age of fifty-four for those who attend church weekly. Catholics are a bit younger, but only by a few years. The average never-attending Catholic is fifty-two years old, which is no different than the age of weekly attending Catholics.

However, the average age of weekly attending Orthodox Christians is forty-three years old. That's eight years younger than the most religiously active Catholic and eleven years younger than the weekly attending Protestant. While other Christian churches have a large share of attendees who are far past middle age, that's certainly not the case in Orthodox Christianity. While this age trend did not pay dividends between 2010 and 2020, it's likely that

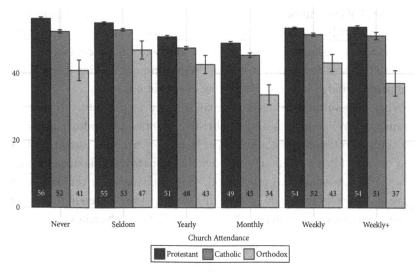

Figure 6.13 Average age by church attendance
Data: Cooperative Election Study

membership could rise in the next decade, given that so many Orthodox Christians are of child-bearing age.

Conclusion

The Orthodox Church in the United States is one that is truly unique. It's obviously much smaller than its Protestant or Catholic cousins, at less than a million members, but its overall composition stands in opposition to other religious traditions. It's notable that over half of all Orthodox Christians are immigrants themselves or are the first generation to live in the United States. However, most of the Orthodox Christian immigrants come from places like Europe, while the overall immigrant population to the United States comes from other parts of the world.

Orthodox Christianity has reported some significant short-term declines in membership, but given their overall age demographics, it seems realistic to assume that the overall Orthodox community will increase in size as those young families have children. However, the issue of retention will be key as those young people who were raised in the church move into adulthood. One aspect of the Orthodox experience that may drive up retention

104 THE AMERICAN RELIGIOUS LANDSCAPE

is the level of commitment it takes to be a member of that faith community. Recall that Orthodox religious gatherings can sometimes last two to three hours and often include a community meal after worship has concluded. The gatherings foster deep ties to others in the community, making it less likely that people will fall away from their religious tradition.

What may sustain the Orthodox community in the future is its true uniqueness. While maintaining a Christian identity, Orthodox Christians are neither Protestant nor Catholic. The beauty of Orthodox worship spaces that are often filled with colorful and detailed icons from Bible stories alongside the liturgy, which has remained largely unchanged for centuries, can serve as a draw for those who are looking for something different than what they grew accustomed to in their Protestant or Catholic churches.

Notes

1. Henry Chadwick. 2003. *East and West: The Making of a Rift in the Church: From Apostolic Times until the Council of Florence.* Oxford: Oxford University Press.
2. Greek Orthodox Archdiocese of America. 2023. "About the Greek Orthodox Archdiocese of America/Greek Orthodox Archdiocese of America/Orthodox Church." Greek Orthodox Archdiocese of America. https://www.goarch.org/about; Pew Research Center. 2017. "Orthodox Christianity in the 21st Century." https://www.pewresearch.org/religion/2017/11/08/orthodox-christianity-in-the-21st-century/.
3. Alexei Krindatch. N.d. "The Greek Orthodox Archdiocese of America (GOA) from 2010 to 2020: Changes in Parishes, Membership, and Worship Attendance." *Orthodox Reality.* https://orthodoxreality.org/wp-content/uploads/2021/09/Report-GOA-From2010To2020Reduced1-1.pdf.

Data References

Grammich, Clifford, Kirk Hadaway, Richard Houseal, Dale E. Jones, Alexei Krindatch, Richie Stanley, and Richard H. Taylor. 2023. 2020 U.S. Religion Census: Religious Congregations & Membership Study. Association of Statisticians of American Religious Bodies. https://www.usreligioncensus.org/node/1639.

Schaffner, Brian, Stephen Ansolabehere, Sam Luks, Shiro Kuriwaki, and Marissa Shih. 2006-2023. Cooperative Election Study Common Content, 2006–2022. Harvard Dataverse. https://cces.gov.harvard.edu/.

7

Catholics

One of the true religion success stories in the United States is the ascendancy of the Catholic Church. It's easy to forget that there was a tremendous amount of animus toward followers of the Catholic faith for a significant portion of American history. In 1700, New York passed a law that barred Catholic priests from entering the colony.[1] It was enforced only once, when John Ury was falsely accused of being a Catholic priest, tried, and sent to the gallows in 1741.[2] The law that ended Ury's life was only repealed in 1784.[3] Thus, Catholics were slow to come to American shores, unsure of what fate would befall them as they stepped foot into the New World.

Thus, Catholicism only played a minor role in American religious history during this period. There were fifty-five signers of the Declaration of Independence in August 1776. Just one of them, Charles Carroll, identified as a Roman Catholic.[4] By 1790, there were only 35,000 Catholics in a country of 4 million people—less than 1% of the population.[5] During the nineteenth and twentieth centuries, many Catholic families decided to remove their children from the local public schools, fearing that they would be indoctrinated by the Protestant school teachers and administrators. This rise in parochial schools was met by Protestant opposition, which culminated in the attempted passage of a Constitutional amendment that would have banned direct government aid from going to religious schools. Proponents for the so-called Blaine Amendment often used anti-Catholic rhetoric to drum up support, but the amendment stalled out in the U.S. Senate after easily passing the House of Representatives and never became law. However, despite its failure at the federal level, thirty-seven states have passed their own version of the Blaine Amendment.[6]

Yet, despite all the opposition to the Catholic Church among Protestants in the early part of American history, the Church has continued to grow in strength and influence. Today, there are over 60 million Catholics spread across every region of the United States, and they make up at least 20% of the U.S. population.[7] It is rare to find a county where there is not a Catholic

The American Religious Landscape. Ryan P. Burge, Oxford University Press. © Oxford University Press 2025.
DOI: 10.1093/oso/9780197762837.003.0008

106 THE AMERICAN RELIGIOUS LANDSCAPE

parish; and thousands of charities, schools, and hospitals are maintained by Catholic dioceses across the United States.

However, in recent years, the Catholic Church has been rocked by a sexual abuse scandal that was first revealed by a series of articles published in the *Boston Globe* in 2002.[8] These reports detailed a series of actions taken by the Roman Catholic Church to cover up sexual abuse that was occurring at the hands of priests in parishes around Boston. Subsequent reporting has further substantiated instances of sexual abuse of children by priests across the United States and the world.[9]

The story of American Catholicism over the last fifty years is one that can best be described as remarkable stability. While the General Social Survey shows that the nonreligious have grown by a factor of six since 1972, and evangelicals have vacillated between 17% and 30% of the American population in the last fifty years, the Catholics' share of the population has been unequivocally steady. In the early 1970s, about 26% of American adults identified as Catholic. By 1990, the number was unchanged. In the next decade, the share of Catholics may have dropped by a single percentage point and stayed at 25% all the way through 2010. Given all the turmoil and change in American religion and the constant drumbeat of stories about abusive priests in the Catholic Church, it's remarkable that between 1972 and 2010, the Catholic Church did not materially change in size.

However, more recent data point to a clear decline, as seen in Figure 7.1. By 2016, the trend line was pointing downward, but only slightly. However, the data collected in 2018 and 2021 both signal a clear conclusion: there are clearly cracks forming in the Catholic foundation. The 2021 General Social Survey puts the number of American Catholics at 21%, a figure that is lower than any other year that the Survey was conducted. Thus, it's fair to say that American Catholicism is declining, but how far and how fast that will occur remains to be seen.

Despite this recent decline in overall population share, it is important to put the size and scope of the Catholic Church in a larger context. According to data from the 2020 Religion Census, contained in Figure 7.2, there are nearly 62 million Americans who are on the membership rolls of Catholic Churches across the United States. This number is orders of magnitude larger than any other religious group. For instance, the Religion Census reports that the second largest religious group is nondenominational Protestants, with just over 21 million members—about one-third the size of the Catholic

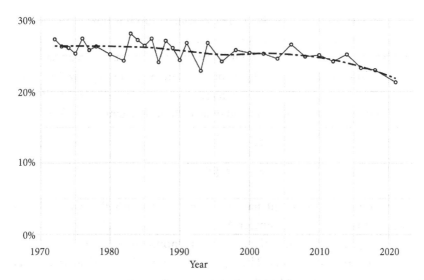

Figure 7.1 Share of Americans who identify as Catholic
Data: General Social Survey

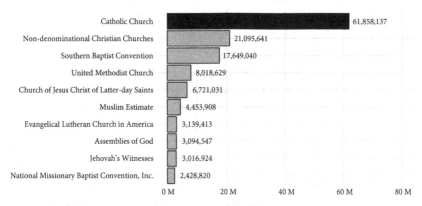

Figure 7.2 The ten largest religious groups in the United States by adherents
Data: Religious Census

Church. In fact, there are more American Catholics than the next five religious denominations in the United States combined.

The primary reason for this huge disparity between the Catholic Church and these Protestant denominations is the incredible amount of fragmentation inside American Protestant Christianity. Of the ten largest religious groups in the United States, seven of them are Protestant denominations.

108   THE AMERICAN RELIGIOUS LANDSCAPE

One of the truly unique facets of the Catholic Church is how unified it has remained. In the United States, Protestants have dozens (if not hundreds) of options within a short drive of their home. For Catholics, they may have different parishes, but they are all part of the same religious organization. The fact that the Catholic Church has managed to stay organizationally unified in a time of increasing atomization and polarization is a tremendous feat.

Age

One of the most important narratives that undergirds the American religious landscape is that younger Americans are less likely to be affiliated with a religious tradition as the ranks of the nonreligious continue to swell among the youngest adults. The rise of the nones is an existential threat facing every religious tradition, from Methodists to Muslims. Generational replacement is the primary means by which American religion changes— older Americans, who tend to be more religious, die and are replaced by young people coming of age who are much less religiously inclined. Thus, if a religious tradition needs to understand where it will be in three or four decades, a good barometer is how many young people it has in attendance on an average weekend.

For Catholics, the picture likely looks a bit more optimistic than what many would expect. For instance, among people born around 1950, about 20% of them identify as Roman Catholic, as can be seen in Figure 7.3. For those born in 2000, which denotes people who are currently in their early twenties, about 15% say that they are Catholic. This is a decline, certainly, but a fairly modest one considering the fifty-year gap between 1950 and 2000.

Comparing Catholics to Protestants in Figure 7.3 makes it clear how much worse things can be. Among the oldest Americans, at least 45% say that they are Protestant—about double the rate of Catholics. However, from that point forward, the share of people who align with a Protestant denomination drops noticeably. Only 28% of those born in 1980 identify as Protestant, down from 33% of those born in 1970. The decline is even more pronounced among those born around the year 2000, with only 20% reporting a Protestant affiliation—just five percentage points higher than the Catholic figure.

The implications of these results are worth considering for American Protestants and Catholics. For Protestants, affiliation drops from 47% among those born in 1940 to 20% among those born in 2000. For Catholics,

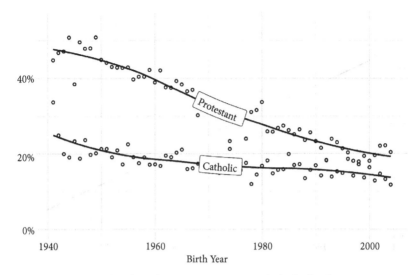

Figure 7.3 Share who identify as Protestant or Catholic by birth year
Data: Cooperative Election Study

the decline is much smaller—about eight percentage points. This indicates that the Catholic Church will experience a decrease because of generational turnover, but this decline will be significantly less pronounced than what is observed in numerous Protestant denominations.

Mass Attendance

While the Catholic Church has benefitted from not having a large age disparity when it comes to affiliation, that is only one metric to understand the future trajectory of any religious tradition. Another essential component is regular worship attendance. Those who gather on a regular basis are more likely to financially support their house of worship and be available to help with other tasks necessary to maintain the facility and the grounds. Having many members with a small percentage regularly attending weekly services could signal concerns for the long-term sustainability of a religious organization.

Catholics clearly stand out on this measure. The General Social Survey has been asking about religious attendance for nearly fifty years. Figure 7.4 illustrates that during the 1970s, Catholics had the highest church attendance

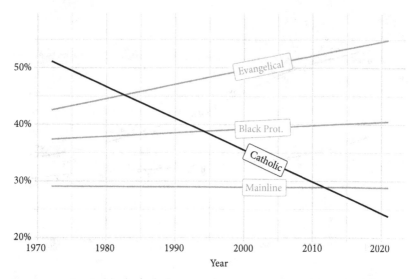

Figure 7.4 Share attending services nearly every week or more
Data: General Social Survey

rates among all religious traditions, with slightly more than 50% indicating they attended services nearly every week or more frequently. Evangelicals were the closest at 42%, while Black Protestants were around 37% and mainline Protestants just below 30%. However, the trajectory of those measures looks vastly different over the last five decades.

For all three types of Protestants, the share who attend nearly every week or more is as high today as it was in the 1970s. Catholics are outliers when it comes to religious attendance. From 1972 to 1992, there was a ten-percentage-point decrease in Mass attendance. This trend continued, with an additional ten-point drop by 2002, and the rate of decline remained consistent through 2012. According to the most recent data, the share of Catholics who attend nearly every week has now dipped below a quarter. Simply stated, a Catholic today is half as likely to attend weekly Mass compared to a Catholic in the 1970s.

The decline in attendance raises the question of its source. If individuals are transitioning from weekly to monthly participation, it's concerning, yet it indicates some ongoing engagement with the Church. These infrequent attenders remain contributors and active in both their religious community and broader societal efforts. However, if these weekly attenders are becoming never attenders in large numbers, it suggests a trajectory where many may

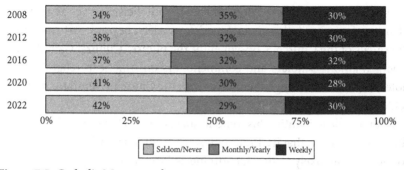

Figure 7.5 Catholic Mass attendance
Data: Cooperative Election Study

disengage from religious practice altogether, signaling a deeper disconnection from the faith community.

In the case of Catholics, the latter is clearly the case, as can be seen in Figure 7.5, using data from the Cooperative Election Study. It's notable that weekly Mass attendance has stayed remarkably consistent between 2008 and 2022 at just around 30%—an estimate that is slightly higher than the percentages reported in the General Social Survey. The biggest shift is among Catholics who describe their attendance as seldom or never. In 2008, that figure was 34%. It rose to 42% by 2022. Thus, it's the middle being squeezed—those who attend monthly or yearly. This percentage dropped from 35% to 29% between 2008 and 2022. In 2008, a Catholic was just as likely to be in the middle category of attendance as in the seldom/never camp. Now, it's much more likely that their Mass attendance is less than once per year.

Cultural Catholicism?

The data surrounding church attendance create an interesting puzzle. Why would religious attendance hold steady among all other Protestant groups but drop so precipitously among Catholics? One potential explanation is that Catholicism holds a different place in American culture than Protestant Christianity. Many Catholics in the United States have strong ethnic ties, such as Irish Catholics in Boston and the Italian Catholic community around New York City and New Jersey. Also, Catholicism is deeply intertwined with the culture of Hispanics who are recent immigrants from countries in Central and South America. Just as Judaism encompasses both an ethnic identity and a religious practice, Catholicism serves as a cultural identifier for many followers in American society, beyond participation in the rituals of the Church. Consequently, the phrase "Cultural Catholic" has emerged among scholars and commentators on American religion to denote individuals who align themselves with the Church's cultural aspects but seldom attend Mass.

Is it possible to identify this trend in survey data? One way to think about this conceptually is that if a Protestant starts to attend very infrequently, they would be more likely to stop identifying as Protestant all together and may choose to be nothing in particular when asked by a survey administrator. For Catholics who are very low attenders, they would be less inclined to jettison their religious affiliation. Thus, if the Cultural Catholicism phenomenon is true, it's reasonable to assume that there is a bigger share of never or seldom attending Catholics compared to Protestants.

The data visualized in Figure 7.6 support that conclusion—the share of Catholics who report very infrequent religious attendance is higher than it is for Protestants. In 2008, 27% of Protestants said that they attended church seldom or never, compared to 34% of Catholics. The gap between Catholics and Protestants goes up and down a little bit but is likely closer to 10% in

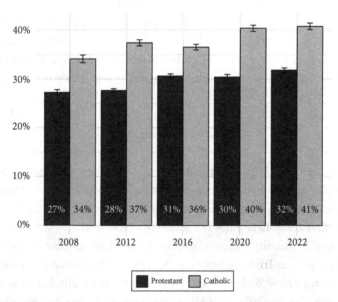

Figure 7.6 Share never or seldom attending church services
Data: Cooperative Election Study

the most recent data. In 2022, 32% of Protestants attended seldom or never, compared to 41% of Catholics. Given that the overall share of Protestants has fallen faster than the share who are Catholics, it makes sense that a lot of those losses for Protestants are the result of low attenders shedding the Protestant label.

There are other ways to use the data to get closer to understanding the phenomenon of Cultural Catholicism, though. For instance, the General Social Survey asks individuals about the religion in which they were raised, and then it asks them about their current religious affiliation. It is an insightful way to understand how movement is occurring across the American religious landscape. If Cultural Catholicism significantly influenced the Church's overall statistics, we would expect the data to reveal that a small number of individuals raised Catholic depart from the Church as they transition into adulthood.

As can be seen in Figure 7.7, among those who indicated that they were raised Catholic, two-thirds are still in the faith tradition. Among those who

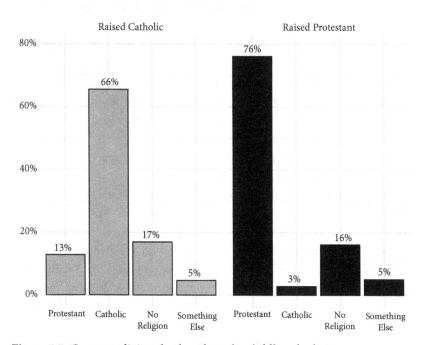

Figure 7.7 Current religious broken down by childhood religion
Data: General Election Study

114 THE AMERICAN RELIGIOUS LANDSCAPE

left, they are fairly evenly split between becoming Protestant (13%) and those choosing no religion at all (17%). Protestants are a much different story, however. Over three-quarters maintain the religious tradition of their youth—ten points higher than Catholics. Among those Protestants who leave, the majority abandon religion all together, while just a small number become Catholic (3%).

If the Cultural Catholic hypothesis were true, the data should indicate that very few people who were raised Catholic switch to another religious group as adults. But that's not what is happening. Instead, Catholics are noticeably more likely to leave the faith behind compared to Protestants, and when they leave, many of them choose to become a Protestant. In comparison, Protestants seem to have more brand loyalty than Catholics. Thus, the results here are mixed when it comes to Cultural Catholicism. Clearly, a Catholic is more likely to report low service attendance without leaving the identity behind, but those who are raised Catholic are more likely to leave Catholicism compared to Protestants.

Racial Composition of American Catholics

One of the most important trends in the Catholic Church, beyond the previously discussed drop in Mass attendance, is the increasing racial diversity found in American Catholicism over the last several decades. One of the defining characteristics of Catholicism is its truly global reach. Most regions of the world have a strong Catholic presence, and when people from those regions of the world migrate to the United States, they bring their Catholic faith along with them. That is having a tremendous impact on the overall composition of American Catholicism.

In the 1970s, the Catholic Church in the United States was almost entirely white, as can be seen in Figure 7.8. According to the General Social Survey, just a bit over 10% of Catholics said that they were not white in 1972. That share has slowly crept up over the last few decades, however. By 1987, it had reached 15% and ten years later had risen to 20%. By 2010, about a quarter of all Catholics were people of color, and the most recent data put that number around 27%. But how much of that is Hispanic Catholics?

The data from the Cooperative Election Study help provide some more granular detail on the racial composition of Catholics in the United States.

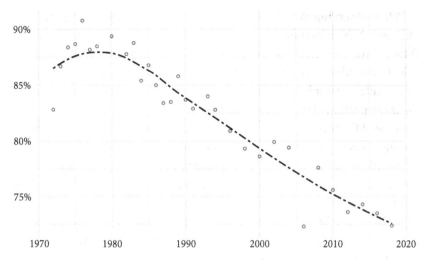

Figure 7.8 Share of Catholics who identify as white
Data: General Social Survey

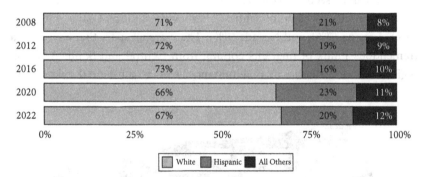

Figure 7.9 The racial composition of Catholics
Data: Cooperative Election Study

The share of Catholics who are white is clearly trending downward at around two-thirds in Figure 7.9. But it's noteworthy that the share of Catholics who are Hispanic has stayed relatively stable at around 20% over the last fourteen years. Where things have shifted is among Black and Asian Catholics. In 2008, 3% of Catholics were Black; that's risen to 6% in more recent data. For Asian Catholics, the increase is from 1.5% to 4%. While it's hard to predict when it will happen, it seems inevitable that the Catholic Church will be less than 50% white at some point in the next fifty years.

When observing the state-level trends in Catholic membership between 2010 and 2020, it becomes clear just how important racial diversity is to the future of the Church in the United States. There are nineteen states that saw a decline in adherence by at least 1% during that decade, and there is an unmistakable geographical pattern displayed in Figure 7.10: they are in the northern portion of the United States.

Some of the biggest declines are in the states that are typically considered synonymous with American Catholicism: Massachusetts is down 9%, Connecticut has experienced a seven-point drop, and New Jersey is down 5%, as well. As previously discussed, these are states that have strong ethnic ties with the Catholic Church, given that those states have large numbers of Italian and Irish Americans. There are other states that have seen dips, but those are much smaller in magnitude. Minnesota and Iowa are down 2% each, while Colorado and California have seen a 1% decline.

It must be pointed out that while Catholicism declined in nineteen states, the change in Catholic share was less than 1% (in either direction) for eighteen states, as can be seen in Figure 7.10. In the thirteen states where Catholicism grew, there are a few commonalities. There were significant gains in Florida (6%), Arizona (7%), and Nevada (8%). These are all states that have seen a tremendous influx of migrants coming from Central and South America, regions where Catholicism is dominant. There is substantial evidence to

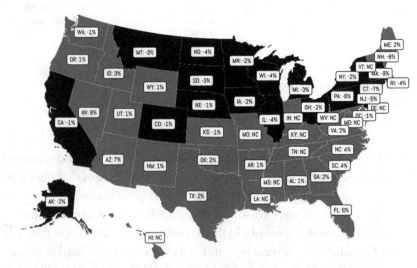

Figure 7.10 Change in share of population that is Catholic, 2020 versus 2010
Data: Religion Census

suggest that the Church is experiencing a decline in regions where White Catholicism predominates while witnessing growth in states with a higher proportion of Hispanic immigrants. Without increasing racial diversity, the Catholic Church would be facing even steeper declines in the United States.

Catholic Beliefs

American religion is dominated by Christian religions, but among the many sects of Christianity, Protestants and Catholics are easily the largest. Both are geographically distributed and racially diverse. The general tenets of their theology are similar. Protestants and Catholics see the Bible as their primary theological document, they believe that Jesus Christ is the savior of the world, and that regular worship gatherings are a necessary part of an active spiritual life. However, Catholics have several theological beliefs that are unique to their faith.

Among the core beliefs is the concept of the magisterium, which posits that Jesus granted the Church the authority to teach and that its leaders are vested with the power to interpret scriptures considering social and cultural developments. The Church's doctrine holds that, under specific conditions, the pope possesses infallibility and serves as the paramount interpreter of scriptures for the Catholic faithful.

However, this viewpoint is not shared by lots of people who identify as Catholic in the United States, as can be seen in Figure 7.11. The General Social Survey has regularly been asking about papal infallibility, and the results indicate how divided Catholics are on this key issue. In an average

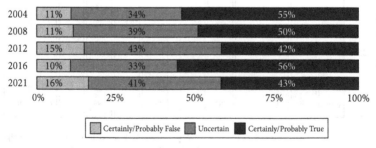

Figure 7.11 Under certain conditions, the pope is infallible when he speaks on matters of faith and morals; among Catholics
Data: General Social Survey

year, about half of Catholics agree with the concept of infallibility, although it does fluctuate a bit from year to year, ranging from a low of 42% in 2012 to a high of 56% in 2016. It's worth pointing out that Benedict XVI was pope during the 2012 survey, while Pope Francis had been installed prior to the 2016 data being collected. Thus, it may be the case that Catholics' view of theological issues is more dependent on the current pope than a bedrock belief in the doctrines of the Church.

Looking at Figure 7.12, there is the distinct possibility that the average Catholic is not completely familiar with many of the theological nuances of the Church, as well. For instance, in a survey conducted in 2019, Catholics were asked to identify the correct description of the term "purgatory." Among those who were infrequent Mass attendees, about a third did not know that it was "where the souls of those who have died undergo purification before they enter heaven." Another question asked about the concept of transubstantiation. Half of Catholics who attended Mass every month did not know that the Catholic Church believes that the bread and wine "actually become the body and blood of Jesus Christ."

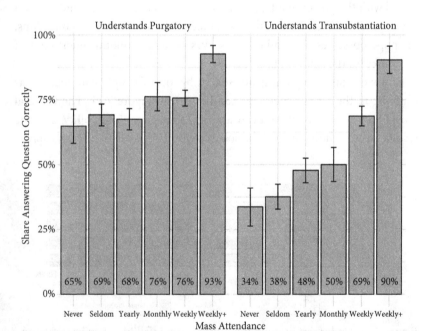

Figure 7.12 How much do Catholics understand Church teachings?
Data: Pew, American Trends Panel 44

Another doctrine that is unique to the Catholic Church surrounds the issue of contraception. An official document from the Vatican states, "The Church has always taught the intrinsic evil of contraception."[10] This stems from the Church's belief that sex is a naturally procreative act and, therefore, anything that impedes the Bible's mandate to "be fruitful and multiply" is prohibited. This doctrine was roundly criticized when it came to how the Church approached the HIV/AIDS crisis on the African continent.[11] While Catholic missionaries were in several countries providing basic needs like food and medicine to those who were suffering from the illness, the official teaching of the Church meant these missionaries could not distribute condoms and instead were told to encourage abstinence among the local population.[12]

As can be seen in Figure 7.13, the average Catholic in the United States does not abide by the teachings of the Catholic Church when it comes to the use of contraceptives. The only means by which a married couple should try and delay children, according to the Vatican, is natural family planning. This

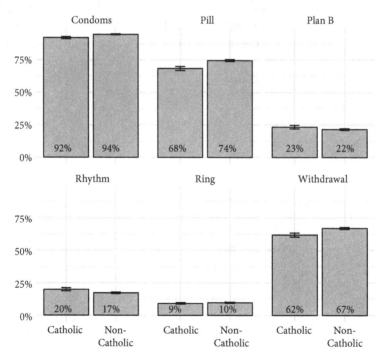

Figure 7.13 Have you ever used the following forms of contraception?
Data: National Survey of Family Growth

approach advises couples to avoid intercourse when fertility is at its peak, but according to data collected by the Centers for Disease Control, just 20% of Catholics have ever used the rhythm method as a form of contraception, which is just three points higher than the non-Catholics.

Conversely, a significant number of Catholics employ reproductive delaying methods that contradict the Church's teachings, at rates comparable to those not affiliated with the Catholic faith. For instance, 92% of Catholics indicate that they have used condoms compared to 94% of non-Catholics, as seen in Figure 7.13. A Catholic is just as likely to have used Plan B to prevent a pregnancy as a non-Catholic. However, the data indicate that Catholics are slightly less likely to use the birth control pill compared to non-Catholics (68% vs. 74%). The overall impression is that the average Catholic takes a similar approach to birth control as non-Catholics, and thus, the majority of Catholics reject the Church's teachings on this matter.

There is some evidence in the data that Catholics' fertility differs little from that of the overall population, as can be seen in Figure 7.14. Between 1972 and the mid-1990s, there was no statistically significant difference in the number of children per Catholic respondent compared to the entire sample. However, that did begin to change in the last twenty years or so. Catholic fertility increased slightly between 1995 and 2010—going from 1.85 children

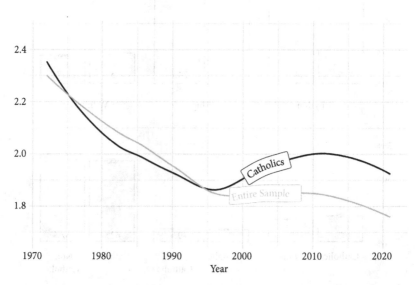

Figure 7.14 How many children have you ever had?
Data: General Social Survey

per respondent to about 2 children. Meanwhile, the fertility rate among the entire sample dropped from 1.85 to 1.75. This could spell good news for the future of the American Catholic Church, but a crucial part of this equation is whether the Church can manage to retain those children born into the faith as they move into adulthood.

Conclusion

The Catholic Church in the United States is, without question, the largest religious denomination in the country. With a membership of 62 million across all fifty states, the Catholic Church, despite experiencing a notable decline in regular Mass attendance, still sees around 15 million Catholics attending services in various parishes throughout the United States. That's more than the population of the fifth largest state in the Union—Pennsylvania.

Yet the Catholic Church is experiencing a tremendous amount of change. The primary shift is in the racial composition of the Church. In the 1970s, nearly all Catholics were white. Historically, the epicenter of the Church's influence was in cities such as Boston, Philadelphia, and New York City, home to substantial Irish and Italian communities with generations of familial ties to some of the country's largest Catholic congregations. Today, one-third of Catholics are non-white, and the only real growth happening in the Church is occurring in states that are experiencing a great deal of immigration from countries in Central and South America. To this point, the Catholic hierarchy has not accurately reflected the shift that is happening in the pews. An embrace of this racial and ethnic diversity will be essential to the growth (or decline) of the Church in the future.

However, there is also a rift in the Catholic Church between the clergy and the laity that has only widened in recent years. The average Catholic is in favor of access to a legal abortion and of allowing same-sex couples to marry.[13] The vast majority of Catholics have used birth control in one form or another in their lives in direct contradiction to the Church's teachings. And, although Pope Francis has closed the door on female priests, most Catholics are in favor of women having access to the priesthood.[14]

These areas of disagreement would have led to the emergence of several new denominations in the world of Protestant Christianity, but the Catholic Church does not have that option. Instead, Catholics have remained unified despite all their internal turmoil. One contributing factor is that numerous

122 THE AMERICAN RELIGIOUS LANDSCAPE

Catholics previously felt they had no alternative. However, with the swift increase in the number of nonreligious individuals, some Catholics might now perceive leaving the Church as their optimal choice. This sentiment could be particularly strong among Hispanic Catholics who feel excluded from the leadership and decision-making processes of the bishops.

Even a casual observer of religion would admit that the Catholic Church has managed to become an indispensable part of American society. They have established thousands of parochial schools in small towns and big cities across the United States. The Catholic Church has built hundreds of hospitals that serve hundreds of millions of patients from a wide variety of faith backgrounds. Some of the finest universities in the United States were established and supported by the Catholic Church for centuries. It seems unlikely that many of these institutions would close if the Catholic Church began to fade, but one must wonder what the United States would look like without the influence of American Catholicism.

Notes

1. Jason K. Duncan. 2005. *Citizens or Papists?: The Politics of Anti-Catholicism in New York, 1685–1821*. 1st ed. New York: Fordham University Press, 15–16, 26–27.
2. Daniel Horsmanden. 1899. *The Trial of John Ury: "for Being an Ecclesiastical Person, Made by Authority Pretended from the See of Rome, and Coming into and Abiding in the Province of New York," and with Being One of the Conspirators in the Negro Plot to Burn the City of New York, 1741*. Philadelphia: M.I.J. Griffin.
3. Duncan, *Citizens or Papists?*, 72–73.
4. Lewis Alexander Leonard. 1918. *Life of Charles Carroll of Carrollton*. New York: Moffat, Yard and Company, 18.
5. Tom Frascella. 2014. "Early U.S. Catholics and Catholic Immigrants 1790–1850." *San Felese Society of New Jersey*. http://www.sanfelesesocietynj.org/History%20Articles/Early_US_Ca tholics_and_immigrants_1790-1850.htm.
6. "Answers to Frequently Asked Questions about Blaine Amendments." 2022. *Institute for Justice*. https://ij.org/issues/school-choice/blaine-amendments/answers-frequently-asked-questions-blaine-amendments/.
7. Clifford Grammich, Kirk Hadaway, Richard Houseal, Dale E. Jones, Alexei Krindatch, Richie Stanley, and Richard H. Taylor. 2023. 2020 U.S. Religion Census: Religious Congregations & Membership Study. Association of Statisticians of American Religious Bodies. https://www.usreligioncensus.org/node/1639.
8. Matt Carroll, Sacha Pfeiffer, Michael Rezendes, and Walter V. Robinson. 2002. "Spotlight: Clergy Sex Abuse Crisis." *The Boston Globe*. https://www3.bostonglobe.com/metro/specials/clergy/
9. David K. Li and Corky Siemaszko. 2023. "Baltimore's Catholic Church Sexually Abused at Least 600 Children over 60 Years, Maryland AG Says." *NBC News*. https://www.nbcnews.com/news/us-news/maryland-ag-documents-widespread-sexual-abuse-least-600-victims-baltim-rcna78378.
10. Pontificium Consilium pro Familia. 1997. *Vademecum for Confessors Concerning Some Aspects of the Morality of Conjugal Life*. Città del Vaticano: Libreria Editrice Vaticana. https://www.vati can.va/roman_curia/pontifical_councils/family/documents/rc_pc_family_doc_12021997_v ademecum_en.html

11. Giuseppe Benagiano, Sabina Carrara, Valentina Filippi, and Ivo Brosens. 2011. "Condoms, HIV and the Roman Catholic Church." *Reproductive BioMedicine Online* 22, no. 7: 701–709.
12. Miller Patricia. 2001. "The Lesser Evil: The Catholic Church and the AIDS Epidemic." *Conscience* 22, no. 3: 6.; Lisa L. Ferrari. 2011. "Catholic and Non-Catholic NGOs Fighting HIV/AIDS in Sub-Saharan Africa: Issue Framing and Collaboration." *International Relations* 25, no. 1: 85–107.
13. Ryan Burge. 2023. "Approval for Same-Sex Marriage Has Stopped Increasing." *Graphs about Religion.* https://www.graphsaboutreligion.com/p/approval-for-same-sex-marriage-has.
14. Ryan Burge. 2017. "Who's Afraid of Female Clergy." *Religion in Public.* https://religioninpublic.blog/2017/10/25/whos-afraid-of-female-clergy/.

Data References

Davern, Michael, Rene Bautista, Jeremy Freese, Pamela Herd, and Stephen L. Morgan. 2023. General Social Survey 1972–2022. Principal investigator, Michael Davern; Co-principal investigators, Rene Bautista, Jeremy Freese, Pamela Herd, and Stephen L. Morgan. Sponsored by National Science Foundation. NORC ed. Chicago: NORC at the University of Chicago. https://gssdataexplorer.norc.org/.

Grammich, Clifford, Kirk Hadaway, Richard Houseal, Dale E. Jones, Alexei Krindatch, Richie Stanley, and Richard H. Taylor. 2023. 2020 U.S. Religion Census: Religious Congregations & Membership Study. Association of Statisticians of American Religious Bodies. https://www.usreligioncensus.org/node/1639.

Schaffner, Brian, Stephen Ansolabehere, Sam Luks, Shiro Kuriwaki, and Marissa Shih. 2006–2023. Cooperative Election Study Common Content, 2006–2022. Harvard Dataverse. https://cces.gov.harvard.edu/.

8

Jews

While the current religious landscape of the United States is dominated by Christian groups, as has been described in previous chapters, there are also other religious groups that have had significant influence on the overall spiritual composition of America. One faith tradition that has had an undeniable influence on the cultural, political, and religious composition of the United States is Judaism. In terms of sheer numbers, Jews make up a larger portion of the population than any other religious group outside of Catholic and Protestant Christianity. This is notable, given their relatively small numbers in the early history of the republic.

According to Hasia Diner, there may have been just about two thousand Jews in the colonies during the Revolutionary period, and Paul Johnson contends that number only reached 15,000 by 1840, with most concentrated in the major population centers around New York City and Boston.[1] However, Jewish immigration would explode in the late 1800s and into the early twentieth century. During this period, almost 3 million Eastern European Jews immigrated to the United States, including half of all those fleeing Russia.[2] In response, Congress passed the Immigration Act of 1924, which severely curtailed the number of Jews who could enter the United States by placing quotas on immigrants from countries with a high concentration of Jewish citizens.[3]

The immigration restrictions put in place in the 1920s would remain throughout World War II, significantly limiting the number of Jews who could escape the Nazi regime. Some estimates indicate that nearly 200,000 additional lives were lost during the Holocaust because of American immigration policy.[4] The quota system that was implemented in 1924 remained in force until 1965 when Congress passed the Immigration and Nationality Act, which prohibited immigration officials from considering race, national origin, or ancestry when making visa decisions, thus ending de facto segregation against Jews trying to enter the United States.[5]

The American Religious Landscape. Ryan P. Burge, Oxford University Press. © Oxford University Press 2025.
DOI: 10.1093/oso/9780197762837.003.0009

The Share of Americans Who Are Jewish

Just a few years later, the General Social Survey began trying to assess the share of American adults who identify as Jewish, displayed in Figure 8.1. In the earliest wave of the survey conducted in 1972, about 3% of all respondents said that their current religion was Judaism. That was clearly the high watermark over the last five decades. In those first three years, estimates of Jews ranged from 2.6% to 3%, but those numbers have not been repeated in any subsequent survey estimate.

It's fair to say that the overall trend of Americans who identify as Jewish has been on a very slow decline since the late 1970s. The point estimates each year typically range between 1.5% and 2.2% of the overall sample. The smoothed average was below 2% through the 1990s and 2000s. However, in the most recent data collection, it's clear that the Jewish share of the population has continued to drop. According to the 2021 General Social Survey, about 1.5% of Americans identify as Jewish.

How does this compare to other survey estimates? The Cooperative Election Study also has been asking about religious affiliation since 2008, and the results from this instrument deviate slightly from the General Social Survey. The consistent results from the Cooperative Election Study are that

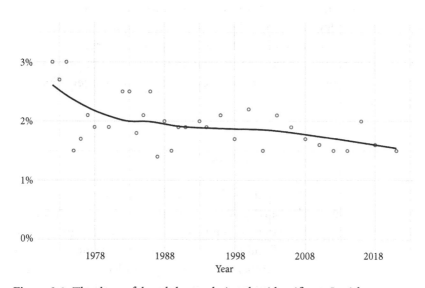

Figure 8.1 The share of the adult population that identifies as Jewish
Data: General Social Survey

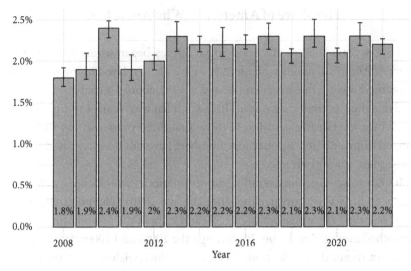

Figure 8.2 The share of the adult population that identifies as Jewish
Data: Cooperative Election Study

just about 2% of adults indicate that they are Jewish, as can be seen in Figure 8.2. That number has not changed in a noticeable way in the last ten years of the survey.

Taken together, it seems appropriate to say that the share of Americans who identify as Jewish is somewhere between 1.5% and 2% of the overall population. For comparison, that's twice as many Jews as there are Latter-day Saints or Muslims in the United States. Given that the total population was about 332 million in 2021, there are likely about 6–7 million Jews living in the United States currently.[6]

Why Are Jews in Decline?

The decline of a religious group can happen for a variety of reasons. One of the primary culprits when a religious group is trending downward is defection. For a religious group to maintain its size or even possibly grow in the future, it must have a significant number of young families who are raising their children to be active members of their faith group. However, a key part of this strategy is that a religion must keep young people in the fold as they move into adulthood. If the share who leaves their childhood faith rises,

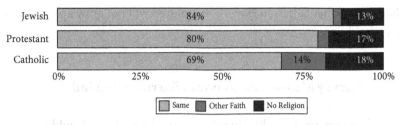

Figure 8.3 Religion as adult based on religion raised in
Data: General Social Survey

then they must be replaced by religious conversion—which is much more difficult.

For American Judaism, this is clearly a concern. The General Social Survey asks individuals about the religion in which they were raised along with their current religion. Figure 8.3 shows data collected since 2010 indicating that Judaism has a relatively high rate of retention with 84% of individuals who were raised Jewish still identifying as a Jew into adulthood. It's noteworthy that among those Jews who change religions, almost all of them become nonreligious.

The Jewish rate of defection has been noticeably lower when compared to both Protestants and Catholics over the last ten years. Only 69% of people raised Catholic were still members of the Church into their adult years. Among those who left, it's interesting that nearly half went to another faith tradition and about the same share reported that they had left religion behind entirely. Protestants look more like Jews on this measure—about 20% defect and almost all of them become religiously unaffiliated.

These data do not seem to point toward defection as the primary cause for the decline, but there are other survey results that do point toward a possible reason—religious intermarriage. According to data from the Pew Research Center—about two-thirds of Jews in their sample were married or living with their partner.[7] Among those who were currently married, 42% said that they had married a non-Jewish spouse, and of those who married a fellow Jew, 93% were raising their children in that faith tradition.[8] For those who married a non-Jew, just 28% indicated that their children were being raised to be a religious Jew and another 29% said that their children would be raised only ethnically Jewish without any of the trappings of the religion.[9] Thus, the data from the General Social Survey may miss this dynamic. While the individual may be raised Jewish and still feel personally

128   THE AMERICAN RELIGIOUS LANDSCAPE

aligned with that faith tradition, their children will not grow up in a Jewish household.

Survey Measurement Issues Surrounding Judaism

One of the primary difficulties in measuring Judaism through public opinion surveys is that it is like no other faith tradition in the world. The scholar Marshall Sklare once wrote:

> Being Jewish involves two complementary aspects: membership in the ethnic group and membership in the religious community. The extent to which the individual exercises his prerogatives by participating in the ethnic group affairs, and particularly in the life of the religious community, is a matter of choice. But no matter to what extent the prerogatives of birth are exercised, all Jews are essentially equal members of the ethnic group and of the religious community.[10]

Thus, for some Jews, their understanding of Judaism is entirely nonreligious. Instead, they understand Judaism to be about culture— holidays, food, and shared history. For other members of the community, Judaism is primarily seen from a theological perspective with a focus on the Torah's instructions about diet, Sabbath, and all manner of other rules handed down by God in the Pentateuch. Thus, there's no inherent contradiction for an individual to describe oneself as a Jewish atheist. The first descriptor describes their social identity (horizontal orientation), while the second one is indicative of their theological beliefs (the vertical dimension).

Trying to parse what share of American Jews are primarily ethnically Jewish from those who are also practicing Jews is obviously difficult. It's inadvisable to ask the question directly, but other queries on surveys can provide helpful insights into how the religiosity of Jews differs from groups like Protestants and Catholics. For instance, the Cooperative Election Study asks individuals how important religion is to them, with response options ranging from "not at all" to "very important."

Figure 8.4 clearly shows the average Jew places a lot less importance on religion compared to Christian groups. For instance, 17% of Jews say that religion is "not important at all," and another quarter indicate that it is "not too important." For comparison, only 10% of Protestants and 21% of Catholics

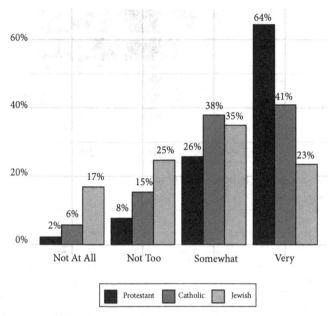

Figure 8.4 How important is religion in your life?
Data: Cooperative Election Study

chose those bottom-two categories. Among Protestant Christians, 64% said that religion was very important to them; that's nearly three times the rate of Jews at just 23%. There's a strong probability that the primary reason for this is that when Protestants become less religious, they also shed the Protestant label. In Chapter 7 we discussed the issue of cultural Catholicism—which is why the average Catholic scores lower on religious importance than Protestants, as well. However, many Jews retain the social identification without the religious component.

There is another way to get at this phenomenon, as well. The General Social Survey asks about religious identification as well as religious belief with options ranging from God doesn't exist to believing in God without a doubt, and the results are displayed in Figure 8.5.

It should come as little surprise that the majority of Protestants say that they believe in God without a doubt (73%), while just 3% say they take the atheist/agnostic view of God. Catholics are a bit less certain with 60% expressing a sure belief, but only 3% take the atheist/agnostic view of God. However, the distribution of answers for Jewish respondents is much more diverse than that of Protestants or Catholics. Only about a quarter of Jews

130 THE AMERICAN RELIGIOUS LANDSCAPE

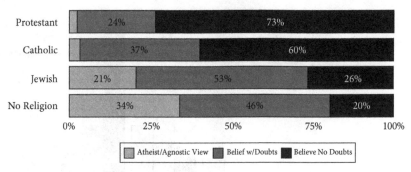

Figure 8.5 What do you believe about God?
Data: General Social Survey

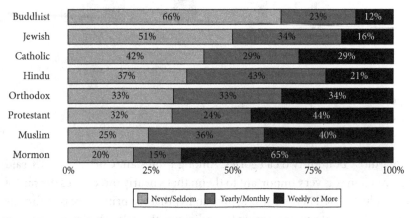

Figure 8.6 Religious service attendance
Data: Cooperative Election Study

express a certain belief in God, which is nearly the same share as the religiously unaffiliated at 20%. However, only 21% of Jews take the atheist/agnostic view of God, which is noticeably lower than the nonreligious. Therefore, it can be said with statistical confidence that Jewish theological perspectives are more closely aligned with those of the nonreligious than with Protestant or Catholic beliefs.

This different understanding of religion among Jews comes through when looking at the data in Figure 8.6 through the lens of religious attendance, as well. For instance, just one in five Latter-day Saints reported that they attend services seldom or never. It's slightly higher among Protestants at 32%. For Jews, synagogue attendance looks much different. For instance, over half of

Jews say that they attend services less than once a year, and only 16% report going to synagogue every Sabbath. The only group that scores lower on this metric are Buddhists who do not have communal worship as a key component of their faith tradition.

The Divisions inside Judaism

Judaism, like most major religions, is not a monolith, as can be seen in Figure 8.7. Just as there are conservative and liberal denominations among Protestant Christians, there are different sects of Judaism, as well. The Cooperative Election Study asks Jews to identify their specific denomination, and it is consistently the case that one subgroup is the dominant voice in American Judaism. The plurality of Jews indicate that they are from the Reform tradition—in the last few years of the Cooperative Election Study that share runs between 40% and 45%. The next most popular selection is Conservative Jews who typically comprise 25%–30% of all Jewish respondents on surveys. About one in ten Jews identifies with the Orthodox tradition, and about half that many say that they are Reconstructionist.

However, the difficulty in measuring American Judaism comes through clearly when comparing the results of a random sample survey with the work compiled by the Association of Statisticians of American Religious Bodies for the Religion Census. This group collects its data by contacting religious groups directly and asking them to pass on records about where they have congregations and how many members are on the rolls of each house of worship. This approach to data collection obviously differs significantly from just asking people about their religious affiliation as a part of a survey battery.

The reasons for the divergence between these estimates are numerous. For instance, a person may have been part of a synagogue when they were

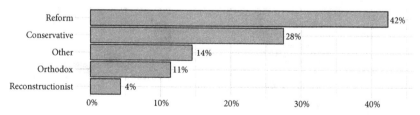

Figure 8.7 Denominational composition of Jewish respondents
Data: Cooperative Election Study

younger and just completed their bar/bat mitzvah, but has subsequently stopped worshiping and no longer feels connected to the larger Jewish community. This could lead them to declare no religious affiliation on a survey while still showing up as a member of a synagogue. Or the opposite could be the case—someone just got involved in a religious community but still has not become a member of any house of worship.

There are a myriad of reasons why approaching the task of religious measurement from two different methodologies would lead to some disparate results. That's most certainly the case when it comes to Chabad, who are often referred to as Hasidic Jews in the United States. According to the teachings of their religion, those who belong to Chabad Judaism believe that they should not be counted in a traditional census.[11] Also, this prohibition means that many Hasidic Jews refuse to take part in a public opinion survey, as well. Thus, it's very likely that any attempt at assessing the Jewish population in the United States will lead to an undercount.

With that caveat in place, it's interesting to look at Figure 8.8, which visualizes the numbers provided in the Religion Census for Jewish denominations. While on surveys, Reform is the most popular response option, that's not the case when looking at membership rolls. The Religion Census reports that there are 914 Orthodox congregations in the United States boasting a total membership of 941,000. That's nearly 50% higher than the number of Reform Jews in the United States. Recall that in the Cooperative Election Study, there were nearly four times as many Reform Jews as there were Orthodox (42% vs. 11%).

The other thing worth dwelling on a bit is the Chabad sect of Judaism. As previously mentioned, they prohibit a counting of their actual membership.

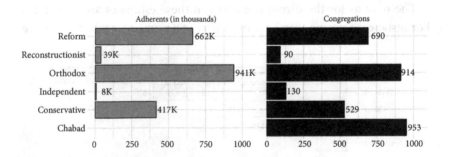

Figure 8.8 Number of congregations and adherents in American Judaism
Data: Religion Census

But that did not preclude statisticians from finding the names and addresses of Hasidic synagogues in the United States. What the Association of Statisticians of American Religious Bodies uncovered were nearly a thousand houses of worship, which is the largest number of any sect of Judaism. In other Jewish traditions, the average house of worship has about a thousand members each. This means that there are likely at least a million Hasidic Jews in the United States. However, given the penchant for Hasidic families to have many children, it's very likely that there are twice as many Jews in the Chabad tradition than there are those who align with the Reform sect.[12]

Notice also that the total number of Jews counted through the Religion Census is just less than 2.1 million people. That number diverges significantly from that which can be extrapolated by looking at data from several surveys. The General Social Survey reports that about 1.5% of American adults are Jews—that generates an estimate of 6–7 million. Given the aforementioned issues with measuring American Judaism, it stands to reason that neither estimate may be accurate, and it is likely impossible to get to the correct estimate given the varying ways that individuals define a Jewish affiliation.

Where Do Jews Live in the United States?

When one thinks about the geography of American Judaism, the most likely image they conjure is an urban environment, which makes sense, given the immigration patterns previously discussed in the introduction. When Jewish families fled Europe during the 1930s and 1940s, they first landed on American shores in the Northeast, particularly around New York City. Many settled into established Jewish enclaves and began to build a life in their new home. Thus, Judaism in the United States has always been deeply intertwined with an urban existence.

The data largely reinforce that perception in Figure 8.9. Individuals in the Cooperative Election Study were asked to describe the place in which they live, given options running from urban to rural. Thirty-five percent of Jews said that they lived in an urban environment—the only religious group that is more urban is Muslims. However, when the urban and suburban options are combined, it's clear that Jews are an outlier with 85%. Just 6% of Jews say that they live in a rural setting, which is one of the lowest shares of any religious group in the United States.

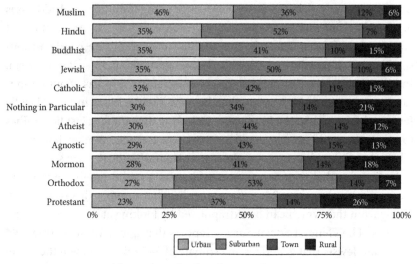

Figure 8.9 How would you describe the place you live?
Data: Cooperative Election Study

When looking at Figure 8.10, which utilizes data from the 2020 Religion Census, the same general conclusion emerges: Jews tend to live in parts of the country with high levels of population density. New York City and the surrounding counties all have at least one Jewish congregation reported in the data. That also includes most of New Jersey as well as a significant portion of Connecticut and Massachusetts. There is also a nearly unbroken line of counties with a synagogue that extends south through the areas surrounding Philadelphia, Baltimore, and Washington, DC.

There are other areas of the country with a significant Jewish presence, as well. For instance, thirty of the sixty-seven counties in Florida have Jewish synagogues. There are also Jewish congregations in many counties throughout California, especially in the Bay Area and continuing south into populated spaces around Los Angeles and San Diego. In addition, Arizona's cities (Tucson and Phoenix) report a Jewish presence, as well. There are huge swaths of the United States that have no organized Jewish community, however. For instance, there are only three Jewish synagogues in the state of South Dakota, four in Montana, and five in Oklahoma.

It's important to point out that even in places where there are a lot of Jewish adherents, they still do not make up a significant portion of the overall population of that country. There are only two counties in the United States

Figure 8.10 Counties that have a Jewish congregation
Data: Religion Census

where Jews make up at least 10% of the population, both in New York. One is Rockland County, which is on the Hudson River just north of New York City, and the other is Kings County, which is the borough of Brooklyn. Additionally, there are only ten total counties where Jews make up at least 5% of the population. Nine of those are on the East Coast. The only exception is Saint Louis County in Missouri.

The geographic pattern of Jewish Americans seems to mirror that of other smaller religious groups like Muslims, Hindus, and Buddhists. They tend to be found most prominently on the coasts, but even in areas where they are in significant numbers, they never are the dominant religious group in their region. Given the overall decline in the number of Jewish Americans, it seems unlikely that Jews will ever have large numbers outside the aforementioned places on the East Coast, Florida, and California.

The Socioeconomic Success of American Jews

There are a number of Jewish stereotypes that exist in American society that are demonstrably false and incalculably harmful to the Jewish community.

The Anti-Defamation League fielded a survey about those tropes against the Jewish community in 2020. That data found that 15% of Americans thought that Jewish people had too much power in the business world, and 17% said that the film and television industries are run by Jews.[13] Another 10% said that "Jews are more willing than others to use shady practices to get what they want."[14] Those statements are clearly untrue, but those sentiments persist among an alarmingly high number of Americans.

However, it is statistically true that American Jews have managed to climb their way up the economic and social ladder in the United States. When looking at just the educational attainment and household income of religious groups in Figure 8.11, that becomes clear. In recent data, 63% of American Jews reported having a college degree. That's nearly twice the national average, which is 33%. In addition, about a third of Jews indicate that their household income is at least $100,000 per year. In the United States as a whole, about 18% of households earn at least six figures in income.

The only religious group that comes close to the educational attainment and high level of income is Hindus, which are a very small religious group that is made up almost entirely of recent immigrants to the United States. Jews do much better on these socioeconomic metrics than larger groups like Protestants, Catholics, and even atheists.

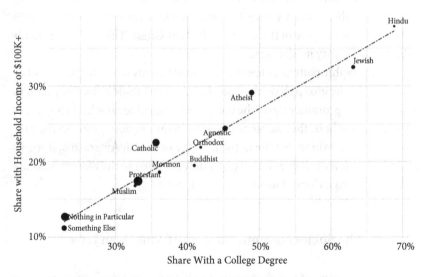

Figure 8.11 The education and income of religious groups
Data: Cooperative Election Study

Part of this may be a function of something that was discussed previously—the Jewish population in the United States is concentrated in the Northeast in metropolitan areas like New York City and Philadelphia, which have easy access to institutions of higher education. Also, the cost of living in that part of the country is far above average, and thus a six-figure income may make someone financially comfortable in rural Iowa, but would only afford a middle-class existence in Manhattan.

Positive Signs for the Future of American Judaism

Although there is a tremendous amount of anti-Semitism in the United States, there are survey results that provide support for the notion that the average American views Judaism in the United States in a similar light as other larger religious groups such as Catholics or Protestants. In 2023, YouGov asked people if they had a favorable or unfavorable view of a variety of religious groups—the results are illuminating, as can be seen in Figure 8.12.

For instance, about 35% of Americans have a favorable view of Protestants and Catholics in the United States. That same share also has a favorable view of Buddhists, as well. Jews score just below that at 32% favorable. Then, there is a tremendous drop-off. Just 24% of Americans have a favorable view of atheists. Latter-day Saints and Muslims score much lower at 19% and 15%, respectively. From this perspective, American acceptance of Judaism is much higher than most other smaller religious groups. While there are still a tremendous number of hate crimes against Jewish Americans, those behaviors

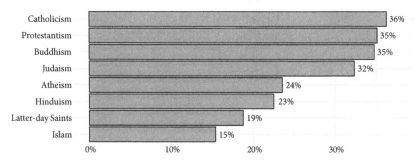

Figure 8.12 Share of Americans with a favorable view of each religious group
Data: YouGov

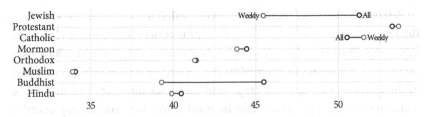

Figure 8.13 Average age of weekly attenders versus all attenders
Data: Cooperative Election Study

do not represent the views of mainstream America. Instead, there's a level of acceptance that rivals some of the largest religious groups in the country.

There also may be some optimistic news when looking at religious attendance among Jews in the United States through the lens of age. It seems logical to assume that the average weekly attender in a religious group is older than the average member of that group. When one looks over a synagogue on Friday night or a Catholic Mass on Sunday morning, there is often a large contingent of retired members in the pews.

The data reinforce that viewpoint, as well. The average weekly attending Protestant or Catholic is two to three years older than the average member of those respective religious traditions. In many cases, however, there's not a huge age variation between the most active and the overall average. That's not the case with American Judaism, as can be seen in Figure 8.13.

In data collected between 2020 and 2022, the average Jew in the sample was fifty-one years old. That's three years older than the average American in the sample. However, the average Jew who attends synagogue weekly is just forty-five years old. That's six years younger than the average weekly attender from any religious tradition. That's a very hopeful sign for the future of American Judaism. While both Protestants and Catholics are facing a looming demographic cliff because of their ever-increasing age, the Jews who are attending synagogues are trending younger. This suggests that the Jewish community has managed to nudge its younger members toward greater religious devotion, which should forestall a numeric decline in the near future.

Conclusion

The story of Judaism in the United States is a complicated one that began with a tremendous amount of immigration in the first hundred years of the country and has recently seen a slow and steady decline over the last several decades. What complicates that narrative is how difficult it is to measure Jews in the United States because of the unique nature of Judaism, which is both an ethnicity and a religion. Survey data indicate that a significant number of Jewish respondents seem to embrace the ethnic component of Judaism while only being marginally attached to the religious tradition.

However, there are signs in the data that American Jews may be able to reverse those declines. Some sects, like Chabad, seem to be growing rapidly and have a deep commitment to the religious component of the Jewish identity. The fact that the average weekly attending Jew is six years younger than the average Jew is a clear indication that younger individuals in this tradition want to hold more strongly to the theological components of their community.

That's not to say that Jews do not face a number of obstacles in the United States. There is still an alarmingly high number of hate crimes toward Jewish people and anti-Semitism still exists among a small subset of the American populace. Additionally, because of the geographic concentration of Jews on the coasts, many Americans have never built personal relationships with Jewish people. Exposure to different groups has often led to a measurable increase in warm feelings toward others.[15]

Despite those challenges, there is little doubt that Judaism in the United States will remain a significant force in politics and culture. Jewish Americans have high levels of educational attainment and household income, two factors that are clearly connected to being influential in several sectors of the American economy. Also, their geographic concentration in some of the cultural centers of the United States ensures that they will continue to be a vital part of the religious discourse in America for decades to come.

Notes

1. Hasia R. Diner. 2004. *The Jews of the United States, 1654 to 2000*. Berkeley: University of California Press, 43; Paul Johnson. 2001. *History of the Jews*. London: Phoenix, 366.
2. Diner, *Jews of the United States*, 96, 115; "A People at Risk." *Library of Congress*. https://www.loc.gov/classroom-materials/immigration/polish-russian/a-people-at-risk/.
3. Diner, *Jews of the United States*, 78–79.
4. "Breckinridge Long (1881–1958)." 2019. *PBS American Experience*. https://www.pbs.org/wgbh/americanexperience/features/holocaust-long/.
5. Muzaffar Chishti, Faye Hipsman, and Isabel Ball. 2015. "Fifty Years on, the 1965 Immigration and Nationality Act Continues to Reshape the United States." *Migration Policy Institute*. https://www.migrationpolicy.org/article/fifty-years-1965-immigration-and-nationality-act-continues-reshape-united-states.

140 THE AMERICAN RELIGIOUS LANDSCAPE

6. United States Census Bureau. 2021. "New Vintage 2021 Population Estimates Available for the Nation, States, and Puerto Rico." Census.gov. https://www.census.gov/newsroom/press-relea ses/2021/2021-population-estimates.html.
7. Pew Research Center. 2021. "Jewish Americans in 2020." https://www.pewresearch.org/relig ion/2021/05/11/jewish-americans-in-2020/#:~:text=In%20absolute%20numbers%2C%20 the%202020,adults%20and%201.3%20million%20children.
8. Pew Research Center, "Jewish Americans in 2020."
9. Pew Research Center, "Jewish Americans in 2020."
10. Marshall Sklare and Jonathan D. Sarna. 1993. *Observing America's Jews.* Waltham, MA: Brandeis University Press, 26.
11. Mendy Kaminker. 2011. "Why Do We Not Count Jews?" *Chabad.org.* https://www.chabad.org/library/article_cdo/aid/1635539/jewish/Why-Do-We-Not-Count-Jews.htm.
12. Mendel Dubov. 2019. "Why Do Observant Jews Have So Many Kids?" *Chabad.org.* https://www.chabad.org/library/article_cdo/aid/4372320/jewish/Why-Do-Observant-Jews-Have-So-Many-Kids.htm.
13. Anti-Defamation League. 2020. "Anti-Semitic Stereotypes Persist in America, Survey Shows." *ADL.* https://www.adl.org/resources/press-release/anti-semitic-stereotypes-persist-america-sur vey-shows.
14. Anti-Defamation League, "Anti-Semitic Stereotypes Persist."
15. Donald P. Green and Janelle S. Wong. 2009. "Tolerance and the Contact Hypothesis: A Field Experiment." *The Political Psychology of Democratic Citizenship*: 1–23.

Data References

Davern, Michael, Rene Bautista, Jeremy Freese, Pamela Herd, and Stephen L. Morgan. 2023. General Social Survey 1972–2022. Principal investigator, Michael Davern; Co-principal investigators, Rene Bautista, Jeremy Freese, Pamela Herd, and Stephen L. Morgan. Sponsored by National Science Foundation. NORC ed. Chicago: NORC at the University of Chicago. https://gssdataexplorer.norc.org/.

Grammich, Clifford, Kirk Hadaway, Richard Houseal, Dale E. Jones, Alexei Krindatch, Richie Stanley, and Richard H. Taylor. 2023. 2020 U.S. Religion Census: Religious Congregations & Membership Study. Association of Statisticians of American Religious Bodies. https://www.usreligioncensus.org/node/1639.

Schaffner, Brian, Stephen Ansolabehere, Sam Luks, Shiro Kuriwaki, and Marissa Shih. 2006–2023. Cooperative Election Study Common Content, 2006–2022. Harvard Dataverse. https://cces.gov.harvard.edu/.

YouGov. 2022. Daily Survey: Favorability of Religions, November 22–26, 2022—1,000 US Adult Citizens.

9

Latter-day Saints

The January 2021 issue of *The Atlantic* included an article with the most intriguing title, "The Most American Religion."[1] It was written by McKay Coppins, staff writer for the magazine, who is a member of the Church of Jesus Christ of Latter-day Saints (LDS). Using the Mormon bicentennial as the backdrop, Coppins makes the argument that the history, beliefs, and practices of the Mormon Church have been deeply impacted by American culture and ideology. Coppins writes that the founder of the LDS Church, Joseph Smith, revered the U.S. Constitution as a "quasi-canonical work of providence."[2] Smith also contended that the reason that God decided to begin this church in the United States was because of the freedom afforded to its citizens.[3] Thus, it is impossible to fully extricate the characteristics of members of the Church of Jesus Christ of Latter-day Saints from the larger story of the United States' rise to power and prominence over the last 240 years.

The data about the Mormon Church paint a fascinating portrait of a religious tradition that has grown at a breathtaking rate over the last century and possesses many of the hallmarks of a healthy religious tradition. Yet, at the same time, there are aspects of Mormon life that pose serious threats to the future direction and vitality of the LDS Church.

The Origins of the Church of Jesus Christ of Latter-day Saints

The Church of Jesus Christ of Latter-day Saints was founded by Joseph Smith in 1830 in upstate New York. At the age of fourteen, Smith was deeply intrigued by religion and was wrestling with which sect to join when he wandered into a grove of trees near his family farm and asked for God's guidance. According to Smith, he encountered divine beings among the trees who told him that he was to lead a new religious movement. Over the next decade, Smith and some of his early followers reported that they had

The American Religious Landscape. Ryan P. Burge, Oxford University Press. © Oxford University Press 2025.
DOI: 10.1093/oso/9780197762837.003.0010

142   THE AMERICAN RELIGIOUS LANDSCAPE

uncovered some golden plates containing sacred writing and then translated those into English. This effort became known as the Book of Mormon, which detailed a story of how a small group of Israelites fled the Middle East and settled in the Americas about six hundred years before the birth of Jesus of Nazareth.

What followed for Smith and the earliest group of Mormons was persecution, ridicule, and ostracism. The Mormon Church was founded in Seneca County, New York, in the spring of 1830, but less than a year later, Smith and his followers had to flee the state due to threats of violence, with some followers venturing to northwest Missouri and others ending up in Kirtland, Ohio. Their stint in Missouri ended when the governor of the state issued an extermination order for the LDS in 1838, and the Kirtland settlement was largely abandoned at the same time.

The Mormon Church reported membership of nearly 18,000 as it relocated to Nauvoo, Illinois, in hopes of finding a community willing to embrace a new religious movement. Yet their hopes were dashed when an angry mob killed Joseph Smith in 1844. Smith's death led to a succession crisis, but many Mormons accepted Brigham Young as the rightful prophet to lead them away from Illinois. Young believed that the only way to truly practice the Mormon faith without fear was to move to the sparsely populated western part of the continent. In the summer of 1847, the Mormon Church had doubled in size to nearly 35,000 members, and Young directed his followers to settle in the Great Salt Lake Valley of Utah. Given the undeveloped nature of the American West, members of the Church of Jesus Christ of Latter-day Saints were given a great deal of latitude to practice their religion as they saw fit and to develop a community that would nurture the Mormon faith and allow it to flourish.[4]

The Growth of the Church of Jesus Christ of Latter-day Saints

There's little doubt that the stability afforded the LDS Church in the American West was a tremendous boon to the membership rolls, as can be seen in Figure 9.1. When the earliest Mormons were forced to move because of threats of violence, the number of LDS rose only at a modest rate. Even upon settling in Utah territory, the overall membership gains were relatively minuscule. The church reported about 50,000 members in 1850, with

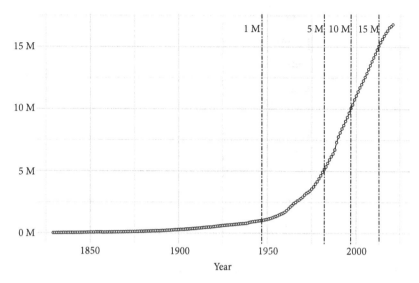

Figure 9.1 Reported membership of the Church of Jesus Christ of Latter-day Saints
Data: Church records

that number doubling to 100,000 by 1873. By 1919, there were half a million Mormons recorded, and it took until 1947 for the membership to reach 1 million.

But from that point forward, growth can only be described as exponential. It took 118 years to get to a million members; the next million would be added in just fifteen years. Nine years later, the LDS faith would add another million. By 1982, the Church of Jesus Christ of Latter-day Saints had over 5 million members on its rolls. That number eclipsed 10 million by 1997 and reached 15 million by 2013—5 million new members in just sixteen years. According to data released in 2021, the total membership of the LDS Church was 16.8 million members.

To put that number in perspective, the state of Pennsylvania is the fifth largest in the United States by population, and it has 12.9 million residents.[5] The largest Protestant denomination, the Southern Baptist Convention, reported a membership of 16.3 million at its peak in 2006.[6] While estimating the number of people who attend weekly worship services is methodologically difficult, there's ample reason to believe that in terms of actual number of attendees, the Church of Jesus Christ of Latter-day Saints may have more people in the pews each weekend than all other religious groups except for

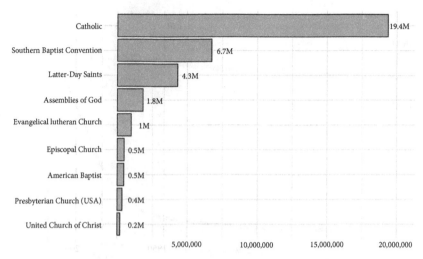

Figure 9.2 Number of people in the pews each weekend
Data: Denominational records

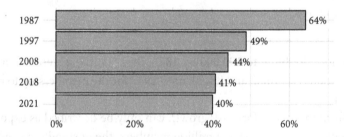

Figure 9.3 Share of Latter-day Saints in the United States
Data: Denominational records

Roman Catholics and Southern Baptists, with 4.3 million attending services each week, as can be seen in Figure 9.2.

Many may not realize that the majority of Mormons reside outside the United States. According to Figure 9.3, out of 16.8 million Mormons worldwide, only 6.8 million, or 40%, are in the United States. However, this wasn't always the case. As recently as 1996, at least half of all Mormons resided in the United States, but this percentage has been declining slowly and steadily for the last twenty-five years. If current trends persist, by 2050, two-thirds of all Mormons will reside outside the United States.

Where do these non-American Mormons live? The majority are living in Central and South America. Data from 2017 indicate that there are about

1.5 million in the country of Mexico and nearly the same number in Brazil (1.4 million).[7] Additionally, there are at least half a million LDS living in Peru and Chile and 450,000 in the country of Argentina.[8] Outside of this region, there are 765,000 Mormons in the Philippines.[9] How did Mormonism, a faith that is "the most American religion," become popular so far from the United States? It's likely due to the robust missionary program employed by the Church of Jesus Christ of Latter-day Saints.

In the LDS community, members are strongly encouraged to become a missionaries for the Church after they complete their high school education. These missions, which typically last between eighteen and twenty-four months, are considered a rite of passage for young Mormons as they become active members of the local church. These missions are focused on trying to win new converts to the Church, with LDS members assigned to countries all over the world. According to data released by the LDS Church, there were over 54,000 proselytizing missionaries throughout the world at the end of 2021.[10] The author David Stewart estimated that in 2004, the average missionary baptized 4.5 converts during their mission.[11]

There are other reasons to believe that future growth may occur outside the United States, as well. One significant impediment for LDS is the perception that their religious tradition struggles to be truly multiracial. For instance, Mark E. Peterson, who served as one of the Quorum of Twelve Apostles (the leadership body of the LDS), stated in a speech at Brigham Young University in 1954 that "if a Negro is faithful all his days, he can and will enter the celestial kingdom. He will go there as a servant, but he will get a celestial resurrection."[12] For most of the history of the LDS, the church prohibited those of African descent from being allowed entry into the priesthood, and it barred Black members from attending several types of rituals in the LDS faith. These bans were lifted by an Official Declaration in 1978.[13] However, in recent years the church has been intentional about working with groups like the National Association for the Advancement of Colored People (NAACP) to raise awareness of issues related to race in the United States and to fund scholarships for African American students to attend college.[14]

Thus, it should come as little surprise that those who identify as LDS on surveys are overwhelmingly white. According to data from the 2020 Cooperative Election Study, visualized in Figure 9.4—just 20% of Mormons indicate that they are a racial minority, compared to 31% in the overall sample. Just 7% of LDS are Black, which is about half the rate of the general population, and only 5% are Hispanic—while it's 10% of the overall

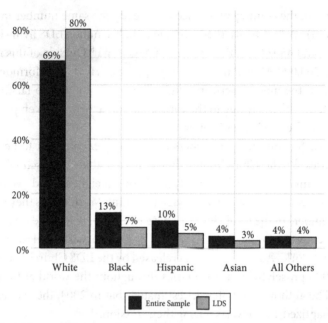

Figure 9.4 The racial composition of Latter-day Saints
Data: Cooperative Election Study

sample. As the United States becomes more racially diverse every year, it behooves the Church of Jesus Christ of Latter-day Saints to become more racially diverse as a means to reach the next generation of Americans. If this is not accomplished, it's likely that membership growth in the LDS faith will only expand through children born into the faith as opposed to conversions of outsiders. This would further isolate the LDS faith from the rest of the U.S. population—making it even more difficult to proselytize—which has always been at the core of the Mormon faith.

The Geographic Distribution of American Mormons

Even those Americans who are relatively unfamiliar with the history and theology of the Church of Jesus Christ of Latter-day Saints are likely to know about the incredible concentrations of Mormons in the state of Utah. That point becomes clear when looking at data from the 2020 Religion Census, visualized in Figure 9.5. About two of three residents in the state of Utah

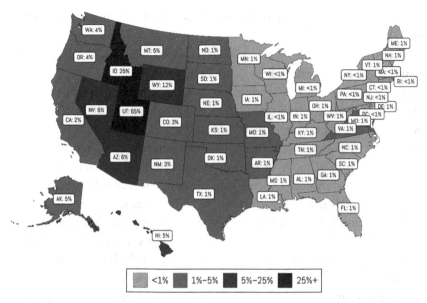

Figure 9.5 Share of the population that is Latter-day Saints
Data: Religion Census

identify as members of the LDS. There is no other religious group in the United States today that has such a high concentration in a single state.

However, outside the state of Utah, Mormons enjoy a much smaller share of any state's population. Idaho is the second, with the second highest concentration of Mormons at 25% followed by Wyoming at 12% and Arizona and Nevada at 6% each. But for the remainder of the United States, Mormons are a very small share of the overall population. In states that make up the Bible Belt, members of the LDS Church make up about one in one hundred individuals—not enough to have a real impact on the culture or politics of a region. Mormons in New England are even scarcer—at less than 1% in places like Massachusetts, Rhode Island, and Connecticut.

It would be entirely fair to describe the Church of Jesus Christ of Latter-day Saints as the most geographically concentrated religious tradition in the United States—with the locus of power in Utah, which quickly diminishes as one moves further and further away from the state. However, even in Salt Lake County, where the headquarters of the LDS Church is located, there has been a precipitous decline in members. According to data from the church itself, LDS fell to less than half the population of Salt Lake County in 2017 and now just 47% of those living in Salt Lake are Mormons.[15] It's telling that even in the heart of Mormonism in the world, the church is losing its grip on the average Utahn.

That's not to say that Mormons don't live, work, and worship all across the United States. If one maps all the counties that report having an LDS congregation, it becomes clear that while the Church is obviously strongest in the West, it still has houses of worship in many counties across the United States. According to data from the 2020 Religion Census, displayed in Figure 9.6, there is an LDS house of worship in 1,900 counties of 3,033 across the fifty states. This means if one were to choose a county at random, they would have a 63% chance of choosing one with an LDS presence. Clearly, the Mormon Church is well distributed throughout the United States.

Although the Church of Jesus Christ of Latter-day Saints has a small footprint in New England, it's interesting to note that every county in Maine, Connecticut, and Delaware has members of the LDS Church. The church is less pervasive in the Midwest and the Great Plains. For instance, just 30% of Nebraska counties have an LDS Church—it's slightly higher in Kansas at 37%. Most of the counties in Illinois, Iowa, and Kentucky don't have a measurable Mormon community either. But there are notable outliers. For instance, the Mormon Church is pervasive in Florida, with 88% of counties having a recorded church in the 2020 Religion Census.

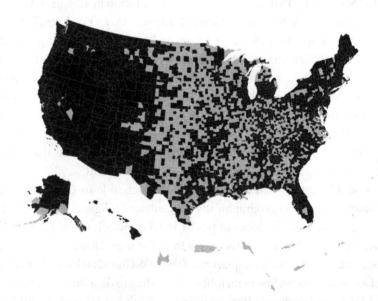

Figure 9.6 Counties that have a Latter-day Saint congregation
Data: Religion Census

Indicators of Growth in the LDS Church

Although the percentage of the population of Utah that is Mormon is declining and more and more Mormons are not living in the United States, there are plenty of reasons to believe that the overall health of this religious community is strong and growing stronger. One clear indicator of future increases in a demographic group is that the average age of a member is younger than the overall population. Looking at Figure 9.7, that's obviously the case when it comes to Latter-day Saints.

In 2008, the average adult American (eighteen and older) was about forty-five years old, while the average member of the Church of Jesus Christ of Latter-day Saints was two and a half years younger than that. Over the last decade that age gap has persisted—with Latter-day Saints consistently reporting a younger overall age than the general population. In 2021, the average Latter-day Saint adult was forty-five years old, which means that a significant portion of those who align with the LDS Church are still of childbearing age, which is an important factor for any religious group. Having children (and keeping those children in the faith) is the surest way to maintain congregational health for decades to come.

Other data about Latter-day Saints makes it clear just how much of an outlier the group is in terms of fertility. The Cooperative Election Study

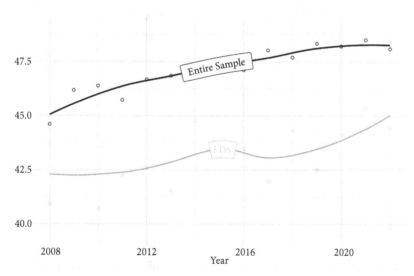

Figure 9.7 Average age of Mormon adults compared to the general population
Data: Cooperative Election Study

asks individuals if they are a parent or guardian of any children under the age of eighteen years old. The most likely time in one's life when that would be true is between the ages of thirty and forty-five years old. For those who had children in their teens or early twenties, those children would still be under the age of eighteen. For those who waited a bit longer to become parents, it would be unlikely for them to have their first child after the age of forty-five.

When calculating the share of people from each religious group who had children during this time, it's clear that Latter-day Saints are much more family-centered than other religious traditions. In Figure 9.8, among Mormons between the ages of thirty and forty-five years old, 71% of them report having children under the age of eighteen. The only other group that comes close to this level of parenthood are Hindus. For Catholics and Protestants, only a slim majority report being parents during this time of their lives. For Jews, just 42% are parents and for atheists/agnostics, they are half as likely as Latter-day Saints to report having children at home.

Thus, the image that many people conjure in their heads of Latter-day Saint communities filled with young families is confirmed by this data.

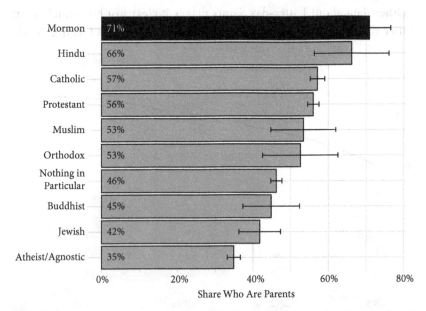

Figure 9.8 Are you the parent or guardian of any children under the age of eighteen? (age thirty to forty-five)
Data: Cooperative Election Study

Latter-day Saints are younger than the average American and are significantly more likely to be parents than those who identify with another religious tradition. These are hallmarks of a religious group that has a bright future ahead of it.

That supposition is only bolstered when looking at the number of children that Mormon families have compared to other religious traditions, as can be seen in Figure 9.9. Again, the sample is restricted to just those between the ages of thirty and forty-five years old and limited to those people who have at least one child. But, according to data collected in 2020, the average Mormon family has 2.8 children. The only religious group that comes close to Latter-day Saints in terms of family size is Muslims with 2.5 children. Major Christian groups like Protestants and Catholics fall far behind at just 2.1 children per family.

When demographers think about issues of fertility and the future, they use 2.1 children per woman as "replacement level fertility." This means that if the average woman has slightly more than two children, then the overall population of a country will not decline. But the replacement level must be higher for religious groups, because defection is a real concern for many faith

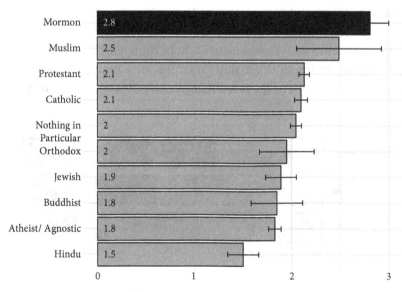

Figure 9.9 Average number of children by religious tradition, age thirty to forty-five

Data: Cooperative Election Study

communities. For Protestant families, 2.1 children are likely insufficient to maintain a replacement level—for Mormons, there is a great deal more room for defection before the overall size of the tradition begins to decline.

The Religious Intensity of Latter-day Saints

Beyond the previously mentioned characteristics of the Latter-day Saints—their overall youthful, large families, desire to proselytize, and geographic concentration in the Utah area—the other hallmark of Mormons is their devotion to their religious faith. This is not a faith group that claims an affiliation on a survey but never engages in the practices of that tradition. Instead, Mormons are likely one of the most religious active groups in the United States today.

According to survey data collected in 2020, displayed in Figure 9.10, nearly two-thirds of Latter-day Saints report attending religious services at least once a week. That's 20% more than the weekly attendance of Protestants and thirty-six percentage points more than Roman Catholics. What's especially noteworthy about this reported level of religious service attendance is how much of a time commitment that Mormon worship requires. Until just a few years ago, the leadership of the Mormon Church required that Sunday morning worship last a total of three hours—much longer than the average worship service in most Protestant or Catholic churches.[16]

Issues like the length of worship gatherings are a crucial detail when it comes to the goals of a religious tradition. Services that are over in forty-five

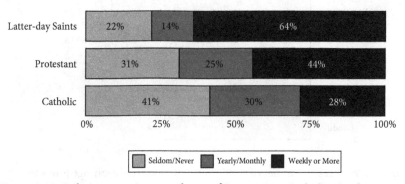

Figure 9.10 Religious service attendance of Protestants, Catholics, and Latter-day Saints

minutes to an hour make it easier for members to fit religious attendance into their regular schedule. However, that may not provide the time necessary for individual members to strengthen relational ties to others in the faith tradition. Having more time at the house of worship can allow single members to find a potential partner or for widows to find social support among people in similar circumstances.

However, a longer worship service is clearly a high barrier to entry for potential new converts. If one were choosing what religion to join, a possible consideration is how much time will be needed to devote to this new endeavor. Facing the possibility of spending an entire Sunday morning in worship may turn off some individuals who live fast-paced lives or have many commitments. Yet spending that much time with other members of the faith community will make it even more difficult for an individual member to leave the fold, even if their faith waivers. It will be interesting to see if this change in policy for the LDS Church will have any appreciable impact on new members or individuals leaving the church entirely.

Beyond religious service attendance, it's also been true that Latter-day Saints are more likely to report an active prayer life than Catholics or Protestants. Figure 9.11 shows that in 2008, 62% of Mormons said that they prayed multiple times per day—a rate that far exceeded their Protestant

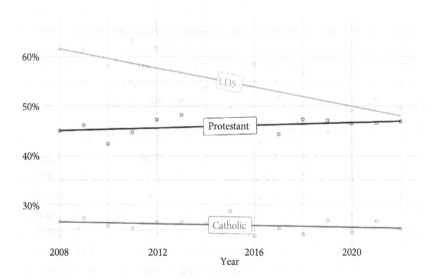

Figure 9.11 Share who indicate that they pray several times a day
Data: Cooperative Election Study

154 THE AMERICAN RELIGIOUS LANDSCAPE

(45%) or Catholic counterparts (27%). However, that gap in prayer frequency between Latter-day Saints and Protestants has narrowed significantly over the last decade. By 2015, the share of Latter-day Saints who prayed multiple times a day was below 55%, and in the most recent data, it dropped below a majority for the first time. Now, there's not a statistically significant difference in prayer frequency between Protestants and Latter-day Saints.

This significant decline in prayer frequency may be a cause for concern for those in the leadership of the Church of Jesus Christ of Latter-day Saints. While attendance at religious services is still notably robust for Mormons, a drop in prayer frequency may proceed a drop in other types of religious involvement like weekend services and tithing to the Church. When these data are seen in concert with the reports from the LDS Church that Mormons are losing ground in Salt Lake County and in the State of Utah, it should serve as a warning that the Church may truly decline in both size and influence in the United States in the near future.

Perceptions of Latter-day Saints

Strategies employed by the Church of Jesus Christ of Latter-day Saints over the last decade have made it clear that image management is an issue when it comes to winning new converts to the church in the United States. In 2011, the Church funded a significant public relations campaign entitled "I'm a Mormon." The focus of the ads was to normalize Latter-day Saints to those who were not familiar with the church.[17] They featured both celebrities and everyday members of the Church and included links to resources about the beliefs and practices of the LDS Church.

However, given data collected in 2022 and displayed in Figure 9.12, there's empirical evidence that the American public is still skeptical of the Mormon Church. YouGov, a polling firm, asked respondents to indicate whether they had a favorable or unfavorable view of a variety of religious groups. Just 18% of Americans said that they had an unfavorable view of Protestants, and only 26% took a dim view of Catholics. Latter-day Saints did not fare so well, though. Just 19% of Americans described their view of Mormons as "somewhat" or "very favorable," compared to 20% who said their views of the Church were "very unfavorable," and another 21% who reported a "somewhat unfavorable" perception.

LATTER-DAY SAINTS 155

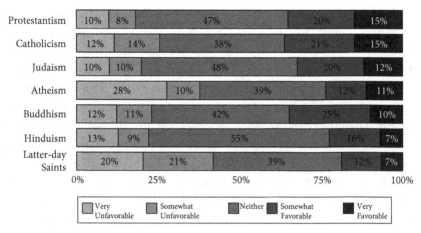

Figure 9.12 Do you have a favorable or unfavorable view of the following groups?
Data: YouGov

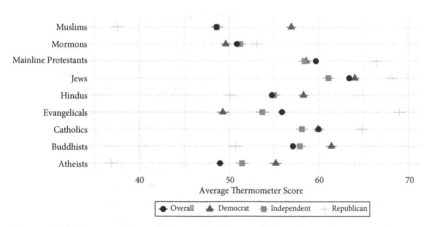

Figure 9.13 Score each group between 0 (very cold) and 100 (very warm)
Data: Pew, American Trends Panel 44

There are other survey data that shed more light on how Latter-day Saints are viewed by the American public. In 2019, the Pew Research Center asked respondents to rate several religious groups using a feeling thermometer where zero represents very cold feelings and one hundred represents a great deal of warmth toward a group. Thus, a score of fifty represents ambivalence. When the data are broken down by political partisanship, a fascinating pattern emerges in Figure 9.13.

156 THE AMERICAN RELIGIOUS LANDSCAPE

There are certain religious groups that have a polarized perception among the general public. For instance, Muslims are viewed relatively warmly by Democrats at 57 but less favorably by Republicans at 38. The same is true for atheists: 55 for Democrats and 37 for Republicans. However, Republicans view evangelicals very warmly at 69, while Democrats take a cooler view at 49.

Latter-day Saints see almost no variation when it comes to political partisanship. Their overall score in the entire sample was 51—basically a neutral view. For Democrats, the mean score was 50; for Republicans, the average was 53. There was no other religious group in the sample where the mean score for Republicans and Democrats was as close as it was for members of the Church of Jesus Christ of Latter-day Saints. The overall impression that is derived from these data is that no single group feels that negatively about Mormons, but there's also no group that clearly has a positive view of the LDS Church, either.

The Future of the Church of Jesus Christ of Latter-day Saints

Throughout its two-hundred-year history, if there's a common thread that runs through the story of the Church of Jesus Christ of Latter-day Saints, it's that they have always been seen as outsiders. From their very beginnings in upstate New York to their current base of operations in Utah, Mormons have always been viewed with an air of suspicion by those who are not that familiar with the Latter-day Saint faith. This sense of social isolation may have actually served to their benefit once they put down roots in the American West. Creating a relatively insular community that focused on family and faith led to a high fertility rate and made it difficult for children raised as Mormons to leave the faith behind.

However, those engines of growth may be losing some steam in the United States over the last few years. The Internet has provided an easy forum for Mormons who are considering leaving the faith to exchange information and offer moral support. The social media site Reddit has a forum specifically for ex-Mormons that boasts 265,000 members—an impressive number in comparison to the overall membership of the Church. It may be that these lines of exchange have emboldened younger members to question some of the doctrines and practices of the LDS Church.

Additionally, it's clear that Mormons have a perception problem in the United States. They are a group that is viewed with deep suspicion, if not outright hostility, by a significant portion of the general population. Given their often conservative values, it would seem that the LDS Church should be embraced by members of the Republican Party, but prominent leaders in the evangelical movement called the Mormon Church "a cult" when Mitt Romney was running for president in 2012.[18] And Democrats are increasingly becoming the party of nonreligious Americans—making them hesitant to embrace any religious tradition, especially one that is often aligned with Republican politics.

Given these impediments, it seems prudent for members of the Church of Jesus Christ of Latter-day Saints to seek growth in regions outside North America. They have made impressive inroads in Central and South America by devoting significant time and resources to missionaries in those regions. But, given the spread of information via the Internet, the same forces that may be driving young people away from organized religion in the United States may also throw up roadblocks for the growth of the Mormon Church outside American shores.

One term that is often used when it comes to members of the Church of Jesus Christ of Latter-day Saints is "a peculiar people," a phrase that occurs in several passages in the Bible. While some outsiders have used it as a pejorative, many Mormons seem to embrace the fact that they practice a faith that is distinct from most other Americans.[19] This peculiarity comes as a double-edged sword. It can serve as a way to stand apart from the larger culture, which makes it easier to keep people inside the faith community. But it can also make it more difficult for curious outsiders to join the fold. How the Church navigates this tension will dictate the future of the Church of Jesus Christ of Latter-day Saints in the United States and throughout the world.

Notes

1. McKay Coppins. 2021. "The Most American Religion." *The Atlantic* January/February. https://www.theatlantic.com/magazine/toc/2021/01/
2. Coppins, "The Most American Religion."
3. Coppins, "The Most American Religion."
4. Matthew Burton Bowman. 2012. *The Mormon People: The Making of an American Faith.* New York: Random House.
5. U.S. Census Bureau. 2022. QuickFacts, Pennsylvania. V2022. Suitland, Suitland-Silver Hill, MD: U.S. Census Bureau, 2022.

6. Aaron Earls. 2023. "Southern Baptists Decline in Membership, Grow in Attendance, Baptisms." *Lifeway Research*. https://research.lifeway.com/2023/05/09/southern-baptists-decline-in-mem bership-grow-in-attendance-baptisms/
7. Matthew Martinich. 2018. "Percent LDS by Country—2017." Growth of The Church of Jesus Christ of Latter-day Saints (LDS Church) [blog]. Blogger, April 25. http://ldschurchgrowth. blogspot.com/2018/04/percent-lds-by-country-2017.html
8. Martinich, "Percent LDS by Country—2017."
9. Martinich, "Percent LDS by Country—2017."
10. The Church of Jesus Christ of Latter-Day Saints Newsroom. "2021 Statistical Report for the April 2022 Conference." *The Church of Jesus Christ of Latter-Day Saints Newsroom*. https:// newsroom.churchofjesuschrist.org/article/2021-statistical-report-april-2022-conference.
11. David G. Stewart Jr. 2007. *The Law of the Harvest: Practical Principles of Effective Missionary Work*. Henderson, NV: Cumorah Foundation, 23.
12. Elder Mark E. Peterson. 1954. *Race Problems—As They Affect the Church*. August 27. In Jerald Tanner and Sandra Tanner's, *Curse of Cain?: Racism in the Mormon Church*. Sandy, UT: Utah Lighthouse Ministry. http://www.utlm.org/onlinebooks/curseofcain_appendix_b.htm
13. The Doctrine and Covenants of The Church of Jesus Christ of Latter-day Saints. 2013. Official Declaration 2. Salt Lake City, UT: The Church of Jesus Christ of Latter-day Saints. https://www. churchofjesuschrist.org/study/scriptures/dc-testament/od/2?lang=eng
14. The Church of Jesus Christ of Latter-Day Saints Newsroom. 2023. "On Juneteenth, How the NAACP and the Church Are Carrying Out a Prophet's Vision." *The Church of Jesus Christ of Latter-Day Saints Newsroom*. http://newsroom.churchofjesuschrist.org/article/juncteenth-naacp-church-of-jesus-christ-2023.
15. Lee Davidson. 2021. "Salt Lake County Keeps Losing Latter-Day Saints, and There Are Multiple Theories as to Why." *The Salt Lake Tribune*. https://www.sltrib.com/religion/2021/01/14/salt-lake-county-keeps/
16. Peggy Fletcher Stack. 2018. "Mormons Rejoice at News of Shorter Sunday Services, but the Move Will Pose Challenges to Some, Especially Single Members." *The Salt Lake Tribune*. https://www.sltrib.com/religion/2018/10/06/mormons-rejoice-news/
17. Keith Coffman. 2011. "Latter-day Saints Launch 'I'm a Mormon' Ad Campaign." *Reuters*. October 2. https://www.reuters.com/article/us-mormons-media/latter-day-saints-launch-im-a-mormon-ad-campaign-idUKTRE7911CM20111002.
18. Richard A. Oppel Jr. and Erik Eckholm, 2011. "Prominent Pastor Calls Romney's Church a Cult." *The New York Times*. https://www.nytimes.com/2011/10/08/us/politics/prominent-pas tor-calls-romneys-church-a-cult.html.
19. Kevin Barney. 2006. "A Peculiar People?" *By Common Consent* [blog]. https://bycommoncons ent.com/2006/07/17/a-peculiar-people/.

Data References

The Church of Jesus Christ of Latter-Day Saints Newsroom. 2014. "2013 Statistical Report for 2014 April General Conference." *The Church of Jesus Christ of Latter-Day Saints Newsroom*. https://newsroom.churchofjesuschrist.org/article/2013-statistical-report-2014-april-gene ral-conference.

The Church of Jesus Christ of Latter-Day Saints Newsroom. 2015. "2014 Statistical Report for 2015 April General Conference." *The Church of Jesus Christ of Latter-Day Saints Newsroom*. https://newsroom.churchofjesuschrist.org/article/2014-statistical-report-for-2015-april-general-conference.

The Church of Jesus Christ of Latter-Day Saints Newsroom. 2016. "2015 Statistical Report for April 2016 General Conference." *The Church of Jesus Christ of Latter-Day Saints Newsroom*. https://newsroom.churchofjesuschrist.org/article/2015-statistical-report-april-2016-gene ral-conference.

LATTER-DAY SAINTS 159

The Church of Jesus Christ of Latter-Day Saints Newsroom. 2017. "2016 Statistical Report for 2017 April General Conference." *The Church of Jesus Christ of Latter-Day Saints Newsroom.* https://newsroom.churchofjesuschrist.org/article/2016-statistical-report-2017-april-con ference.

The Church of Jesus Christ of Latter-Day Saints Newsroom. 2018. "2017 Statistical Report for 2018 April Conference." *The Church of Jesus Christ of Latter-Day Saints Newsroom.* https:// newsroom.churchofjesuschrist.org/article/2017-statistical-report-april-2018-general-con ference.

The Church of Jesus Christ of Latter-Day Saints Newsroom. 2019. "2018 Statistical Report for 2019 April Conference." *The Church of Jesus Christ of Latter-Day Saints Newsroom.* https:// newsroom.churchofjesuschrist.org/article/2018-statistical-report.

The Church of Jesus Christ of Latter-Day Saints Newsroom. 2020. "2019 Statistical Report for 2020 April Conference." *The Church of Jesus Christ of Latter-Day Saints Newsroom.* https:// newsroom.churchofjesuschrist.org/article/2019-statistical-report.

The Church of Jesus Christ of Latter-Day Saints Newsroom. 2021. "2020 Statistical Report for the April 2021 Conference." *The Church of Jesus Christ of Latter-Day Saints Newsroom.* https://newsroom.churchofjesuschrist.org/article/april-2021-general-conference-statisti cal-report.

The Church of Jesus Christ of Latter-Day Saints Newsroom. 2022. "2021 Statistical Report for the April 2022 Conference." *The Church of Jesus Christ of Latter-Day Saints Newsroom.* https://newsroom.churchofjesuschrist.org/article/2021-statistical-report-april-2022-con ference.

The Church of Jesus Christ of Latter-Day Saints Newsroom. 2023. "Facts and Statistics." Salt Lake City, UT: The Church of Jesus Christ of Latter-day Saints. https://newsroom.churchof jesuschrist.org/facts-and-statistics.

Davern, Michael, Rene Bautista, Jeremy Freese, Pamela Herd, and Stephen L. Morgan. 2023. General Social Survey 1972–2022. Principal investigator, Michael Davern; Co-principal investigators, Rene Bautista, Jeremy Freese, Pamela Herd, and Stephen L. Morgan. Sponsored by National Science Foundation. NORC ed. Chicago: NORC at the University of Chicago. https://gssdataexplorer.norc.org/.

Deseret News. 2013. *Deseret News Church Almanac 2012.* Salt Lake City, UT: Deseret News.

Grammich, Clifford, Kirk Hadaway, Richard Houseal, Dale E. Jones, Alexei Krindatch, Richie Stanley, and Richard H. Taylor. 2023. 2020 U.S. Religion Census: Religious Congregations & Membership Study. Association of Statisticians of American Religious Bodies. https://www. usreligioncensus.org/node/1639.

Masci, David. 2019. "In U.S., Familiarity with Religious Groups Is Associated with Warmer Feelings toward Them." *Pew Research Center.* https://www.pewresearch.org/short-reads/ 2019/10/31/in-u-s-familiarity-with-religious-groups-is-associated-with-warmer-feelings-toward-them/.

Orth, Taylor. 2022. "Americans' Views on 35 Religious Groups, Organizations, and Belief Systems." *YouGov.* https://today.yougov.com/society/articles/44850-americans-views-religi ous-groups-yougov-pol.

Schaffner, Brian, Stephen Ansolabehere, Sam Luks, Shiro Kuriwaki, and Marissa Shih. 2006-2023. Cooperative Election Study Common Content, 2006–2022. Harvard Dataverse. https://cces.gov.harvard.edu/.

10

Muslims

For those who study world religions, the primary way that they are divided is into Western religions and Eastern religions. Eastern religions include faith groups like Hinduism, Buddhism, and Confucianism. And Western religions are almost always defined as being from the Abrahamic faith tradition: Christianity, Judaism, and Islam. In the United States, Christianity is undoubtedly the dominant expression of religion, with the General Social Survey reporting that at least 70% of Americans describe themselves as Protestant, Catholic, or Jewish in recent years. Judaism, as previously discussed, is smaller at around 2% of the country, but it still plays a prominent role in American religious conversation. However, the third branch of the Abrahamic faith, Islam, does not feature so prominently in the American discourse when it comes to religious traditions.

The story of American Islam is a completely unique one—it's not easy to draw parallels between the trials and travails of Muslims and other religious groups, whether they be a Western or Eastern tradition. While American society has always provided a privileged position to Christianity and frequently tried to marginalize and ostracize other religious groups to varying degrees, it's fair to say that Muslims have faced a significant amount of opposition, especially in the last several decades. Yet, despite these headwinds, Islam in the United States is experiencing substantial growth over the last several years, and Muslims are taking on more prominent roles in various facets of American society.

This chapter traces the contours of American Muslims—where they live and how they worship—and tries to sketch out the future of the religious tradition in the United States. There are many reasons to believe that Islam will continue to grow from a demographic perspective. Even a cursory look at the data indicates that they are benefitting from growth through immigration and this growth will be sustainable for the near future as Muslims tend to be a very young religious tradition. However, they still face a tremendous amount of skepticism, if not outright hostility in some corners of American society. It's undoubtedly true that the United States is experiencing a significant shift

The American Religious Landscape. Ryan P. Burge, Oxford University Press. © Oxford University Press 2025.
DOI: 10.1093/oso/9780197762837.003.0011

MUSLIMS 161

in religious composition and Islam is certainly one of the driving factors for those changes.

A Brief History of Islam in the United States

Scholars of American religious history argue that while Islam was in the New World soon after Columbus's voyage to the continent, it did not reach significant numbers until the importation of hundreds of thousands of enslaved people from the continent of Africa. However, while many of these slaves came to North America as practicing Muslims, they were forced to assimilate to the Christianity of their slaveholders soon after their arrival on the plantations throughout the South.[1] Thus, Islam was still a relatively small segment of the American religious landscape even in the years after the Civil War.

Muslims began to appear in the United States in the latter half of the nineteenth century and the early twentieth century through significant waves of immigration from countries with Islamic ties such as Syria, Turkey, and Palestine.[2] In 1965, the passage of the Immigration and Nationality Act eliminated immigration quotas, making it much easier for people to come to the United States from countries with a high concentration of Muslims.[3] Edward E. Curtis IV analyzed immigration records from 1965 to 1997 and concluded that 1.1 million immigrants to the United States during that time period were Muslim.[4] A report from the *Seattle Times* published in 2005 found that nearly 96,000 Muslims became permanent legal residents of the United States, which was a higher level of naturalization than at any point in the prior two decades.[5]

However, it's essential to note that Muslims have faced a tremendous amount of political backlash in the last two decades in the wake of the tragedy of September 11, 2001. In the aftermath of the attack on the World Trade Center and the Pentagon, there was an organized and sustained attempt to marginalize Islam in the United States. In the data below, we will see that despite the efforts of some politicians, antipathy toward Muslims is fairly low in the general population.

For instance, Donald Trump was a vocal proponent of the falsehood that President Barack Obama was secretly a Muslim. His rhetoric against Islam only intensified when he began his run for president. In December 2016, Trump called for "a total and complete shutdown of Muslims entering the United States until our country's representatives can figure out what is going on."[6] When elected to the White House, Trump signed an executive order that became known as the Muslim Travel Ban, which restricted travel from several majority-Muslim countries, including Iran, Iraq, Syria, and Yemen. President Biden revoked the order when he took office in January 2021. Undoubtedly, the last several decades have been fraught for Muslim families in the United States and for those who are trying to come to American shores.

The Growth of Islam in the United States

It's incredibly difficult to track the size of a relatively small religious group by using survey estimates. This is clearly the case when looking at the trajectory of Muslims in the United States. The General Social Survey began in 1972, and it has been asking about the religion of respondents since its inception. However, it took until 1998 for the General Social Survey to specifically provide "Muslim/Islam" as a response option. While the General Social Survey tends to vary in overall sample size, a typical year polls a bit over 2,000 respondents. Very few Muslims show up in these waves of the survey.

For instance, in Figure 10.1, there were just fifteen Muslims in both the 1998 and 2002 surveys. The variability of the number of Muslims that appear

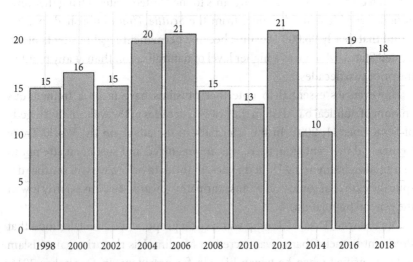

Figure 10.1 Total number of respondents in the General Social Survey who identify as Muslim
Data: General Social Survey

in the General Social Survey is not large. The number never falls below ten (as it did in 2014) but never rises above twenty-one, which happened in both 2006 and 2012. What's notable is that the highest raw number of Muslims was followed by the fewest. However, this one result is not enough evidence to conclude that Islam has dramatically increased or decreased in size. Thus, when dealing with such a small portion of the population, Figure 10.1 makes it clear why it's inadvisable to use this data as a way to extrapolate to the general population.

This is a primary reason why there has been so little quantitative scholarship about Muslims in the United States—until recent years, there just was not a sufficient sample to do any type of demographic breakdown. In a case like this, the only options that a survey researcher has at their disposal are to do a very large random sample of the population to yield a significant number of Muslims (which is cost-prohibitive) or do a convenience sample that specifically seeks out Muslims and asks them to take part in a survey (which introduces a number of methodological issues).

However, in recent years, scholars have benefitted from several large data collection efforts that have been made available to the scholarly community. One of them is the Cooperative Election Study, which often samples over sixty thousand American adults. What this means is that now the sample size goes from 10–15 to 200–300. This unlocks a number of possible avenues for statistical analysis and the ability to track trends with significantly more confidence.

The Cooperative Election Study does hint at a noticeable rise in the share of Americans who self-identify as Muslims, as can be seen in Figure 10.2. In the early waves of the Cooperative Election Study, about one-half of 1% said that they were Muslims, but that has clearly risen in the last several years. By 2016, about three-quarters of 1% were Muslims, and it has steadily increased from this point forward. It seems appropriate to say that about 1% of all American adults are Muslims, although that estimate may be off slightly in either direction. That would put the current number of Muslims in the United States at right about 3.5 million. This comports with a Pew Research Center estimate of the American Muslim population of 3.45 million in 2017.[7]

This estimate derived from the Cooperative Election Study dovetails nicely with an analysis conducted using the 2020 Religion Census. The Religion Census was based on both a mail survey of mosques around the United States followed by a telephone call to a random sampling of mosques. Using this sampling procedure, the estimate of the total number of Muslims

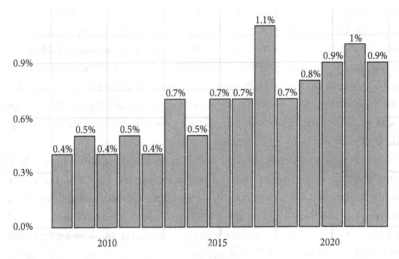

Figure 10.2 The share of the population that identifies as Muslim
Data: Cooperative Election Study

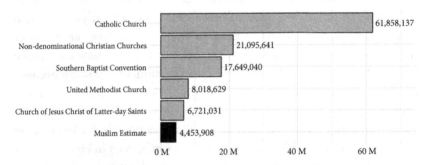

Figure 10.3 The six largest religious traditions in the United States
Data: Religion Census

is nearly 4.5 million, as seen in Figure 10.3. Thus, it's fair to assume from both survey data and the information from the Religion Census that the number of Muslims is likely in the 3–5 million range in the United States.

In a similar fashion to Protestant Christianity, Islam also has denominations (oftentimes referred to as sects) that differ on key theological points. According to the Pew Research Center, the majority of Muslims identify as Sunni, 87%–90%, and Shia Muslims make up 10%–13%.[8] The primary difference between these two sects is the events that immediately followed the death of the prophet Muhammad. Shiites believe that the

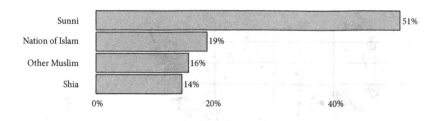

Figure 10.4 Breakdown of Muslim denominations in the United States
Data: Cooperative Election Study

rightful leader should come from the family of Muhammad, while Sunnis argue that the new leader of Islam should be chosen by consensus.

In the United States, Figure 10.4 shows that Sunnis are clearly the largest branch of Islam, with nearly half of all Muslims living in the country, while those who identify as Shia make up about 14% of the country. The Shiite share is clearly in line with the overall composition of Muslims worldwide, but the Sunni percentage is much lower. One primary reason for that is a notable share of Muslims in the United States who identify as members of the Nation of Islam (NOI). This sect of Islam began in the United States in the 1930s. While the NOI does hold to some teachings of mainstream Islam, what makes this sect unique is its politics. The NOI is a Black nationalist organization that advocates for a separation of the Black and white races and has argued for the creation of a separate Black state.[9] The famed civil rights activist, Malcolm X, was one of the most prominent members of the NOI in the 1950s until he grew disillusioned with the organization in the 1960s.[10] Today, 16% of Muslims in the United States align with the NOI.

Where Do Muslims Live in the United States?

As previously mentioned, the Religion Census, which is compiled by the Association of Statisticians of American Religious Bodies, went to great lengths to collect membership information about Islam in the United States between 2010 and 2020. In total, they identified 2,771 congregations around the country. They determined that about 1.3% of the country identifies as Muslim and 2.8% of all people who are adherents of any religious faith are

Figure 10.5 Counties that have a Muslim congregation
Data: Religion Census

aligned with the Islamic faith. Visualizing the geographic distribution of Islam in Figure 10.5 yields some interesting insights.

In total, the Religion Census found a Muslim congregation in 670 counties in the United States. That means that just over 21% of all counties report having a place of worship for Muslims. However, they clearly are not evenly distributed across the country. Like many other non-Christian faiths, there are significant pockets of Muslims on both the East and West Coasts of the United States. There is an especially strong contingent in what is known as the Northeast Corridor, which runs from Boston to Washington, DC, and includes such cities as New York, Philadelphia, and Baltimore.

There are significant pockets of Muslims to be found in Florida, as well. According to this data, thirty-four counties in the state have an Islamic mosque. Broward County, which is in the Miami metro area, reports twenty-one Muslim congregations and nearly 20,000 adherents. Southern California and Arizona have a significant Muslim community, too. Besides their coastal presence, it's notable how there are mosques scattered throughout the middle of the United States, too. While a majority of these can be found in more population-dense areas, there are some more rural counties that are home to Islamic houses of worship, as well.

However, while Muslims might enjoy a significant level of religious dispersion, that does not mean that they achieve a high level of concentration at the state level—that is clear when looking at the most recent Religion Census, visualized in Figure 10.6. In fact, Muslims make up less than 1%

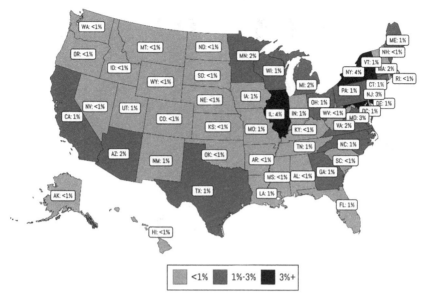

Figure 10.6 Share of the population that is Muslim
Data: Religion Census

of the population in thirty-two states. There are only four states in which Muslims are at least 3% of the population: Illinois, New York, New Jersey, and Maryland. Again, notice how three of those states can be found in the Northeast portion of the United States. Across most of the country's midsection, Islam is just a fraction of a percentage of the overall population of the state. There are just not many states where it would be commonplace to find an Islamic house of worship.

However, there are several counties in which Muslims make up a significant share of the overall population; this is displayed in Figure 10.7. The county with the highest overall number of Muslims is Cook County, Illinois, which comprises the city of Chicago with 311,000 Muslims. DuPage County, which is in suburban Chicago, also has another 71,000 Muslims. Added together, it's highly likely that one in ten Muslims in the United States lives in northern Illinois. But even in those areas, Muslims only make up 6%–7% of the population.

The county with the highest concentration of Muslims is Wayne County, Michigan, whose county seat is Detroit. About 8% of the entire county is Muslim, and over 17% of all religious adherents follow the Islamic faith

County	State	Congregations	Adherents	% of Adherents Who Are Muslim	% of Population Who Are Muslim
Cook County	Illinois	68	311,223	10.9%	5.9%
Queens County	New York	83	178,323	13.6%	7.4%
Kings County	New York	69	154,120	12.0%	5.6%
Wayne County	Michigan	64	145,494	17.2%	8.1%
Los Angeles County	California	74	142,661	2.8%	1.4%
Bronx County	New York	48	111,936	19.6%	7.6%
Harris County	Texas	63	91,156	3.3%	1.9%
Maricopa County	Arizona	26	90,826	4.3%	2.1%
DuPage County	Illinois	18	71,090	12.0%	7.6%
Philadelphia County	Pennsylvania	41	70,065	10.1%	4.4%

Figure 10.7 Countries with the most Muslim adherents

in Wayne County. Beyond Detroit, one of the major population centers is Dearborn, which boasts the largest mosque in the United States, the Islamic Center of America.[11] In 2021, Dearborn elected the first Arab American mayor, largely because at least 42% of the population in Dearborn, Michigan, is Arab American, with many being members of the local mosques in the community.[12]

There are also significant concentrations of Muslims in other urban counties, as well. The New York City metropolitan area has a significant Islamic presence, with more than half a million Muslims spread across several counties and boroughs. But there are also a notable number of Muslims in places further west such as Phoenix, Houston, and Los Angeles. Thus, Islam is a religion that has gained a foothold in more densely populated parts of the country while not just being segregated into one specific region.

Age and Race among Muslims

One truly unique characteristic of Muslims in the United States is their tremendous amount of racial diversity. Many religious groups have strong ties to one race, like Latter-day Saints, for instance, who are overwhelmingly white, while nearly 80% of all Hindus are Asian. However, Muslims occupy an interesting racial space in that some come from Middle Eastern and Southeast Asian countries while others, like those of the Nation of Islam, are African American. These data bear this out when it comes to Muslims in the United States, which can be seen in Figure 10.8.

In the Cooperative Election Study, the plurality of Muslims indicates that they are Black at 37%. The second most popular response option was white

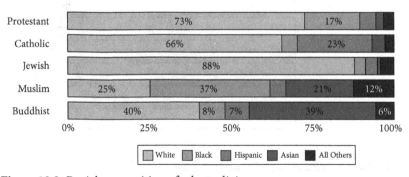

Figure 10.8 Racial composition of select religious groups

at 25% followed closely by Asian at 21%. It's notable that three different racial groups make up at least 20% of all Muslims. No other religious group that is highlighted in this volume can boast such a claim. In fact, for many groups, the largest racial group makes up two-thirds or more. That's certainly the case for Protestants, Catholics, and Jews. But there's no doubt that Muslims exhibit a kind of racial diversity that is unmatched by other religious groups.

One other interesting demographic fact about Muslims, as seen in Figure 10.9, is their overall age. The Cooperative Election Study only polls those who are at least eighteen years old, so it can only provide an estimate of the age of adult Americans, but on this measure, no one is younger than the average Muslim at just thirty-four years old. The religious group that is the closest in average age to Muslims is Hindus, but they are nearly 6.5 years older than Muslims on average. It's clear that followers of Islam in the United States are an incredibly young group.

In the recent waves of the Cooperative Election Study, the average adult respondent (regardless of religious tradition) was forty-eight years old. That's fourteen years older than the average Muslim. Most of the larger religious traditions in the United States like Protestants and Catholics are slightly

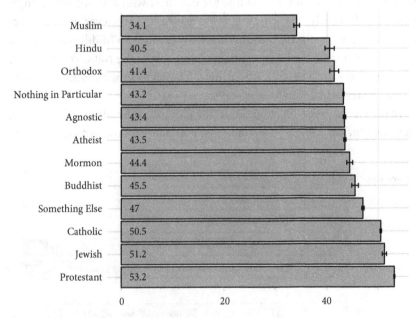

Figure 10.9 Average age of religious traditions
Data: Cooperative Election Study

older than the average adult American. Thus, there's ample reason to believe that the future trajectory of Islam is a positive one. With such a low mean age, it means that most adult Muslims are in the stage of life when having children is still a very real possibility. These children will presumably be raised in the faith of their parents, and many will maintain that into adulthood. This is an extremely positive indicator of the future vitality of Islam in the United States.

What is an even more positive indicator is looking at the relationship between age and religious attendance. One would assume that older adults are the ones who are the most likely to be attending mosque on a regular basis and attendance levels are lower for those who are in their twenties and thirties. However, the data displayed in Figure 10.10 reveal a pattern that goes against this assumption for Muslims.

Among the youngest adults, those between the ages of eighteen and thirty-five years old, 42% of Muslims report going to a mosque at least once a week. That is eleven percentage points higher than Catholics and just slightly less than Protestants. When looking at the next age category, the numbers look strikingly similar, with Protestants and Muslims attending at a similar rate and Catholics lagging behind. There's a bit of a drop among Muslims between the ages of forty-five and fifty-four, but then mosque attendance shoots back up to nearly half of Muslims between the ages of fifty-five and

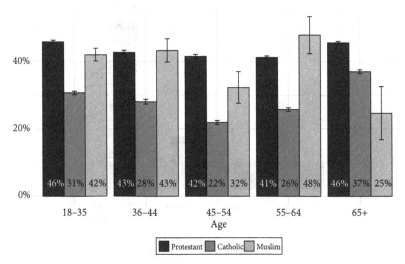

Figure 10.10 The share attending religious services weekly
Data: Cooperative Election Study

sixty-four. But the big takeaway here is that younger Muslims are fairly active in their faith community—they are not drifting away. This points to a future in which Muslims who are having children are raising them with a strong association with their local mosque. This increases the likelihood of retention and the future health of the religious tradition.

Immigration and American Muslims

One important facet of understanding Muslims in the United States is the issue of immigration. As previously mentioned, federal immigration policy made it difficult, if not impossible, for Muslims to come to the United States based on the quotas imposed by Congress at several points in American history. When those quotas were lifted, it made it easier for followers of Islam to enter the United States. The end result is that a significant share of Muslims living in the United States have recently immigrated to the country or have living relatives who made the journey themselves.

This experience is validated in survey data visualized in Figure 10.11. Among the general population, less than 10% of people say that they

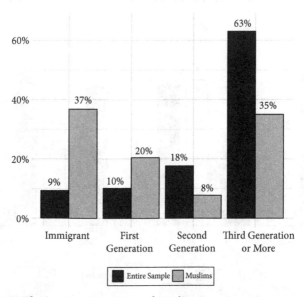

Figure 10.11 The immigration status of Muslims
Data: Cooperative Election Study

immigrated to the United States themselves. Among Muslims, the percentage is over four times higher (37%). In fact, nearly three in five Muslims either immigrated to the United States themselves or their parents came to the country as immigrants. That experience is only shared by one in five Americans in the full sample. Just over a third of Muslims in the United States say that their family has been in the country for at least three generations. It's nearly two-thirds of Americans overall. Without a doubt, Islam is making gains in part due to the rapid increase in immigrants.

But this surfaces an interesting question: Are recent Muslim immigrants more religiously active than those who have been in the country for several generations? It's a possibility that recent immigrants move to a community with a significant Islamic presence as a way to make quick connections. Thus, mosque attendance is a way to build a social network as a means to find friends, employment, and other basic needs. But the opposite may happen as well. It's possible that recent immigrants want to assimilate into the larger community by not going to mosque but instead attending nonreligious social events on the weekends and making friends outside the bounds of Islam.

The data seem to support the conclusion that recent Muslim immigrants are slightly less likely to go to mosque on a regular basis compared to those who have been in the United States for generations, as can be seen in Figure 10.12. Among recent immigrants, just 34% say that they attend religious services at least once a week. For those who are at least third-generation immigrants, regular mosque attendance is 42%. However, note that the share who attend never/seldom is exactly the same for recent immigrants and those who have been in the country for generations.

Along with fairly robust religious attendance, especially among Muslims across age and immigration categories, there is evidence in the data (see

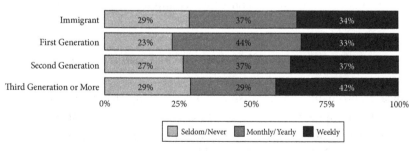

Figure 10.12 The religious attendance of Muslims based on immigration status
Data: Cooperative Election Study

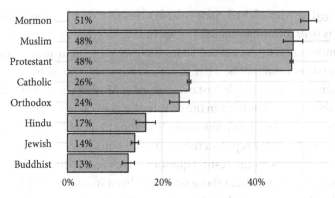

Figure 10.13 Share praying multiple times a day
Data: Religion Census

Figure 10.13) that the average Muslim is more engaged in regular prayer than many other religious traditions that have large shares of immigrants like Hindus and Buddhists. Regular prayer plays an especially integral role in the Islamic faith with Muslims being called to prayer five times a day, a practice that obviously requires a tremendous time commitment from its adherents but also has the effect of building social cohesion among followers of Islam.

The Cooperative Election Studies data indicate that about half of Muslims report praying multiple times per day, which is statistically tied for the highest rate of any religious group (along with Latter-day Saints). Prayer frequency is much lower among any other religious group. For instance, just a quarter of Catholics report praying multiple times per day, and it's even lower among groups like Hindus (17%) and Buddhists (13%). Again, this is an incredibly positive sign in terms of retention for Muslims. Those who are actively engaging in faith practices are more likely to stay in the Islamic tradition throughout their lives and raise their children in a similar fashion.

Perceptions of Muslims in the United States

However, no chapter about Muslims would be complete without discussing a significant impediment to the growth of Islam within the United States—negative views of Muslims that are held by a significant portion of the American population. While it's possible to trace anti-Muslim sentiment in the United States for centuries, these discriminatory views increased rapidly in the wake of the terrorist attacks on September 11, 2001. In the immediate aftermath of those events, a narrative began to emerge that the hijackers were motivated by talk of jihad and the blessings that they would receive in the afterlife for sacrificing their lives for the cause of Islam.

Many Americans were looking for a possible motivation for such horrific acts, and the lack of knowledge of Islam among the average American made it easy to blame the events of 9/11 on religion, not necessarily a political conflict that had been brewing for decades. When former Speaker of the House, Newt Gingrich was running for president in 2010, he made the encroachment of sharia law in the United States a central theme. He stated that the goal of Islam was "to replace Western Civilization with a radical imposition of Shariah."[13] When President Obama was in the White House, there was a concerted effort to convince the American public that he was, in fact, a Muslim, even though he had been baptized in a Protestant church on Chicago's South Side as an adult. This view was held by 43% of Republicans in polling conducted in 2015, near the end of his second term.[14]

Some of the animus toward Islam persists even in survey data collected many years after the events of September 11, as seen in Figure 10.14. For instance, the General Social Survey asked respondents about their personal attitudes toward Muslims in 2018. Overall, 40% of those taking the survey said that they had a positive view of Muslims, 43% were ambivalent, and 17% said that they held a negative view.

When looking at individual religious groups, there are some noticeable variations. Protestants look almost the same as the overall population, with just a slightly larger share saying that they have a negative view—22%. Catholics feel much more warmly toward Muslims than the rest of the sample, with about half having an overall positive view. The nonreligious

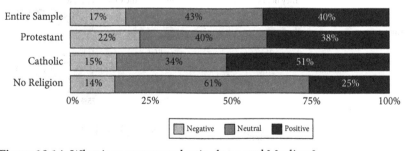

Figure 10.14 What is your personal attitude toward Muslims?
Data: General Social Survey

are at the other end of the spectrum with just a quarter expressing a positive view. Note that three in five describe their position as neutral, and only 14% have a negative perception of Muslims.

There are, of course, two ways to look at this data. One is that very few Americans express true negative feelings about followers of Islam, less than 20%. But the other way to view this is that a majority of Americans do not express positive feelings toward Muslims. One problem that is always prevalent in survey data is social desirability bias. This is the tendency for individuals to not tell the truth when being questioned about sensitive topics. Survey respondents know that their true feelings are not socially acceptable and thus they fudge their answers a bit. When looking at data from Figure 10.14, it's wise to assume that a significant percentage of "neutral" responses are probably negative. Calculating that share precisely is not possible, however.

There are other surveys that try to get at this question about the perception of Muslims. In 2017, the Baylor Religion Survey included a section where participants were asked to read and react to three distinct statements concerning Muslims and conservative Christians. These statements asked if respondents felt personally threatened by either group, whether they thought that those groups were morally inferior, or if they wanted to limit the respondent's personal freedom. Those results are displayed in Figure 10.15.

In terms of personal safety, there is some evidence that the average American feels more threatened by Muslims than they do by conservative Christians. Twenty-five percent of Americans agreed with that statement,

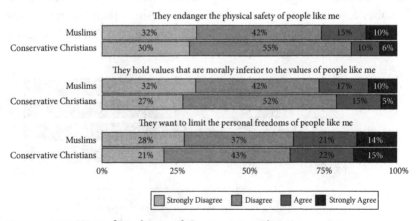

Figure 10.15 View of Muslims and Conservative Christians
Data: Baylor Religion Survey, 2017

MUSLIMS 177

compared to only 16% for conservative Christians. Twenty-seven percent of Americans believe that Muslims "hold values that are morally inferior to the values of people like me"; when Muslims are replaced with conservative Christians, the share agreeing drops to 20%. On the issue of whether these groups want to limit personal freedoms, there's not much difference. About 36% of Americans agree with that statement. Overall, there's some evidence here that Muslims are more marginalized in American society but not by a significant margin.

Conclusion

When thinking about the future of the population in the United States, one way to consider it is through the metaphor of headwinds and tailwinds. There are certainly both in great measure right now for Muslims. The headwinds were just discussed—the significant amount of animosity against Islam in the United States. Consider the fact that 60% of Americans do not report a positive view of Muslims and a quarter say that Muslims endanger their physical safety. That's a difficult public relations problem that is not easily or quickly solved.

However, there are also a lot of demographic tailwinds that can bolster the Muslim population in the United States. The biggest factor is that the average adult Muslim is just thirty-four years old. That's fourteen years younger than the average adult in the United States. That means that a significant share of Muslims is still of childbearing age. Among those younger Muslims, the frequency of mosque attendance is relatively robust, as well. This means that those children will be raised in a religious community and retention will be fairly high. Also, half of Muslims in the United States report that they pray multiple times a day. This all points to the same conclusion: followers of Islam in the United States are deeply rooted in their faith tradition.

The stigma against Islam in the United States will obviously put a damper on the ability of adherents to bring new members into the fold, while the low average age and devotion will make those who are born into the faith much more likely to stick around. What may be the most likely outcome is that Islam flourishes in pockets where it has already gained a significant foothold. It seems plausible that cities like Dearborn, Michigan, may be majority Muslim in the decades to come. However, that geographic concentration

178   THE AMERICAN RELIGIOUS LANDSCAPE

means that many Americans will likely not live in a county with a mosque. This lack of familiarity can drive up suspicion and intolerance.

Every minority religious group in the United States faces the tradeoff between staying in communities with a significant number of people of the same faith group or venturing out into other areas where there is no established house of worship. Followers of Islam will likely face this tension repeatedly in the years to come. As the events of 9/11 continue to fade in the American consciousness and the younger generations come of age after the anti-Islamic protests, it seems that some of the prejudice toward Muslims will fade. If the Islamic community can find ways to interact with the average American, there's a good chance the feelings of warmth will continue in the future.

Notes

1. Jane I. Smith. 2010. *Islam in America*. New York: Columbia University Press, 78–79.; "The First American Muslims." *The Pluralism Project*. Harvard University. https://pluralism.org/the-first-american-muslims.
2. Smith, *Islam in America*, 51–53.
3. Edward E. Curtis IV. 2009. *Muslims in America: A Short History*. New York: Oxford University Press, 72–73.
4. Curtis, *Muslims in America*, 73.
5. Andrea Elliott. 2006. "Muslim Immigration Has Bounced Back." *The Seattle Times*.
6. Jenna Johnson and Abigail Hauslohner. 2017. "'I Think Islam Hates Us': A Timeline of Trump's Comments about Islam and Muslims." *The Washington Post*.
7. Besheer Mohamed. 2018. "New Estimates Show U.S. Muslim Population Continues to Grow." *Pew Research Center*. https://www.pewresearch.org/short-reads/2018/01/03/new-estimates-show-u-s-muslim-population-continues-to-grow/.
8. Pew Research Center. 2011. *The Future of the Global Muslim Population: Projections for 2010–2023*, 153. https://www.pewresearch.org/religion/2011/01/27/the-future-of-the-global-muslim-population/.
9. Dawn-Marie Gibson. 2012. *A History of the Nation of Islam: Race, Islam, and the Quest for Freedom*. Santa Barbara, CA: Praeger, 17, 34; Clifton E. Marsh. 2000. *The Lost-Found Nation of Islam in America*. Lanham, MD: Scarecrow Press, 37, 41–42, 46–47; Martha F. Lee. 1988. *The Nation of Islam, an American Millenarian Movement*. Lewiston, NY: The Edwin Mellen Press, 44–45.
10. Gibson, *A History of the Nation of Islam*, 60; Marsh, *The Lost-Found Nation of Islam in America*, 60.
11. *Islamic Center of America*. https://www.icofa.com/founders/.
12. CBS Detroit. 2021. "Dearborn's First Arab-American Mayor Has a Message for Its Youth: 'Be Proud of Your Name.'" https://www.cbsnews.com/detroit/news/dearborns-first-arab-american-mayor-has-a-message-for-its-youth-be-proud-of-your-name/.
13. Scott Shane. 2011. "In Islamic Law, Gingrich Sees a Mortal Threat to U.S." *The New York Times*. https://www.nytimes.com/2011/12/22/us/politics/in-shariah-gingrich-sees-mortal-threat-to-us.html.
14. Sarah Pulliam Bailey. 2015. "A Startling Number of Americans Still Believe President Obama Is a Muslim." *The Washington Post*. https://www.washingtonpost.com/news/acts-of-faith/wp/2015/09/14/a-startling-number-of-americans-still-believe-president-obama-is-a-muslim/.

Data References

Davern, Michael, Rene Bautista, Jeremy Freese, Pamela Herd, and Stephen L. Morgan. 2023. General Social Survey 1972–2022. Principal investigator, Michael Davern; Co-principal investigators, Rene Bautista, Jeremy Freese, Pamela Herd, and Stephen L. Morgan. Sponsored by National Science Foundation. NORC ed. Chicago: NORC at the University of Chicago. https://gssdataexplorer.norc.org/.

Froese, Paul. 2017. Baylor Religion Survey, Wave V (2017). Baylor University. Waco, TX: Baylor Institute for Studies of Religion. https://www.thearda.com/data-archive?fid=BRS5.

Grammich, Clifford, Kirk Hadaway, Richard Houseal, Dale E. Jones, Alexei Krindatch, Richie Stanley, and Richard H. Taylor. 2023. 2020 U.S. Religion Census: Religious Congregations & Membership Study. Association of Statisticians of American Religious Bodies. https://www.usreligioncensus.org/node/1639.

Schaffner, Brian, Stephen Ansolabehere, Sam Luks, Shiro Kuriwaki, and Marissa Shih. 2006–2023. Cooperative Election Study Common Content, 2006–2022. Harvard Dataverse. https://cces.gov.harvard.edu/.

11
Buddhists

If the average American were asked to describe the term "karma," they would likely be able to describe the word with some specificity. The same may be true of the concept of reincarnation. However, it's unlikely that many people living in the United States could tie either concept back to the Buddhist religion. Although central Buddhist principles have become part of the broader conversation in America, the Buddhist faith still remains enigmatic to tens of millions of Americans nationwide.

This is likely because Buddhists, like many smaller religious traditions, arrived on American shores through the process of immigration. Many immigrants, aiming for a smoother adjustment to a new country, often choose to reside in communities where there is a significant presence of individuals from their own country or who share similar religious beliefs and practices. As this chapter will describe, this is certainly the case for Buddhists in the United States.

Buddhism also provides a measurement challenge for social scientists who try to make comparisons about religious behavior among and between various religious traditions. While Western faith groups like Protestants, Catholics, and Jews make regular corporate worship a central part of their faith and practice, the same is not true for Buddhists. This chapter explains that the Buddhist perspective on faith and its application among followers offer researchers a unique framework for understanding how religion functions within its community.

Buddhism is a religious tradition that in some ways fits many of the stereotypes of a minority, largely immigrant-based faith. But on other measures, Buddhists tend to defy conventional wisdom. Quantitative social science reveals that our perceptions of groups can be accurate in certain aspects, yet in other areas, our views may be founded on misinformation or inaccuracies. As Buddhism continues to evolve in the United States, so should our views of this fascinating and vibrant faith tradition.

The American Religious Landscape. Ryan P. Burge, Oxford University Press. © Oxford University Press 2025.
DOI: 10.1093/oso/9780197762837.003.0012

The Size of the Buddhist Community in the United States

It's hard to measure Buddhism, for many of the same reasons why it is a challenge to measure Latter-day Saints, Muslims, or Hindus—there just aren't that many of them in a country of more than 330 million people. Generating an accurate survey estimate of such a small group can prove to be a very difficult task. It's possible to do a random sample survey of several hundred and not have a single Buddhist show up in the results. In fact, fifty years ago there were hardly any surveys that included a response option for groups like Buddhists, Hindus, and Muslims because they were so rare in the general population.

That is certainly the case with the General Social Survey (GSS). The GSS first included Buddhism in its response options in 1998, even though the survey had been conducted every year or two since 1972. The results, visualized in Figure 11.1, provide a glimpse into the distribution of Buddhists in the overall population. The results show the share who identify as Buddhists as somewhere between 0.3% and 1.2%. Results gathered from the 2000s show that Buddhists were likely around 0.5% of the entire sample population. The last several survey waves point toward some growth in the Buddhist population. For instance, the 2014 figure was 1.1%. That dropped a bit in 2016 and 2018 only to rise to 1.2% in the most recent survey conducted in 2021.

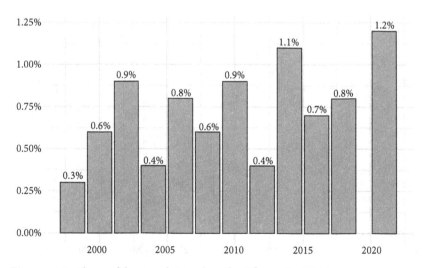

Figure 11.1 Share of the population that identifies as Buddhist
Data: General Social Survey

From this angle, there appears to be some weak evidence that the share of Buddhists in the United States may be increasing slightly over time. The data from the last four survey waves point in that general direction. The issue is simply this: with a group that is such a small fraction of the population, a random sample could easily report an abnormally high (or low) number of Buddhists just by chance. What can mitigate this concern is when several surveys in a row arrive at the same general estimate. That seems to be the case in the GSS since 2014, but it's helpful to corroborate these results with other surveys, as well.

The Cooperative Election Study (CES), with its larger sample size, can help alleviate the issues associated with the volatility of small population groups in a single random sample, as the larger sample provides a more stable and reliable representation. Thus, the results displayed in Figure 11.2 are much more consistent—a typical result when the overall sample size increases. Here, there isn't the up-and-down pattern seen in the results from the GSS. The variation in the CES runs from 0.7% of the total sample to 1% of all respondents. For many years, the percentage was the same: 0.9%.

Seeing these two survey results in tandem helps to provide a much more balanced and comprehensive picture of the share of Americans who identify as Buddhist. There is sufficient evidence here that the percentage of adults in the United States who self-identify as Buddhists is around 1%. It may be

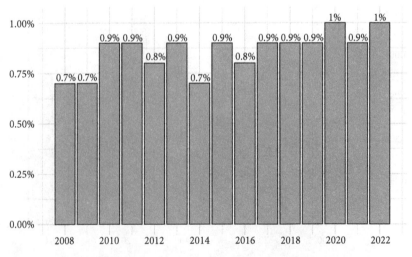

Figure 11.2 Share of the population that identifies as Buddhist
Data: Cooperative Election Study

a bit higher or it could be a bit lower. The trend line in both the CES and the GSS does point upward, as well. This is not a dramatic increase, but it would appear that the share of Buddhists has risen noticeably in the last four or five years.

Where Are Buddhists Located?

Because Buddhists are not an exceedingly large part of the overall population, it logically follows that they are not geographically dispersed across the United States. Data from the Religion Census tracks Buddhists by contacting houses of worship and asking them to provide basic information, such as the number of individuals on local membership rolls. The advantage of this data is that it is much more granular than survey data, making it possible for analysts to look at county-level statistics. That level of specificity would only be possible using incredibly large and cost-prohibitive surveys.

According to the Religion Census, visualized in Figure 11.3, there are 438 counties that have a Buddhist house of worship in the United States. The states with the most Buddhist temples are some of the largest states in the

Figure 11.3 Counties that have a Buddhist congregation
Data: Religion Census

union: California has eighty-two, New York reports fifty-five, Florida has thirty-eight, and Texas has thirty-six. No other state reports more than thirty houses of worship for Buddhist traditions. California easily has the most Buddhist members at 311,273. The next largest is New York at 76,280. For comparison, there are fewer than 1,000 Buddhists in Delaware, Wyoming, Mississippi, and the Dakotas combined.

While there is a Buddhist house of worship in almost every state in the country, there are entire regions where Buddhism is scarce. For instance, there are only eight Buddhist temples in the entire state of Iowa and only nine in South Carolina, Montana, and Kentucky. And, as can likely be understood from the map in Figure 11.3, major metropolitan areas are the places where Buddhists tend to be found in higher numbers. Los Angeles County reports 97,602 adherents—the most of any county. Honolulu County in Hawaii ranks number two at just less than 41,000 Buddhists. There are also large pockets of Buddhists in Chicago, New York City, San Diego, and Seattle.

Figure 11.4 illustrates a significant correlation between the total population of a county and the probability of encountering a Buddhist temple

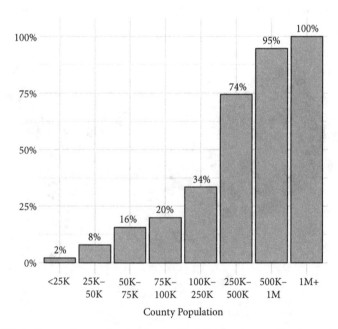

Figure 11.4 Share of counties that have a Buddhist congregation by population size
Data: Religion Census

or center in that area. For instance, among counties with less than 25,000 inhabitants, just one in fifty reports having a Buddhist congregation. As the population rises, so does the likelihood of finding a Buddhist presence. Among counties with between 100,000 and 250,000 residents, about one-third have a Buddhist temple. Thus, even in fairly populated counties, it's still relatively rare to find a significant concentration of Buddhists.

But once a county's population exceeds a quarter million, the chance of finding a Buddhist temple surges sharply, approaching almost 75%. This percentage climbs to 95% of counties with half a million residents, and when a county has at least a million people, one is certain to find a Buddhist house of worship. This trend speaks to the pattern that exists for many of the smaller religious groups in the United States: they tend to be found largely in communities with greater population density and are relatively rare in more rural parts of the United States. This geographic concentration is understandable, given the desire to move into an established religious community with like-minded individuals. However, it means that large swaths of Americans who live in places with lower population density will be less likely to encounter a Buddhist in their everyday life.

Type of Buddhists in the United States

If a respondent indicates that they are a Buddhist on the initial question about religious affiliation, the CES asks a follow-up that tries to sort them into the correct type of Buddhism. The CES offers three options—Mahayana (also known as Zen Buddhism), Theravada (Vipassana), and Vajrayana (Tibetan). While it's hard to get a true sense of the distribution of Buddhism across the world, the Pew Research Center contends that Mahayana is the largest in the world because it is found in high concentrations in places with lots of Buddhists like China and Vietnam.[1] Theravada is seen as the second largest sect and is found in high percentages in Thailand, Laos, and Cambodia.

Data from the Cooperative Election Study conducted in the United States generally align with the broader classifications regarding the predominant types of Buddhists. Figure 11.5 shows that in data collected between 2020 and 2022, about 40% of Buddhists align with Mahayana—easily the largest branch in the United States. There are about half as many Theravada Buddhists at 18%, and an even smaller share are Vajrayana (or Tibetan) Buddhists. It's worth pointing out that about a quarter of Buddhists in the

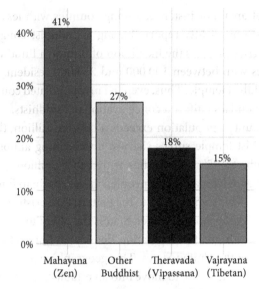

Figure 11.5 Types of Buddhists in the United States
Data: Cooperative Election Study

sample are not able to report which type of branch that they belong to—making them the second largest category of Buddhists in the United States.

Demographic Characteristics of Buddhism

As previously noted, Buddhism is largely an immigrant faith in the United States—like Islam and Hinduism. The data in Figure 11.6 confirm that. Thirty percent of all Buddhists surveyed in the last several years indicate that they themselves had come to American shores. Another 22% report that their parents had immigrated to the United States, but they were born in the country. For comparison, only 9% of the full sample were immigrants and another 10% were first-generation Americans.

These differences come into sharper focus when looking at those respondents who indicate that their family had been in the United States for generations. Nearly two-thirds of all survey respondents said that their family had been American citizens for at least three generations. The same was true for only about a third of Buddhists in the sample. Consider this: a Buddhist in the United States is just as likely to be an immigrant themselves as to be at least a third-generation citizen of the country. In the total sample,

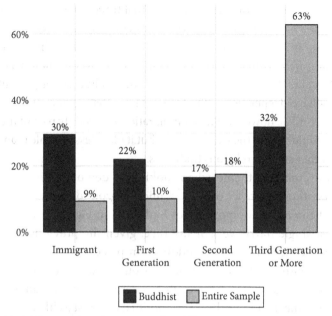

Figure 11.6 The immigration status of Buddhists
Data: Cooperative Election Study

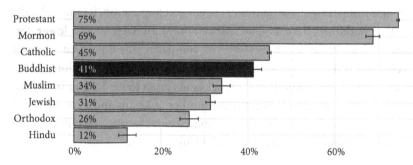

Figure 11.7 Share who are third-generation immigrants or more
Data: Cooperative Election Study

one is seven times more likely to have been in the country for generations than they are to be a recent immigrant. Thus, immigration is a crucial part of the story when it comes to Buddhism in the United States.

However, when comparing the immigration status of Buddhists to other religious groups, it's apparent that they land in the middle of the distribution, as can be seen in Figure 11.7. Given the history of the United States and immigrants, it should come as no surprise that three-quarters of Protestants can trace their lineage back on American shores for at least three generations, with Latter-day Saints not far behind at 69%. However, Buddhists don't look that much different than Catholics when it comes to the share who are at least third generation—41% versus 45%, respectively. A larger percentage of Buddhists have deeper ties in the United States than groups like Muslims, Jews, and Hindus, however. Thus, immigration is certainly part of the larger picture of Buddhists in the United States, but it plays less of a role than it does for some other smaller religious traditions.

That's a common theme when looking at demographic data about Buddhists: they seem to occupy a middle ground. As is clear when looking at the racial composition of Buddhists in Figure 11.8, they don't easily fit a single narrative. For instance, given the previous discussion about large concentrations of Buddhists in places like China, Vietnam, and other Southeast Asian countries, it would make sense that a significant portion of Buddhists in the United States identify as Asian. However, according to the data from the CES, Buddhists are just as likely to identify as white as they are to say that they are Asian (about 40% each). Only 8% of Buddhists say that they are Black, and a similar share report they are Hispanic.

When comparing those figures to the general population, it's undoubtedly true that Buddhists have a higher concentration of Asians and a lower percentage who identify as white. However, comparing the Black and Hispanic percentages reveals only a small gap between the general population and the racial composition of Buddhists. These results point toward a Buddhist community that is made up of a significant number of Asians and a good portion of immigrants, but those two demographic characteristics certainly do not describe the majority of Buddhists in the United States.

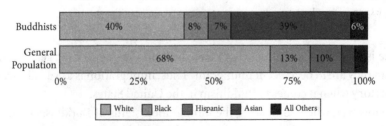

Figure 11.8 Racial composition of Buddhists in the United States
Data: Cooperative Election Study

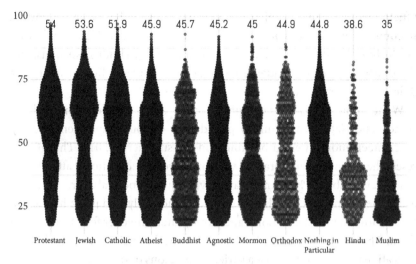

Figure 11.9 Age distribution of the religious traditions in the United States
Data: Cooperative Election Study

What about other basic demographic characteristics, such as age? Figure 11.9 is a beeswarm plot that visualizes the distribution of age for every religious group in the dataset. When the plot is wider, that means that there are more respondents clustered in that area; when it's narrower, there are fewer. Additionally, the mean age for every religious tradition is listed at the top of the graph. It's important to note that this is the mean age for just adults in the sample—as most surveys only query individuals who are at least eighteen years old. Both observing the mean and the distribution of ages helps in understanding not only the present situation but also what the future may look like for these religious groups.

Buddhists land squarely in the middle of the distribution. Protestants are clearly the oldest at fifty-four years old, followed closely by Jews. The average adult Buddhist in the data is about forty-six years old. That puts them on par with atheists and agnostics. For comparison, the mean of the overall sample is forty-eight-and-a-half years old, which means that adult Buddhists are slightly younger than the overall average. However, they are significantly older than Hindus and Muslims, who are the youngest religious traditions in the United States at thirty-nine and thirty-five years old, respectively.

When comparing the distribution of values for Buddhists to Hindus and Muslims, one clear difference emerges: there are lots of Buddhists who are over the age of fifty. In fact, 42% of all Buddhist adults have seen their fiftieth birthday—that's similar to Latter-day Saints, atheists, and agnostics. In comparison, just 20% of Hindus are at least fifty years old, and only 16% of Muslims. While it may seem convenient to group Hindus, Muslims, and Buddhists together, the evidence says that in terms of age, Buddhists are in a different category entirely.

What about other demographic factors such as education and income? The Nationscape Survey polled over 477,000 respondents during an eighteen-month period beginning in the summer of 2019. This affords researchers a much finer-grained view into levels of educational attainment. For instance, about 1% of Americans have earned a doctoral degree. In a typical survey sample of one thousand, one would likely find just a handful of PhDs. However, in the Nationscape Survey, there are over four thousand of them. This provides a great deal more statistical certainty when looking at educational attainment across a variety of religious traditions.

In the overall sample, 11.5% of respondents reported earning a master's or doctoral degree. Figure 11.10 shows that several different groups are clustered right around the mean, including several types of Protestant Christians, as well as atheists and agnostics. The group that is the most likely to have earned a graduate degree are Hindus at 31%, followed closely by Jews at 30% and then Muslims at 24%. No other group is above 20%, including Buddhists. These data report that 15% of Buddhists have a master's

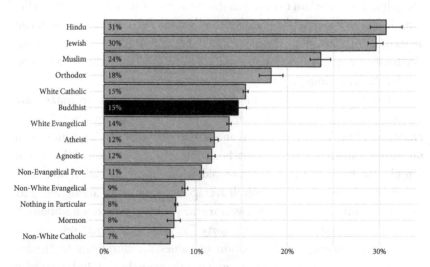

Figure 11.10 Share with a master's or doctoral degree
Data: Nationscape

or doctoral degree—which is just slightly higher than average. However, it is much lower than Muslims and Hindus. Thus, age is not the only demographic factor in which Buddhists stand apart. Buddhists have more education than the national average, but clearly a lower share of graduate degrees compared to other minority religious groups.

Another area in which these differences manifest is annual household income. Obviously, education is highly correlated with how much money one earns, but it's not a perfect linear relationship. Those with graduate degrees tend to make more money than without them, but sometimes people can choose professions that require advanced levels of education and training but do not enjoy high salaries. Also, these metrics are almost always based on household income, which includes money earned by a spouse or children.

In many cases the order for religious groups in terms of household income is exactly the same as it was for educational attainment, as can be seen in Figure 11.11. For instance, Hindus were the most likely to have earned a graduate degree—they also have the highest average household income in the sample at just above $70,000 per year. Jewish respondents were the second most likely to have a graduate degree, and they are second in terms of household income at just below $70,000 per year. Buddhists are clearly in the middle of the pack, with a household income of just about $53,000 per year. Buddhists' household income is just slightly above the overall sample mean of $51,000.

Thus, the data point to Buddhists being surprisingly average on these metrics. They tend to have educational attainment that is just slightly above the national average, and the same is true for their household income. They do not enjoy the incredibly high levels of income and education that are evinced among Hindus or Jewish respondents. Instead, on at least these two demographic factors they tend to look like larger religious groups like Protestant

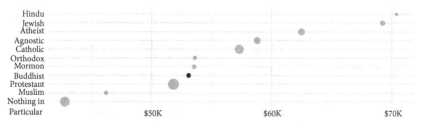

Figure 11.11 Mean household income for religious groups
Data: Cooperative Election Study

192 THE AMERICAN RELIGIOUS LANDSCAPE

Christians or Catholics. Obviously, there is a tremendous amount of difference between Christians and Buddhists when it comes to theology and religious practice, but on basic demographic characteristics, they share many commonalities.

Measures of Religion among Buddhists

One of the most pernicious problems when it comes to survey design is that questions must be written in a highly generalizable way. That means that when researchers are focused on measuring religious behavior, they need to have some type of religious tradition in mind when constructing their queries. Many surveys that have been in constant use for decades rely on questions that were written decades ago when Christianity was the dominant expression of religion in the United States. Thus, these surveys are well-tailored to assess the religiosity of Western religious traditions, but not so useful when considering people from other faith traditions. For instance, regular attendance at a house of worship is a key feature of religious life for Protestants, Catholics, Jews, Latter-day Saints, and Muslims. The surveys that have been in use for decades are well-tailored for these groups.

However, not every religious group has the same perspective on corporate worship as Western faith traditions. For Buddhists, meeting together for worship services is not considered to be an essential part of their religious practice.[2] That's not to say that Buddhists don't have houses of worship— as mentioned previously, there are hundreds of temples across the United States. However, Buddhists are free to worship in their homes, as well. Many Buddhist households will have a special space set aside for this practice, and it may include candles and/or incense and possibly a statue of Buddha or another icon.

Thus, questions about religious practice that originated from a primarily Western understanding of religion tend to make Buddhist respondents look less active because many do not gather for regular corporate worship. That certainly comes through when looking at the data presented in Figure 11.12, which focus on the share of people who say that they never or seldom attend religious services. Only one in five Latter-day Saints attends church less than once a year, and it's a quarter of Muslims. The share of Protestants and Orthodox Christians is higher at about one-third.

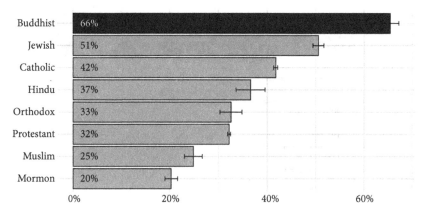

Figure 11.12 Share never or seldom attending religious services
Data: Cooperative Election Study

However, Buddhists are clearly an outlier on this metric. Just one in three Buddhists says that they have attended religious services at least once in the prior year. The next closest group is Jews at a bare majority—51%. For Judaism, the justification for this low rate of religious attendance is likely tied up in the fact that it serves as both a religious tradition as well as an ethnicity. But, for Buddhists, this is likely not the case. Instead, the more logical answer is that Buddhism does not center the practice of regular worship attendance and thus many Buddhists rarely go to a temple to worship. However, because most surveys are only designed to measure a specific type of religious practice, this means that there are no specific questions about worshiping at a shrine in one's own home. Thus, it's not possible to know just what percentage of Buddhists engage in personal religious worship using traditional survey instruments.

Another question in the CES asks respondents about their frequency of prayer, as well. This may be tapping into the idea that many Buddhists engage in a type of prayer ritual in front of their home shrines, but it's not clear whether every Buddhist respondent believes that this question is asking about that specific religious action, especially because this question includes the phrase "outside of religious services." For some, prostrating in front of a home shrine may be a religious service, and thus they believe this question does not apply to how they worship.

On this metric, Buddhists indicate a lower level of prayer frequency than most other religious groups, as can be seen in Figure 11.13. About half of

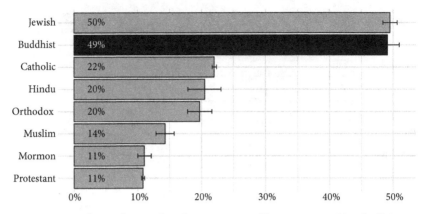

Figure 11.13 Share who say that they never or seldom pray outside of religious services

Buddhists say that they never or seldom pray outside of religious services. That's functionally the same share as Jews in the sample. These two groups clearly stand alone on this metric. For comparison, just 22% of Catholics report praying never/seldom. Just one in ten Latter-day Saints and Protestants reports that low of a frequency of prayer. Thus, from these two metrics (flawed as they are), Buddhists appear to be less likely to be religiously active than any other religious tradition, save for Jews.

Conclusion

Buddhism is a tradition that offers up a bit of a methodological puzzle for those who study religious groups through survey instruments. Their size alone makes it very difficult to come to any certain conclusions when using anything other than the very largest public surveys available. They also don't fit into any neat demographic bucket. In terms of race, they are an even mix of white and Asian members. No other religious group in the United States has such an interesting racial composition. It's clear from that angle that American Buddhism is a mix between East and West—not something that is typically seen with other religious groups. That same pattern emerges when it comes to their immigration status. Buddhists are noticeably more likely to be immigrants than Americans as a whole, but they are not in the same category as the scores of immigrants who are Hindus or Muslims.

In terms of factors related to socioeconomic status, it would be fair to put Buddhists in the "middle of the road" category. They have a level of educational attainment that is slightly higher than the national average when it comes to earning graduate degrees. They also have annual household incomes that score just a bit above the mean, as well. This puts them into the same category as larger, more readily recognized traditions like Protestants and Catholics as opposed to minority religious groups like Hindus and Muslims.

However, when it comes to religious practice, Buddhists are clearly an outlier. Two-thirds of them say that they attend religious services less than once a year. That's fifteen percentage points higher than any other tradition. It also puts them far out of step with larger religious groups like Protestants who are just half as likely to indicate that their attendance is never or seldom. In terms of prayer frequency, Buddhists also report infrequent religious behavior—half say that they pray seldom or never. That is in line with Jews, but it is far out of step with Hindus at 20% and Muslims at 14%. As mentioned above, this may be due in some part to the type of survey questions being asked, but it would be hard to argue that the average Buddhist is incredibly religiously active when compared to other Christian groups, especially.

Buddhists occupy an interesting space in the American social and religious landscape. They don't score particularly high on a number of metrics related to income, education, and the share who are immigrants. They represent the future of other smaller religious groups like Hindus and Muslims. It appears that Buddhists have become a mix of long-time Americans who are often white and many immigrants who come from Asian countries. As will be explored later, Hindus have a much higher level of immigration, but one has to wonder whether they will, over time, begin to look more like the composition of Buddhists.

Notes

1. Pew Research Center. 2012. "Buddhists." https://www.pewresearch.org/religion/2012/12/18/glo bal-religious-landscape-buddhist.
2. Pew Research Center. 2023. "Measuring Religion in China." https://www.pewresearch.org/ religion/wp-content/uploads/sites/7/2023/08/PF_2023.08.30_religion-china_REPORT.pdf; Manitoba Education. 2021. *Buddhism: A Supplemental Resource for Grade 12 World of Religions: A Canadian Perspective*. Winnipeg, Manitoba: Manitoba Education. https://www.edu.gov.mb.ca/ k12/docs/support/world_religions/buddhism/index.html.

196 THE AMERICAN RELIGIOUS LANDSCAPE

Data References

Davern, Michael, Rene Bautista, Jeremy Freese, Pamela Herd, and Stephen L. Morgan. 2023. General Social Survey 1972–2022. Principal investigator, Michael Davern; Co-principal investigators, Rene Bautista, Jeremy Freese, Pamela Herd, and Stephen L. Morgan. Sponsored by National Science Foundation. NORC ed. Chicago: NORC at the University of Chicago. https://gssdataexplorer.norc.org/.

Grammich, Clifford, Kirk Hadaway, Richard Houseal, Dale E. Jones, Alexei Krindatch, Richie Stanley, and Richard H. Taylor. 2023. 2020 U.S. Religion Census: Religious Congregations & Membership Study. Association of Statisticians of American Religious Bodies. https://www. usreligioncensus.org/node/1639.

Schaffner, Brian, Stephen Ansolabehere, Sam Luks, Shiro Kuriwaki, and Marissa Shih. 2006–2023. Cooperative Election Study Common Content, 2006–2022. Harvard Dataverse. https://cces.gov.harvard.edu/.

Tausanovitch, C., and L. Vavreck. 2023. Democracy Fund + UCLA Nationscape Project (version 20211215). Harvard Dataverse. https://doi.org/10.7910/DVN/CQFP3Z.

12

Hindus

Hinduism is one of the oldest religious traditions on Earth. While there is no precise way to date its origin, scholars believe that people were engaging in Hindu religious practices at least four thousand years ago in the Indian subcontinent.[1] Even in the twenty-first century, the geographic center of Hinduism is found in the Asia-Pacific region. According to the Pew Research Center, data from 2010 indicated that 94% of all Hindus in the world lived in the country of India, and less than 1% of all Hindus resided in countries outside the Asia-Pacific region.[2]

Yet, although there are still several million people in the United States who identify as Hindu on surveys, the majority of Americans do not interact with a Hindu on a regular basis. In fact, just two Hindus have ever run for president of the United States—Tulsi Gabbard as a Democrat in 2020 and Vivek Ramaswamy as a Republican in 2024. Given that the majority of Republican primary voters are Christians, Ramaswamy made it a point to connect his Hindu upbringing with that of his potential supporters. He said, "As we say in the Hindu tradition, God resides in each of us. In the Christian tradition, you say we're all made in the image of God."[3] While both the Gabbard and Ramaswamy campaigns failed to gain significant traction in the primary process, they managed to introduce Hinduism to mainstream America.

Hinduism offers a fascinating window into how immigration is changing the overall composition of the country—racially, economically, and religiously. Hindus, by many objective metrics, have attained a great level of success in American society, yet they still face obstacles to being fully integrated in the United States. Yet, despite these obstacles, many Hindus have managed to ascend to leadership roles in many of the most influential sectors of American society. How these high-visibility positions will impact the growth of Hinduism in the United States is yet to be seen.

The American Religious Landscape. Ryan P. Burge, Oxford University Press. © Oxford University Press 2025.
DOI: 10.1093/oso/9780197762837.003.0013

198 THE AMERICAN RELIGIOUS LANDSCAPE

How Many Hindus Are There in the United States?

One of the difficult decisions survey authors must make is to establish an arbitrary number regarding how big a religious group needs to be to merit a response option on a survey. There's a real trade-off that needs to be considered. If a survey respondent is presented with a simple question like "What is your present religion, if any?" and then they are given a list of forty different religious groups, it's highly likely that they won't read through all those options, may inadvertently click the wrong one, or get so fatigued with all the text on the screen that they give up on the rest of the survey.

But, at the same time, a key facet of survey construction is providing enough options so that lots of people taking the survey are not tempted to check the box marked "something else" and then write their answer in a textbox. These "free response" options create hours of work for those cleaning the data and sorting those text fields into one of the previously mentioned categories. Thus, there must be an arbitrary cut point for which religious groups get their own response option and which ones are relegated to the "something else" button at the bottom of the list.

The Pew Research Center has consistently included a Hindu option in its survey for the last fifteen years, and that typology is recreated in the Cooperative Election Study (CES). This allows researchers the opportunity to study this important religious group in a more in-depth way. However, year over year, the data point to the same conclusion: when given twelve different response options, Hindu is the one that is chosen with the least frequency.

The share of respondents to the CES who choose the Hindu option is objectively very small. In fact, there are many years of the survey in which there are just a small number of respondents. For instance, in 2008, there were just forty-four total Hindus in the entire sample of 32,000 respondents. However, the trend line is clear in Figure 12.1: Hindu identification is increasing over time. In surveys conducted a decade ago, the overall conclusion is that about one-quarter of 1% of respondents were Hindu. In more recent surveys, that share has doubled, and now about one in two hundred American adults identifies as Hindu.

But it's important to understand why this makes studying this religious group through surveys incredibly difficult. The average poll that appears on the nightly news during the run-up to a presidential election has about one thousand respondents. Based on Figure 12.1, one could reasonably expect

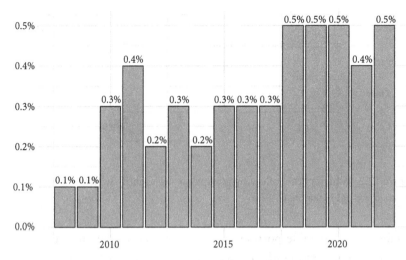

Figure 12.1 The share of Hindus in the adult population
Data: Cooperative Election Study

the survey to have five total Hindu respondents. Some may have ten Hindus, and it would not be that unusual to have no Hindus at all in a sample size of one thousand people.

The only way that quantitative social science can really understand the Hindu population in the United States is because the overall sample size of surveys has gotten much larger in the last fifteen years. For instance, the 2022 CES has a total sample of 61,000 people—of that, 306 people identify as Hindus. While this is obviously much better than the five or ten Hindus that would be found in a typical horse race poll, it's still not enough to do a deep dive into the racial makeup or educational attainment of Hindus. Thus, the rest of this chapter will combine the data from the 2020, 2021, and 2022 waves of the CES, giving us a total sample size of 717 Hindus.

Luckily, the CES also asks Hindus which sect they most closely identify with so that researchers can understand the contours of Hinduism in the United States with a bit more specificity. As can be seen in Figure 12.2, the plurality of Hindu respondents (40%) aligned with Vaishnavism—a group that accepts Vishnu as the supreme manifestation of the Divine. This result aligns with an estimate of Hindus that concluded a majority are Vaishnavites.[4] Figure 12.2 also shows that 21% of Hindus in the United States believe that Shiva is the supreme deity, while just 9% align with Shaktism.

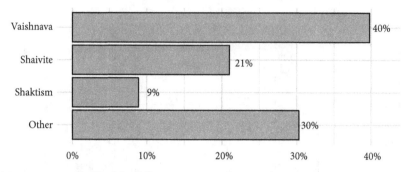

Figure 12.2 Which of the following groups do you identify with?
Data: Cooperative Election Study

Notably, a considerable portion of the Hindu participants in the sample chose the "other" option when asked about their alignment. They were not inclined to identify with any of the three given choices.

Immigration and Hinduism in the United States

As previously noted, Hinduism is a religion of tremendous geographic concentration. According to Pew, 99% of all Hindus on Earth live in the Asia-Pacific region.[5] Thus, it logically follows that there is an inextricable link between immigration and Hinduism in the United States. For Hindus to continue to grow as part of the American population, continued immigration from countries like India is necessary, but that must also be coupled with a resistance to assimilate to the dominant religious traditions of the United States. There's clear evidence for this in the data.

The CES asks individuals about their immigration status with options ranging from "they themselves are an immigrant" to "their family has been in the United States for at least three generations." Comparing the immigration status of Hindus in the United States to the overall population of the country clearly illustrates just how unique the Hindu community is in the United States, as can be seen in Figure 12.3. For instance, 72% of Hindus indicate that they are immigrants to the United States. Among this group, the sample is nearly evenly split between those who have been naturalized American citizens (54%) and those who have not become citizens of the United States (46%). Consider this: 40% of all adult Hindus in the United States were born in another country, immigrated to the United States, and

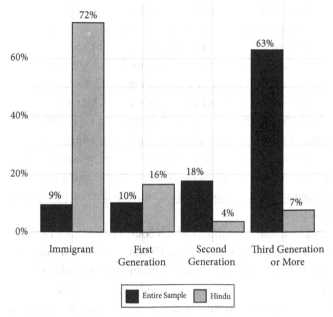

Figure 12.3 The immigration status of Hindus
Data: Cooperative Election Study

have become naturalized citizens. That's nearly seven times the rate found in the overall population (6%).

It's also possible to see with some specificity when the wave of Hindu immigrants came to the United States. Besides the fact that nearly three-quarters of all Hindus are themselves immigrants, another 16% indicate that their parents had immigrated to the United States, but that they were born on American soil. That share is only slightly larger than the overall population, where 10% say that their parents immigrated. But just 4% of Hindus say that their grandparents were immigrants, while their parents were born in the United States, compared to 18% of the overall population. Finally, only 7% of Hindus indicate that their family immigrated to the United States at least three generations ago—it is 63% of those in the total sample.

Looked at in its totality, it's hard to ignore the impact that immigrant status has on Hinduism in the United States. Nearly nine in ten Hindus are either immigrants themselves or their parents were born in a country outside the United States. This simple fact frames a great deal of the discussion about Hindus in the United States in terms of their racial composition, educational attainment, and geographic distribution.

Race, Education, and Income among American Hindus

Given the previous data about immigrant status, it should come as no surprise that the racial composition of Hindus in the United States is vastly different than that of America as a whole. Figure 12.4 shows that over two-thirds of survey respondents indicate that they are white non-Hispanic in the overall sample. It's just 6% of people who reported being Hindus. Seventy-eight percent of Hindus report their race as Asian, which diverges dramatically from the total sample, where only 4% of respondents say that they are Asian. Six percent of Hindus say they are Black, and another 4% report they are Hispanic. In both cases, that's about half the rate that is found in the overall population.

The CES also asked individuals which country they trace their heritage or ancestry. Among those who identify as Hindu and Asian in the 2022 survey, nearly 90% said that they could trace their ancestry to India. Given the Pew estimate that 94% of all Hindus in the world currently live in India, it logically follows that almost all the Hindu immigrants to the United States are Indian as well.[6]

There is no doubt that Indian Americans (and, therefore, many Hindus) have seen tremendous success in many industries in the United States. For instance, many major American technology companies employ large numbers of recent immigrants from the Asia-Pacific region. At one point in 2021, all the heads of Microsoft, Google, and Twitter were of Indian descent.

The reasons for this success in the world of business, medicine, and other industries become clear when looking at the educational attainment of religious groups in the United States. In data collected in 2020, 2021, and 2022, about 12% of American adults said that they had taken courses beyond their

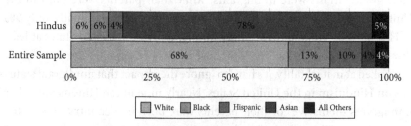

Figure 12.4 Racial breakdown of Hindus
Data: Cooperative Election Study

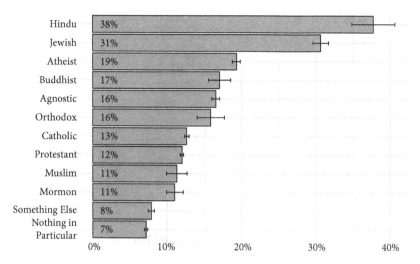

Figure 12.5 Share with a postgraduate degree
Data: Cooperative Election Study

bachelor's degree. Many of the larger religious traditions in the United States fall very close to this average, including Protestants and Catholics.

As can be seen in Figure 12.5, Hindus in the United States are clearly much more likely to have a postgraduate education. Thirty-eight percent have taken graduate-level coursework, which is much higher than any other religious group. Jewish Americans do very well on this metric, but they still trail Hindus by seven percentage points. Note that a Hindu in the United States is twice as likely to have a postgraduate degree compared to an atheist and three times more likely than a Catholic.

This level of education, unsurprisingly, translates to household income. The average household in the recent waves of the CES reports an income that is just about $50,000 per year. The average Protestant is just slightly higher than the average, as are Mormons, Buddhists, and Orthodox Christians.

But, as can again be seen in Figure 12.6, Hindus are far above average. The typical Hindu household in the United States earns just a bit more than $70,000 per year, which is statistically the same as Jewish households. But, again, there is a large gap between these groups and the next closest: atheists. An atheist makes about $63,000 a year, or 10% less than Hindus. It's no exaggeration to say that Hindus enjoy the highest socioeconomic status of any religious group in the United States.

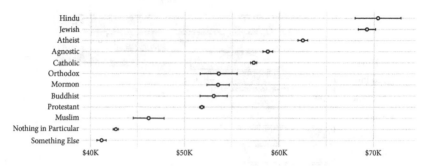

Figure 12.6 Mean income by religious groups
Data: Cooperative Election Study

Age and Fertility among Hindus

The data so far have pointed to the unique position of Hindus in the American religious landscape. Clearly, they are much more likely to be impacted by the issue of immigration compared to other religious traditions, with nearly 90% having come to the United States themselves or being the first generation born in the United States. They also have a very high level of income and education, on average. But will those factors lead to an overall increase in their population share in the United States? The data are somewhat mixed on this point.

To get a good sense of the future of any group, it's helpful to look at their overall age distribution. If a tradition has a high concentration of older people, then there's a real possibility of numerical decline in the near future. However, a tradition that is full of people under the age of forty has several advantages. Not only does it not have to worry about losing lots of members to death, but it also has the possibility of growth through younger couples having children. While the CES only surveys those who are eighteen years or older, the age distribution of Hindus points to a bright future.

Among the twelve religious groups who are included in the CES and shown in Figure 12.7, Hindus rank as the second youngest religious group. The average age of a Hindu adult in the United States is just about forty-one years old. The only group that is younger are Muslims. In comparison, many of the largest traditions, like Protestants and Catholics, have an average age that is above fifty years old.

The distribution in Figure 12.7 is visualized in what is called a beeswarm plot—this makes it easy to understand where the largest number of

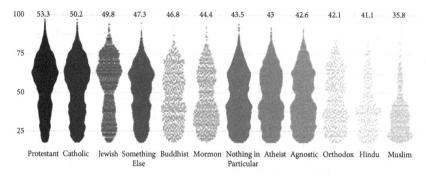

Figure 12.7 Age distribution of the religious traditions in the United States
Data: Cooperative Election Study

individuals in each group can be found in terms of age. For Hindus, the concentration is the largest around those who are between the ages of thirty-five and forty years old. However, there are also a significant number of Hindus who report that they are in their twenties as well. In contrast, there are very few Hindus to be found at the top of the plot. According to the 2022 CES, just 25% of all Hindus in the United States have celebrated their fiftieth birthday; in comparison, 64% of Protestants are at least fifty years old.

Yet average age is just one part of the puzzle when it comes to projecting the future of a religious group. If a tradition has lots of younger members, but those members do not produce many offspring, there will not be a way to easily replace those in the religious community who leave the tradition or are no longer able to attend due to health concerns.

When it comes to Hindus and their likelihood of having children, there is strong evidence that they are more likely to be parents than other groups like Jews or Buddhists. Because the survey question in the CES asks respondents if they are currently the parent or guardian of a child under the age of eighteen, the sample was restricted to just those between the ages of thirty and forty-five years old, when the chances of having children at home are the highest. In these results, shown in Figure 12.8, two-thirds of Hindus are parents—that's statistically the same as Latter-day Saints, at 69%.

The rate shown in Figure 12.8 for Hindus is 66%; in comparison, the share of the overall sample who have children in this age range is just above 50%. This means that Hindus are clearly significantly more likely to have children than other individuals in their same age group. However, being a parent is just one part of the equation—the other is how many children parents have.

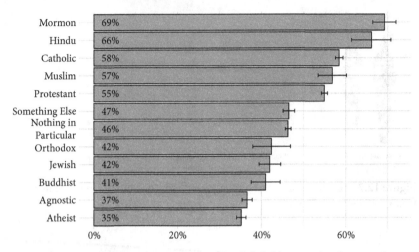

Figure 12.8 Share who are parents/guardians of children under the age of eighteen; respondents between the age of thirty and forty-five
Data: Cooperative Election Study

For instance, if 80% of a religious group indicated that they were parents, but they only averaged one child per family, that would be significantly fewer children than a religious tradition that only had 50% who were parents, but the average family had three children. The CES also asked how many children were in each family, and this metric paints a different portrait.

While Hindus were clearly far above average in the share who are currently parents, the number of children in their family is decidedly below average. The average Hindu parent has just 1.65 children, as can be seen in Figure 12.9. That is statistically the same as atheists, who rank at the very bottom on this metric. The overall average for the entire sample of parents is about 1.9 children per respondent, much higher than Hindus. Comparing Latter-day Saints to Hindus is instructive across the last two graphs. Hindus are just as likely to be parents as Latter-day Saints; however, the average Mormon family has 2.4 children, while the average Hindu has just 1.65—about 50% lower. From a purely numerical standpoint, it's much more likely that the Latter-day Saints tradition grows in size because of the high number of children. For Hindus, they are not reaching replacement level and thus must rely on other means to increase their share in the United States.

Why would this be? There's not a simple way to understand the myriad of factors that go into significant decisions such as when to be parents and how many children to have, but it does seem likely that these choices are linked

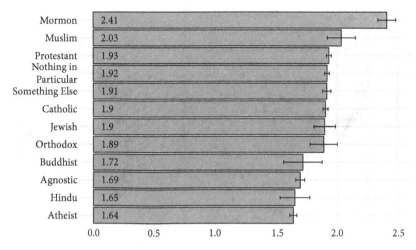

Figure 12.9 How many children do you have under the age of eighteen? (among those who have children)
Data: Cooperative Election Study

with other factors like educational attainment and career choices. As previously mentioned, Hindus have very high levels of education, which tend to lead to careers that may take more time away from family life. In this way, the high socioeconomic status of Hindus may make them less likely to have large families.

Where Are Hindus Located?

Given the overall size of the Hindu population in the United States at about one-half of 1% of adults, it seems likely that Hindus are geographically concentrated. The 2020 Religion Census bears that out. There are 3,143 counties in the United States, and there is a Hindu temple or a Hindu yoga center in 603 of them, about 19%. When those counties with a Hindu presence are visualized in Figure 12.10, it becomes clear that there are large swaths of the central United States where there are no Hindu houses of worship.

Instead, Hinduism seems to be concentrated around the coastal areas of the country. Some of the highest concentrations of Hindus are in areas of the country that have the highest population density. Among the five counties with the most Hindus, two are in the New York City metro area (New York and Queens), while three are in Southern California (Santa Clara, Ventura,

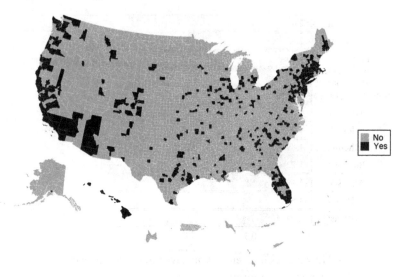

Figure 12.10 Counties that have a Hindu congregation
Data: Religion Census

and Los Angeles). Many of the other counties with a large number of Hindus can be found in the Northeast: New Jersey, Maryland, and Pennsylvania.

However, looking at Figure 12.10, other parts of the country also have a Hindu presence. For instance, there is a Hindu congregation in over half the counties in the state of Florida. There are also several states where nearly a quarter of the counties have a Hindu house of worship, including Illinois, Pennsylvania, and Ohio. Yet there are some states like Montana, Maine, and South Dakota that report less than a thousand total Hindus.

Hindu Religiosity

One of the many difficulties facing scholars studying religion by using surveys is that many concepts are not universal across every religious tradition. For instance, regular worship attendance is encouraged in Christianity, Judaism, and Islam. However, that's not necessarily the case with Hinduism. While Hindus certainly engage in worshipful experiences, they can take on a variety of forms, including engaging in personal reflection at home on a regular basis. While going to a Hindu temple is certainly commonplace for many adherents, traveling to a house of worship does not carry the same importance as it would in other Western religious traditions. Thus, it's likely that the survey questions typically employed in the United States under-report the religious devotion of Hindus because of the way that the questions are structured.

To get a clearer picture of the disconnect between religious attendance and other religious activity, a scatterplot was created in Figure 12.11 with the share of each religious tradition that reported praying at least once a day on the y-axis (vertical) and religious attendance on the horizontal (x-axis). The trend line is clearly positive: those who attend religious services more also indicate that they engage in daily prayer at a high frequency. If a tradition goes from 30% attending weekly to 40%, the expected increase in daily prayer is just about ten percentage points, as well.

There are a few outliers in Figure 12.11. According to the trend line, about 77% of Latter-day Saints should pray daily; it's a bit lower at 71%. Jews and Buddhists should indicate higher levels of daily prayer based on their worship attendance, as well. However, Hindus are clearly the biggest outlier. Just over 20% of Hindus say that they attend religious services at least once per week. The trend line predicts daily prayer rates of 37%. Instead, 51% of Hindus who took the CES say that they pray at least once a day.

What complicates the picture is a question about religious importance. As can be seen in Figure 12.12, nearly two-thirds of Protestants and Latter-day

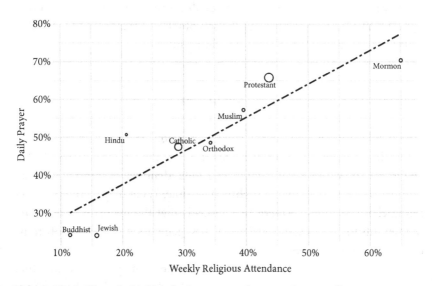

Figure 12.11 The relationship between attendance and prayer frequency
Data: Cooperative Election Study

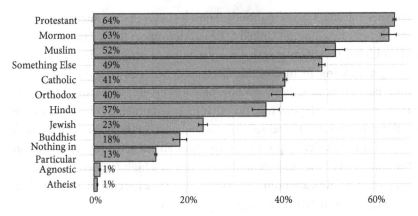

Figure 12.12 Share who say religion is very important
Data: Cooperative Election Study

Saints indicate that they believe it to be "very important." For Hindus, 37% say religion is very important, which could best be described as middle of the pack. Among other religious groups, only Jews and Buddhists score lower. Thus, Hindus are clearly not the most religiously engaged group in the United States. They tend to engage a great deal in an individualized style of religious practice while largely avoiding corporate worship. Their overall orientation to their faith seems to be not all consuming like some other religious traditions. This could be a function of religion survey questions being written for primarily Judeo-Christian faiths, however.

Conclusion

Hinduism represents one of the smallest religious traditions in the United States that can still be accurately measured on the largest surveys. Today, about one in two hundred American adults identifies as Hindu, and that number seems to be growing slightly over time. What may be the most defining characteristic of American Hindus is that the majority of them are immigrants themselves, or they are the first generation of their family to be born in the United States.

This reality bears greatly on some of the other demographic factors that are unique to Hindus in the United States. They have very high levels of educational attainment and also report household incomes at the top of the scale. From this perspective, Hindus enjoy one of the highest standards of living of any religious group in the United States. They also tend to have much smaller families than other religions. It's statistically rare for American Hindus to have more than two children—this fact may be tied up in their educational and career responsibilities.

In terms of their overall religiosity, most Hindus do not go to temple services on a regular basis, while a majority report that they pray daily. Yet when asked how important religion is to them, only 37% say that it is "very important." Based on the analysis of the data, it becomes evident that religion plays a role in the lives of Hindus, yet it doesn't occupy a central role for a considerable number of them.

The influence of Hinduism in American culture and religion seems inextricably tied to the immigration laws that govern the United States. If the federal government makes it easier for people from primarily Hindu countries like India to come to the United States, it seems likely that Hinduism will grow in size and importance. As many of them put down roots here and second- and third-generation American Hindus become more commonplace, it will be worth tracking if these successive generations still identify as Hindus on surveys or if they assimilate to the larger American culture and align with a Christian tradition or chose to identify as nonreligious.

Notes

1. Klaus K. Klostermaier. 2000. *Hinduism: A Short History*. Oxford: Oneworld Publications, 7–10, 44–45, 285.
2. Pew Research Center. 2012. *The Global Religious Landscape: A Report on the Size and Distribution of the World's Major Religious Groups as of 2010*, 10. https://www.pewresearch.org/religion/2012/12/18/global-religious-landscape-hindu/.
3. Deepa Bharath. 2023. "Vivek Ramaswamy's Hindu Faith Is Front and Center in His GOP Presidential Campaign." *AP News*. https://apnews.com/article/vivek-ramaswamy-hindu-republican-presidential-campaign-68a09925f38fb23d69fa31a2271c0ca8.
4. Todd M. Johnson and Brian J. Grim. 2013. *The World's Religions in Figures: An Introduction to International Religious Demography*. 1st ed. Hoboken, NJ: John Wiley & Sons, 26.
5. Pew Research Center, *The Global Religious Landscape*, 10.
6. Pew Research Center, *The Global Religious Landscape*, 10.

Data References

Grammich, Clifford, Kirk Hadaway, Richard Houseal, Dale E. Jones, Alexei Krindatch, Richie Stanley, and Richard H. Taylor. 2023. 2020 U.S. Religion Census: Religious Congregations &

212 THE AMERICAN RELIGIOUS LANDSCAPE

Membership Study. Association of Statisticians of American Religious Bodies. https://www.usreligioncensus.org/node/1639.

Schaffner, Brian, Stephen Ansolabehere, Sam Luks, Shiro Kuriwaki, and Marissa Shih. 2006-2023. Cooperative Election Study Common Content, 2006–2022. Harvard Dataverse. https://cces.gov.harvard.edu/.

13

Atheists/Agnostics

It's hardly an overstatement to suggest that religion has had a more profound impact on America's cultural and political landscape than on any other nation in the West. Every year, the U.S. Mint produces millions of banknotes emblazoned with the phrase "In God We Trust." Countless school children start their day reciting the Pledge of Allegiance, which includes the words "Under God." Also, it's common practice for individuals assuming a public office to take their oath with a hand on a sacred text, concluding with the words "So help me God." These are just three examples of how religion is inextricably linked to the fabric of American society and culture.

Although the United States still imbues so much of civic life with religious undertones, there is a growing group of people who are actively rejecting religious beliefs of any type. In the last several decades, the share of the general public who describe their religious affiliation as atheist or agnostic has increased significantly, even though these groups often face a tremendous amount of ostracism and stigma in American society. Choosing to identify with either of these two religious identities means accepting the potential risk of facing discrimination and social isolation. Nonetheless, the numbers of atheists and agnostics keep rising, despite the potentially significant social repercussions.

The rise of atheists and agnostics will have profound impacts on the future contours of religion, society, and politics in the United States. While becoming a refuge for people who did not fit into the heterosexual, cisgender mold, the atheist and agnostic communities have not managed to achieve the overall diversity of American society when it comes to other factors like race and gender. This chapter aims to depict two social identities that are undergoing rapid transformation, set against the backdrop of a society that appears to be changing direction with increasing frequency. In his first inaugural address in 2009, President Barack Obama told the record-setting crowd that "We are a nation of Christians and Muslims, Jews and Hindus, and nonbelievers."[1] This was the tacit acknowledgment that American religion was changing, and atheists and agnostics are leading the charge to

---

The American Religious Landscape. Ryan P. Burge, Oxford University Press. © Oxford University Press 2025.
DOI: 10.1093/oso/9780197762837.003.0014

214   THE AMERICAN RELIGIOUS LANDSCAPE

create a more inclusive nation for those who embrace faith but also those who reject it entirely.

The Rise of Atheists and Agnostics in the United States

One of the difficulties for those who want to study the trajectory of atheists and agnostics is that most mainstream surveys did not include either choice as a possible response option until the last two decades. For instance, in the General Social Survey (GSS), when someone indicated that their current religion was "no religion," a follow-up question was not included to probe if they were an atheist, agnostic, or something else. However, if a survey respondent indicated that they were a Protestant, additional queries would be posed to sort them into the correct denominational family. Thus, we have little ability to track the number of Americans who took on the social label of atheist or agnostic before the mid-2000s.

However, that's not to say that the GSS does not provide some insight into this question. Beginning in 1988, the team at the GSS included a query that assessed what an individual believed about God. There were six response options that included "I don't believe in God," and "I don't know whether there is a God and I don't believe there is any way to find out." Those two choices map directly onto what the average American would understand to be the worldview of atheists and agnostics, respectively. Thus, it's possible to use these questions to generally assess how many Americans were atheists and agnostics by religious beliefs, but not necessarily social identity.

In the 1988 GSS, contained in Figure 13.1, 1,479 respondents answered the question related to a belief in God. Of that, 23 people said that they believed God didn't exist—about 1.5%. Additionally, 76 individuals chose the agnostic response, for another 3.6%. In total, about one in twenty adult Americans had an atheist or agnostic belief in God in the late 1980s. Interestingly, that is basically the same share of the public who claimed no religious affiliation in the same survey.

From that point forward, the best way to describe the trend lines for both atheist and agnostic views is slow and deliberate. In some years, there would be a one percentage point increase, and in other years there would be no notable change. However, over the period of several decades, those incremental changes piled up and led to large shifts in the overall numbers. By the mid-2010s, about one in ten Americans was in the atheist or agnostic camp—a doubling in about twenty-five years.

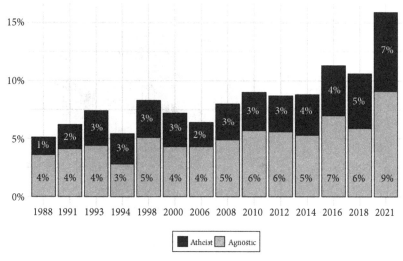

Figure 13.1 The share of Americans who are atheist/agnostic by belief
Data: General Social Survey

The most recent data show a marked increase in these two response choices, reflected in Figure 13.1. In 2021, 7% of the sample said God didn't exist, and another 9% took the agnostic approach. In 2022, those numbers shifted a bit, but the total remained the same—14% of the sample chose one of those two response options. Why the big increase in the last two surveys? One potential cause is that the GSS had to change the method of its survey administration from a face-to-face collection to an online administration. This introduced some very notable changes for religion variables, which scholars have already begun to try and untangle.[2] Despite these methodological issues, it's clearly the case that 10%–15% of the adult public takes an atheist or agnostic stance toward the existence of God, which is at least double the rate from thirty years ago.

When it comes to religious affiliation, a bit of a different story emerges. The Cooperative Election Study (CES) began in 2008, and its approach to assessing atheism and agnosticism diverges from the CES. Instead of asking the question in terms of religious belief, the approach in the CES is toward religious belonging. When folks are asked about their present religion, if any, they are given a menu of choices that include options for both atheists and agnostics. Thus, this survey uses those two words—*atheist* and *agnostic*—which can both describe a religious belief but also a label for a social group.

The 2008 CES reported that 3% of Americans were atheists, and another 4% were agnostic, as seen in Figure 13.2. That combined 7% is statistically

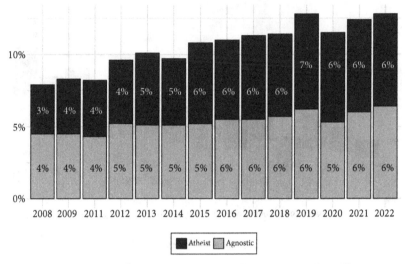

Figure 13.2 The share of Americans who are atheist/agnostic by affiliation
Data: Cooperative Election Study

indistinguishable from the 8% who described an atheist or agnostic belief in God in the GSS. It's helpful to see that measures track these trends in a very similar way. Over time, the share of atheists and agnostics has slowly risen. By 2013, about one in ten adults was atheist or agnostic. From that point forward, it's fair to say that the change has been fairly minimal. Over the past five years, data suggest that approximately 12% of individuals identify as either atheist or agnostic, with the distribution between the two categories being roughly equal. Again, this is fairly consistent with the data from the GSS about religious belief. Statistically speaking, the share of Americans who claim to be an atheist or agnostic by belief or affiliation is somewhere between 12% and 15%.

However, that's not to say that religious belief and religious behavior perfectly mirror each other in surveys. In the 2021 GSS, respondents who indicated that they had no religion on the broad question were asked a follow-up question about what type of none they were and given several options which included atheist and agnostic. What is helpful about this addition is it is possible to take the response to this query and check it against the religious belief question that was visualized in Figure 13.1.

As can be seen in Figure 13.3, about seven in ten self-described atheists say that they don't believe that God exists, which means that 30% of atheists are still open to the possibility of the Divine. However, just 9% say that they

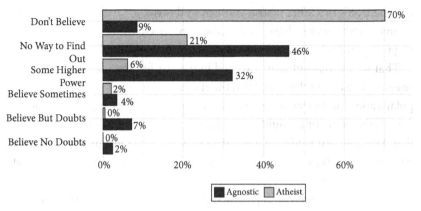

Figure 13.3 View of God among atheists and agnostics
Data: General Social Survey

do believe in God at some level. For agnostics, the responses are much more evenly distributed across several options. Nine percent of agnostics say that God doesn't exist, and another 46% say that there is no way to find out if God exists or not. Thus, just a bare majority of agnostics say they don't believe in God. One-third believe in some kind of Higher Power, while 13% say that they believe in God at least sometimes.

Thus, there is evidence here that identity and belief are correlated but not perfectly. The fact that 30% of atheists by identity are not atheists by belief and 54% of agnostics did not choose the agnostic option when it comes to belief in God is clearly evidenced in Figure 13.3. This is another example of the multifaceted nature of religion in the United States. One can socially identify as an atheist while not necessarily rejecting the existence of God—or the opposite can be true.

The Demographic Factors Driving Atheist/Agnostic Growth

Given the dramatic increase in the share of Americans embracing these two identities, it's worth investigating what factors are driving such a noticeable increase in those who choose the atheist or agnostic options on surveys. When it comes to nonreligion, there is little doubt that age plays a factor. Older Americans grew up in a country where the word *atheist* was often used in a pejorative sense—referring to people living in communist countries

218   THE AMERICAN RELIGIOUS LANDSCAPE

like the USSR or China whose aim was to destroy the American way of life. Younger respondents have been raised in an environment in which the stigma against atheists and agnostics has faded considerably.

That stigma has noticeably waned in the last few decades for a variety of reasons. The end of the Cold War, the rise of the Internet, and the increasing polarization of American politics have undoubtedly changed the calculus for whether someone would willingly embrace the atheist or agnostic moniker. There is clear evidence in the data that atheism and agnosticism tend to be more attractive options for younger adult Americans in the survey data visualized in Figure 13.4.

Among college-aged young adults, about 7.5% identify as atheist, and the same portion indicate that they are agnostic. What's interesting, however, is that neither trend line clearly drops from this point. Instead, it stays relatively steady at around 8% for atheists until at least forty years old. For agnostics, it does dip very slightly, getting down to about 7% among forty-year-olds. From forty to sixty years old, there is a clear and unmistakable decline. By the time that trend line gets to sixty years old, slightly less than 5% identify as atheist, and about the same share are agnostic. Among those in their seventies, it's just below 4% for both identities.

It's noteworthy that the American public is more likely to indicate that they are atheist than agnostic at most ages in Figure 13.4. But it's also worth

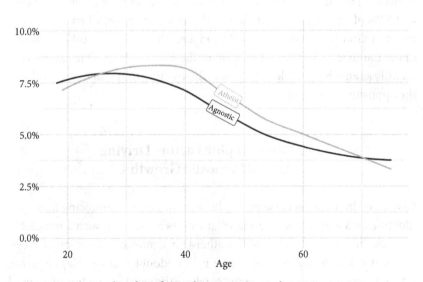

Figure 13.4 Share who identify as atheist or agnostic by age
Data: Cooperative Election Study

considering how even the oldest Americans still indicate some affinity toward the two terms. Among those who are well into their retirement years, about 7% still indicate they are atheist or agnostic. While that's about half the rate of those who are in their thirties, it's evidence that while atheists and agnostics tend to be younger, it's possible to find both identities affirmed even among older Americans.

Another important piece of this puzzle is educational attainment. The prevailing view of atheism is that it is often inculcated in university-level philosophy courses. There's a perception that when young people who were raised Christian, Jewish, or another faith tradition first encounter Nietzsche or Derrida in their required readings, many of them are swept away from a religious belief and become atheists or agnostics. Do the data support such a claim?

They do, actually, as can be seen in Figure 13.5. Among those who completed no more than a high school diploma, about 7% are atheist or agnostic, evenly split between the two. As education increases, so does the share who identify with either term. Among those who have completed a four-year college degree, 9% are atheists, and another 8% claim to be agnostic. That

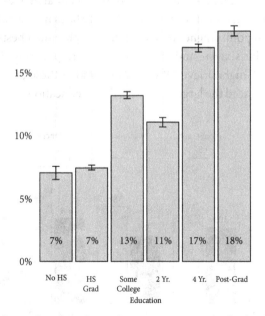

Figure 13.5 Share who identify as atheist or agnostic. HS, high school
Data: Cooperative Election Study

same statistic is essentially true for those with graduate degrees as well—10% are atheists, and 8% are agnostic.

Therefore, the expansion of secularism among Americans appears to be fueled by two key factors: the younger population and individuals with higher education levels. Whether these demographics will continue to drive the rise in secular identification in the future remains an open question. For instance, maybe those who are the most likely to gain higher education are more likely to be atheists in the first place. But, as education becomes more widespread in society, those who will pursue a bachelor's degree come from backgrounds that make them less inclined to be atheist or agnostic.

Another interesting facet of the education story relates to increases in educational attainment over the last fourteen years, shown in Figure 13.6. In the entire sample, about a quarter had earned a bachelor's degree in 2008. In 2022, that number had increased to 34%. For Protestants, the jump in bachelor's degrees is more modest at just 5%. Catholics have done better than the overall sample with a twelve percentage point increase.

Agnostics have also outpaced the national average, with an eleven percentage point increase in the previous fourteen years, as can be seen in Figure 13.6. But atheists are on another level entirely. In 2008, one-third had a college degree. In 2022, that had risen to 51%—a total increase of eighteen points. Now, over half of atheists in the United States have a college degree. That's seventeen points higher than the total sample, and it bests Protestants and Catholics by sixteen and thirteen points, respectively. Not only do atheists have the highest level of education among these groups, but they have also experienced the largest overall gains in education.

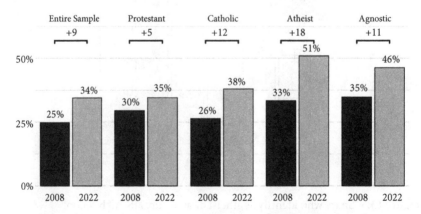

Figure 13.6 Share with a bachelor's degree in 2008 versus 2022

In addition to education, household income is another factor that has predictive power when it comes to which individuals choose to identify as atheist or agnostic. Among those with a high school diploma or less, the rates of atheism/agnosticism are clearly lower, as previously demonstrated. But as household income rises, so does the likelihood of choosing one of those two secular identities. As income rises from less than $10,000 per year to at least $100,000 per year, the likelihood of an atheist or agnostic identity doubles from 5% to 10%.

For those with a college degree, that baseline starts much higher, as can be seen in Figure 13.7. At least 15% of those who finished college identify as atheist or agnostic, which is a much greater percentage than those with a high school diploma, regardless of income. There is a positive relationship between income and embracing a secular identity here. The rate, as previously mentioned, starts at 15% and rises to about 20% among those who are the very highest earners. However, this is a more modest relationship than for those with lower levels of education, where the overall share doubles from the bottom of the income spectrum to the top.

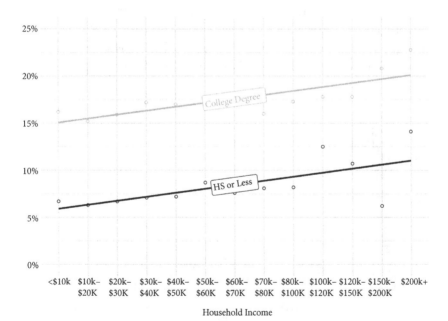

Figure 13.7 Share who identify as atheist or agnostic by education and income. HS, high school

Data: Cooperative Election Study

Other Demographic Characteristics of Atheists and Agnostics

The growth in atheism and agnosticism is influenced by variables such as income and education, leading to demographic profiles that differ from the broader population in several respects. A significant disparity is observed in racial composition, as illustrated in Figure 13.8.

For a baseline, the 2022 CES's overall sample was 68% white. In comparison, 80% of atheists and 76% of agnostics identified as white. One of the primary reasons for such a difference is that atheists and agnostics have much smaller shares who identify as African American compared to the general public. In fact, just 4% of atheists are Black compared to 13% of the population overall. The representation of other racial groups among atheists and agnostics closely aligns with their proportions in the general population.

There is also some evidence of divergence when looking at this through the lens of gender, displayed in Figure 13.9. Obviously, the overall sample is evenly split between men and women, but that's not the case for atheists specifically. In fact, nearly three out of five atheists indicate that they are male, which is one of the highest ratios of any religious group. In comparison, just 52% of agnostics are male, which is slightly above the baseline. While atheists and agnostics tend to look demographically similar, this is an area in which there is a noteworthy difference in the composition of these two groups.

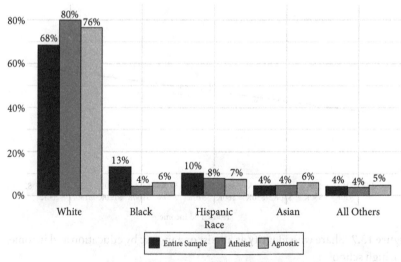

Figure 13.8 Racial composition of atheists and agnostics

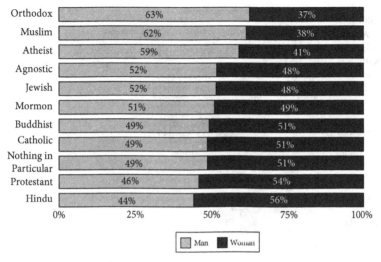

Figure 13.9 Gender composition of religious groups
Data: Cooperative Election Study

What is notable about this is that atheists and agnostics typically pride themselves on liberal political values and are especially vocal about issues related to gender and racial equality. Both groups vote for Democrats in high numbers, and they feel especially warm to candidates who tend to be more liberal on the political spectrum. For instance, Bernie Sanders was supported by 30% of atheists and 36% of agnostics in the 2020 Democratic primaries, compared to just 12% and 16%, respectively, for Joe Biden.[3] Thus, while atheists and agnostics have consistently pushed for legislation that would help gender and racial minorities, they have not managed to diversify their own ranks to match their ideals. This could potentially be rectified as younger atheists, who tend to be more racially diverse, move into adulthood. However, that has not yet emerged in the data.

Atheists and Agnostics: A Refuge for LGBTQ+

There are some areas, however, where the composition of atheists and agnostics looks much different than other religious traditions. For instance, when it comes to the topic of sexual orientation, there's ample evidence that they are far more diverse than the general public or other religious traditions. For a sense of comparison, about 14% of the general public did not say that

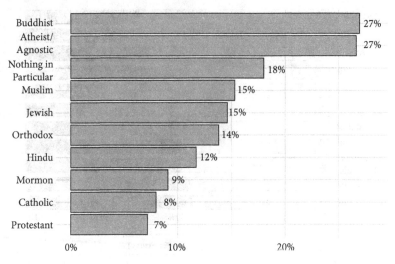

Figure 13.10 Share who say their sexuality is not heterosexual/straight
Data: Cooperative Election Study

they are heterosexual when asked in the CES in 2022. As can be seen in Figure 13.10, Protestants are the least likely group to not identify as heterosexual, followed closely by Catholics, at 7% and 8%, respectively.

In comparison, over a quarter of atheists and agnostics do not identify as heterosexual, which is the same share as Buddhists, but much higher than nothing in particulars or any other religious tradition. The distinct position of gay, lesbian, and bisexual individuals in relation to atheism and agnosticism can be attributed to several compelling factors. Over the past two decades, many of the largest religious organizations in the United States have actively opposed same-sex marriage, and various religious traditions continue to view homosexuality as contrary to their ethical teachings. Consequently, numerous individuals from the LGBTQ+ community have opted to distance themselves from religious affiliations, instead embracing atheism or agnosticism.

That same general pattern shows up in the data, displayed in Figure 13.11, when looking through the lens of gender identity. In the most recent wave of the CES, the question about gender has four response options: man, woman, nonbinary, or other. In the overall sample of 60,000, about 480 responses were nonbinary or other—which represents 0.8% of the population. There are only three religious groups that scored above the mean. About one in

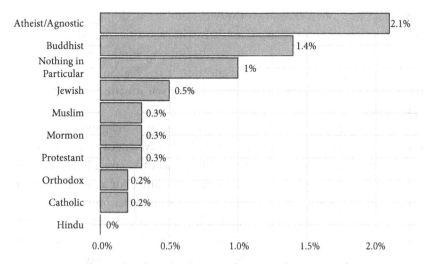

Figure 13.11 Share who describe their gender as nonbinary or other
Data: Cooperative Election Study

one hundred nothing in particulars were nonbinary/other. It was 1.4% of Buddhists and 2.1% of atheists and agnostics.

Again, this is clear evidence that secular identities are increasingly being chosen by those who do not identify as cisgender and/or heterosexual. As younger Americans continue to embrace diverse expressions of sexual orientation and gender identity, it stands to reason that this will swell the ranks of atheists and agnostics. However, there is the possibility that this impact will be somewhat muted if some liberal Protestant traditions become open and affirming to the LGBTQ+ population.[4] To date, many mainline Protestant churches have been vocal in their support of this community, but it has not translated to any appreciable membership gains, as can be seen in the chapter about mainline Protestants (Chapter 4).

Religious Belief and Behavior among Atheists and Agnostics

One of the key identifying features of atheists and agnostics is that they do not engage in religious rituals like worship attendance or prayer, but it's helpful to attach actual statistics to these assumptions. The CES asks every

226   THE AMERICAN RELIGIOUS LANDSCAPE

individual how often they attend services outside weddings and funerals. It's certainly noteworthy that some atheists and agnostics occasionally need religious services. Figure 13.12 shows that among atheists, 89% never attend religious services, while for agnostics, it is 72%. So there is clearly more aversion to religious attendance among self-identified atheists than agnostics.

Comparing the survey about prayer frequency to religious attendance reveals some interesting patterns, as well. Obviously, atheists are more likely to say that they never pray. In the middle panel of Figure 13.12, less than one in ten atheists says that they pray at least a little. For agnostics, prayer is much more commonplace. Only three in five agnostics indicate that they never pray, which means that a significant portion pray at least once a year. It's notable that the differences in religious attendance were fairly small for atheists and agnostics at seventeen percentage points. They are much larger for never praying at thirty-one points. There's no doubt about this in the data—atheists have created much more distance between themselves and religion compared to agnostics.

That's also the case when asking a question that focuses more on religious belief, "How important is religion to you?" Response options ranged from "very important" to "not important at all." Ninety-three percent of atheists said that religion was not important at all. For agnostics, it was twenty percentage points lower. Obviously, those two groups are significant outliers on this metric. Very few Americans who align with a religious tradition say that their faith is not important at all. But, again, there is a clear difference between atheists, who are almost completely detached from any type of religious behavior and belief, and agnostics, who are a bit more likely to behave and/or believe.

What these results point to is a reality that emerges when one works with survey data on a frequent basis: it's hardly ever the case that one specific subgroup is completely unified on any type of belief or behavior. In this case, 11% of atheists report going to religious services more than never. Human nature often works that way—someone could identify as very liberal but still vote for a Republican or identify as a lesbian and think that sexual relationships between two adults of the same sex is morally wrong. While atheists are clearly much farther away from religion than the average American, some of them are still connected to faith in one way or another.

ATHEISTS/AGNOSTICS 227

(a)
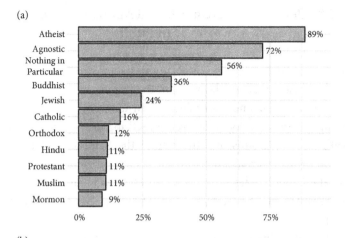

(b)
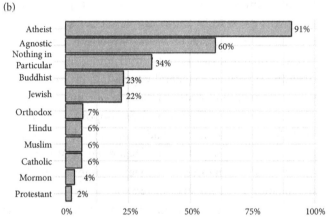

(c)
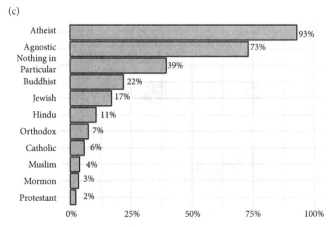

Figure 13.12 (a) Share who never attend religious services, (b) share who never pray, and (c) share saying religion is not important at all
Data: Cooperative Election Study

The Perception of Atheists and Agnostics among the American Public

The trajectory of atheists and agnostics in this data is clearly in the direction of growth. Atheists made up about 3% of the population in 2008. By 2022, that had doubled to 6%. The share of American agnostics has grown from 4% to 6% during the same period. However, something may significantly hinder the growth of both groups into the future: the persistent stigma against atheism and agnosticism in American society. As previously described, the culture of the United States presupposes a religious inclination in terms of many of the rituals that are performed around events like holidays and professional sports.

This level of animus shows up in data about perceptions of religious groups, too. Figure 13.13 shows the results of a survey by YouGov in November 2022. It asked a thousand American adults about their perceptions of several religious groups from all points on the spectrum, from Satanists to Southern Baptists.[5] Generally speaking, the public often takes a neutral stance, rating a group neither favorable nor unfavorable. However, certain groups certainly face some significant opposition from the public. For instance, half of the respondents had an unfavorable view of Satanism, and nearly the same share wasn't fond of Scientology. At the same time, a quarter of Americans had an unfavorable view of atheists, and 15% said the same about agnostics. For comparison, 13% of the public had an unfavorable view of the largest Protestant denomination in the United States—the

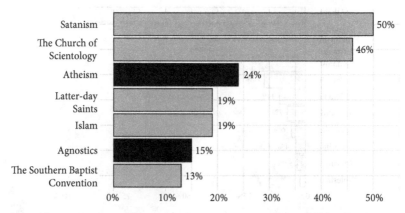

Figure 13.13 Share of Americans with a very unfavorable view of each group
Data: YouGov

ATHEISTS/AGNOSTICS

Southern Baptist Convention. It's fair to say that atheists and agnostics are not universally beloved by Americans.

However, there are other questions that tend to be a bit more negative when it comes to the perception of atheists, specifically. For instance, the Pew Research Center asked respondents if they would be happy, unhappy, or have no opinion if a person in their immediate family married someone who didn't believe in God.[6] Figure 13.14 shows that about half of the overall sample said that they would be unhappy if an atheist joined their family. Among Protestants and Catholics, that share was higher. For instance, 77% of white evangelicals wouldn't want someone in their family to marry an atheist. Even 13% of atheists and agnostics expressed displeasure with the scenario.

However, when the new addition to the family was a born-again Christian instead of an atheist, there was a lot less resistance. Less than one in ten Americans would be unhappy if someone in the family married an evangelical. That's a far cry from the 49% who would be unhappy if an atheist joined the family. Of course, very few Protestants would take issue with an evangelical marrying a close family member. Even among atheists and agnostics, just 28% would bristle if a born-again Christian married a close family member. This is fairly compelling evidence that animus toward atheists is much higher

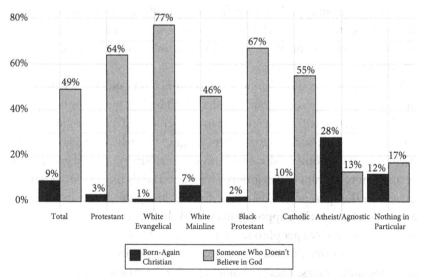

Figure 13.14 Share saying they would be unhappy if a member of their immediate family married an atheist

Data: Pew, 2014 Political Polarization in the American Public

230 THE AMERICAN RELIGIOUS LANDSCAPE

than it is for evangelicals, despite the fact that each group represents what is often perceived to be the two poles of American religion and politics.

The Future of Atheists and Agnostics

There are ample reasons to believe that atheists and agnostics will continue to grow in their share of the American population. Recall that among the youngest adult Americans, about 15% identify as atheist or agnostic. It's very likely that this number represents the future size of these groups and would effectively double their overall proportion of the adult population. To put these numbers in context, that would likely make atheists/agnostics the same size as the Catholic population and maybe even larger than white evangelicals at some point in the next several decades.

However, these groups do face some considerable headwinds when it comes to explosive growth. The average American still seems to be deeply skeptical of atheists and agnostics when it comes to issues like marriage. A helpful thought experiment is this: "Could a person become the president of the United States if they openly declared they did not believe in God?" Right now, the answer is clearly no. Presidential candidates from both major political parties espouse a belief in God, and many tout their deep religious ties when trying to appeal to voters from other faith backgrounds. When Pew Research Center compiled the religious composition of the 117th Congress, they found just one member who identified as a humanist, with no clear atheists among the members.[7]

That may change, though, and it could happen very quickly. As more and more Americans openly declare that they don't believe in God or take an agnostic stance, that will inevitably lead to a lower level of social stigma among the general public. Social contact theory argues that when a person builds a friendship with another individual from a typically marginalized group, they become more tolerant of that group. This was certainly the case for LGBTQ+ rights.[8] In the span of less than two decades, the public went from strong opposition to majority support. This was likely due, in no small part, to an increasing number of people openly identifying as LGBTQ+.

It seems plausible that the future trajectory of atheists/agnostics will run along the same tracks. There are more openly atheist/agnostic people in the United States today than at any point in the country's history. This makes it much more likely for other people to come into close personal contact with these two groups. If the social contact theory is true, then this should, in turn, lead to more acceptance and tolerance. This stigmatization will likely lead more people to openly declare that they don't believe in God, which will perpetuate the cycle of acceptance and toleration.

At this stage, it's likely too early to know if there will be widespread support for atheists and agnostics in a decade or two. However, it does not seem like the perceived discrimination against these groups will increase in the future. It's likely that as society continues to shift its mores and values, a person declaring that they are an atheist will carry no more stigma than aligning with any other minority religious belief. This will certainly lead to a more diverse and pluralistic American society.

Notes

1. Barack Obama. 2009. "President Barack Obama's Inaugural Address." Transcript. Washington, DC: National Archives. https://obamawhitehouse.archives.gov/blog/2009/01/21/president-Barack-obamas-inaugural-address#.
2. Landon Schnabel, Sean Bock, and Mike Hout. 2022. "Switch to Web-Based Surveys during Covid-19 Pandemic Left out the Most Religious, Creating a False Impression of Rapid Religious Decline." *SocArXiv*. https://osf.io/g3cnx/download.
3. Michael Lipka and Gregory A. Smith. 2020. "Among Democrats, Christians Lean toward Biden, While 'Nones' Prefer Sanders." *Pew Research Center*. https://www.pewresearch.org/short-reads/2020/01/31/among-democrats-christians-lean-toward-biden-while-nones-prefer-sanders/.
4. Evangelical Lutheran Church in America. "Resources for the LGBTQIA+ Community." *ELCA.org*. https://www.elca.org:443/LGBTQ.
5. Taylor Orth. 2022. "Americans' Views on 35 Religious Groups, Organizations, and Belief Systems." *YouGov*. https://today.yougov.com/society/articles/44850-americans-views-religious-groups-you gov-pol.
6. Michael Lipka and Jessica Martínez. 2014. "So, You Married an Atheist . . ." *Pew Research Center*. https://www.pewresearch.org/short-reads/2014/06/16/so-you-married-an-atheist/.
7. Aleksandra Sandstrom. 2021. *Faith on the Hill: The Religious Composition of the 117th Congress*. Pew Research Center, 8. https://www.pewresearch.org/religion/wp-content/uploads/sites/7/2021/01/01.04.21_faith_on_the_hill_fullreport.update.pdf.
8. Daniel DellaPosta. 2018. "Gay Acquaintanceship and Attitudes toward Homosexuality: A Conservative Test." *Socius* 4: 1–12.

Data References

Davern, Michael, Rene Bautista, Jeremy Freese, Pamela Herd, and Stephen L. Morgan. 2023. General Social Survey 1972–2022. Principal investigator, Michael Davern; Co-principal investigators, Rene Bautista, Jeremy Freese, Pamela Herd, and Stephen L. Morgan. Sponsored by National Science Foundation. NORC ed. Chicago: NORC at the University of Chicago. https://gssdataexplorer.norc.org.
Schaffner, Brian, Stephen Ansolabehere, Sam Luks, Shiro Kuriwaki, and Marissa Shih. 2006–2023. Cooperative Election Study Common Content, 2006–2022. Harvard Dataverse. https://cces.gov.harvard.edu/.

14

Nothing in Particular

Almost all the chapters in this volume focus on people who affirmatively identify with one type of religious group. They look at all the survey options presented to them and choose to be called a Protestant, a Buddhist, an atheist, or one of the other possibilities. That's a key part of how social science understands how surveys work—people willingly aligning themselves with a faith tradition, a political party, or a racial group. But what about people who read through all those response options for the question about religion and don't feel an affinity toward any of them? What about the people who just opt out of this discussion entirely?

Pew Research Center began giving those people a choice on their surveys about twenty years ago. It was labeled "nothing in particular" and denotes those individuals who look over all those choices and declare that they are "none of the above." For them, it's a simple act of rebellion—opting out of the traditional understanding of religion. However, these people who are just shrugging their shoulders at other faith groups have become the fastest growing segment of society over the last decade. In fact, among the youngest adults, they are more likely to declare that they are "nothing in particular" than they are to affirm a Protestant or Catholic affiliation.

It's important to understand how scholars think about the concept of "nothing in particular" before the discussion moves to their size, growth, and composition. Social scientists typically use the term "none" to encompass the share of Americans who do not identify with any theistic tradition. Inside the nones, there are three subgroups: atheists, agnostics, and nothing in particulars. In the prior chapter, atheists and agnostics were detailed and described. These two groups could best be described as "secular," according to Campbell, Layman, and Green.[1] What this means is that atheists and agnostics have cast aside a religious worldview and replaced it with a secular one that is based on science, logic, and rationality.

People who identify as nothing in particular are not classified as secular. Instead, they are seen as nonreligious. They have walked away from a religious worldview but have not replaced it with anything else. Nothing in

The American Religious Landscape. Ryan P. Burge, Oxford University Press. © Oxford University Press 2025.
DOI: 10.1093/oso/9780197762837.003.0015

particulars are defined by what they are not, not by what they are. The upshot of this is that nothing in particulars tend to be slightly warmer toward religion than their atheist/agnostic counterparts. There are also several demographic factors that separate atheists/agnostics from nothing in particulars, as you will see in this chapter.

The Explosive Growth of Nothing in Particular

One issue that arises when talking about the growth of nonreligion or the increasing secularization of the United States is that people tend to believe that this is about a rapidly expanding number of atheists or agnostics. This is not the case, however, when one looks at the data. In fact, most nones are not actually atheists or agnostics; they are nothing in particular. While it varies a bit from year to year, it's fair to say that at least 60% of the nonreligious are nothing in particular. In some years, there are two nothing in particulars for every atheist/agnostic.

In Figure 14.1, though, there is a clear growth trajectory for both groups. In 2008, atheists/agnostics were 8% of American adults. In 2022, that had risen to 13%. For nothing in particulars, the growth was even more significant. In

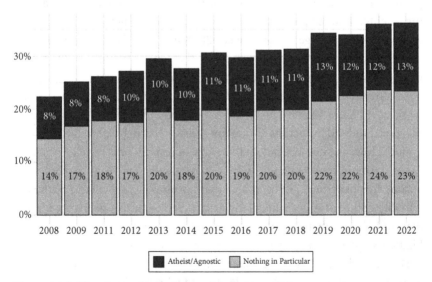

Figure 14.1 The share of Americans who are nonreligious
Data: Cooperative Election Study

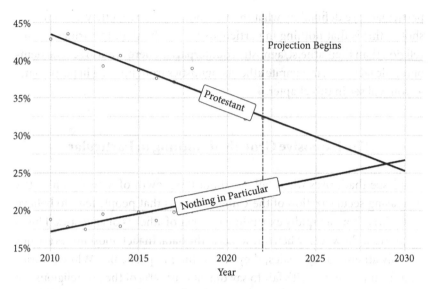

Figure 14.2 Projecting the size of nothing in particular
Data: Cooperative Election Study

2008, 14% of adults were nothing in particular, which has risen to 23% in the most recent survey estimates. While Protestants and Catholics have both posted noticeable declines in their overall adherents, just the opposite is happening with nothing in particulars, who are seeing their ranks swell at an unprecedented rate. To put this in perspective, the nothing in particulars have gained nine percentage points between 2008 and 2022. That share represents a larger number of Americans than all the Latter-day Saints, Orthodox Christians, Jews, Muslims, Hindus, and Buddhists combined.

Another reference point is the size of other religious traditions, as can be seen in Figure 14.2. In 2022, 32% of all respondents to the Cooperative Election Study identified as Protestant—easily the most popular response option. However, just a decade earlier, 42% of respondents were Protestants. At the current growth rate for nothing in particulars and the current rate of decline for Protestants, it's probable that nothing in particulars will be the plurality choice of Americans in the next fifteen or twenty years. One factor that could have a demonstrable impact on these trend lines is age, as seen in Figure 14.3. If lots of younger Americans are nothing in particular and a large portion of older adults are Protestants, that means that generational replacement will speed up the decline of Protestant Christianity and accelerate the rise of the nonreligious.

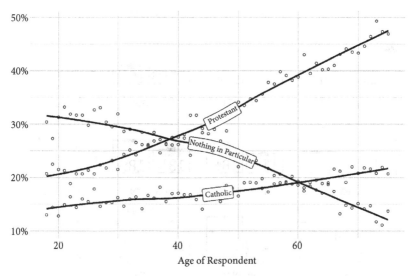

Figure 14.3 Religious tradition by age
Data: Cooperative Election Study

Among the youngest Americans, nearly one in three identifies as nothing in particular. In comparison, 20% say that they are Protestant and 14% are Catholic. Nothing in particulars are a larger share than Protestants at every age from eighteen to thirty-eight years old, when those trend lines intersect. From that point forward, the Protestant share increases rapidly. Nearly 40% of sixty-year-olds are Protestants, and just 18% are nothing in particulars. For nothing in particulars, the line slowly drops over time. Less than a quarter of fifty-year-olds are nothing in particular. It's less than 20% of sixty-year-olds.

This is fairly strong evidence of a sea change happening in American religion over the next two decades. It's likely that the teenagers who move into adulthood over the next five years will be 35% nothing in particular, compared to less than 20% who are Protestant and less than 15% who are Catholic. This generational replacement will shift the overall percentages very quickly as many Baby Boomers move toward the end of their lives and are replaced by less religious young people. From this angle, it seems more appropriate to say that the future of America is not secular; it's primarily nonreligious.

However, that's not to say that the growth in nothing in particulars is not driven entirely by generational replacement. Instead, there's clear evidence in Figure 14.4 that more and more Americans are choosing to be nonreligious

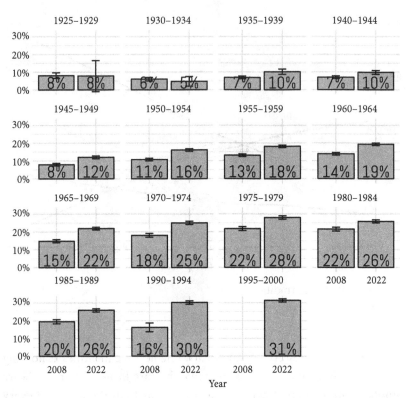

Figure 14.4 Share who are nothing in particular by birth cohort
Data: Cooperative Election Study

at every age level. Even among those born in the 1940s, the share who are nothing in particular has risen a few percentage points between 2008 and 2022. That growth in nothing in particulars is larger among the younger birth cohorts, however. For instance, among those born in the 1970s, the share who are nothing in particular has risen six to seven percentage points between 2008 and 2022. In fact, there's no age cohort after those born in the late 1930s, where nothing in particulars are less prevalent today than they were a decade ago.

Thus, there are two major sources of the growth of the nothing in particulars. One is simply the fact that older Americans are less likely to be nonreligious, while younger adults are more likely to identify as nothing in particular. The other factor that is driving the growth is people moving away from organized religion and choosing nothing in particular as they age. If anything, this means that the growth trajectory of nothing in particulars will only accelerate as new folks arrive by multiple methods.

The Demographics of Nothing in Particular

It's undoubtedly true that nothing in particulars have very little that holds them together as a cohesive group, beyond the fact that they all checked the same box when taking a survey. Obviously, religious groups are united around a shared theology and culture, and even atheists and agnostics are largely unified in how they view the possibility of the Divine. Nothing in particulars don't have any of those things in common. As you will see in the next section, their approach to religion seems to be unique compared to atheists and agnostics; however, they are clearly less religiously engaged than other theistic groups, too. That's not to say that there aren't some findings in the data that help us to understand the contours of this rather amorphous collective of people.

One of the most prominent findings regarding nothing in particulars is their very low level of educational attainment, as can be seen in Figure 14.5. In the overall sample, about 37% of American adults finished their education when they received a high school diploma. Many religious traditions report a much higher level of education than that baseline. For instance, just 15% of Hindus and 16% of Jews finished their education in the twelfth grade, whereas 22% of atheists and agnostics never completed any courses beyond high school.

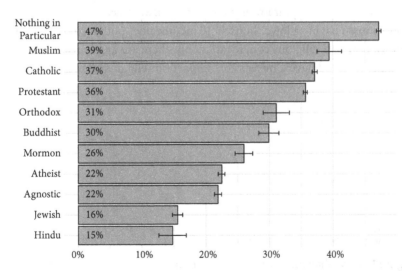

Figure 14.5 The share with a high school diploma or less
Data: Cooperative Election Study

Nothing in particulars are clearly an outlier here. Nearly half of them finished their education with a high school diploma (47%). The next closest group is Muslims at 39%. Overall, one-third of Americans have completed a four-year college degree. Among nothing in particulars it was just 23%—which is ten percentage points lower than any other religious group. A clear and unmistakable point from this data is that nothing in particulars are easily the least educated religious group in the United States today, by a significant margin.

The fact that nothing in particulars easily have the lowest level of education is key in understanding some of the other characteristics of this seemingly amorphous group. In social science research, higher levels of education are often related to increased household income, the likelihood of marriage, and other life choices that can have significant impacts on things like religious affiliation and regular worship attendance. All those factors are evident when looking at nothing in particulars.

In terms of household education, the average respondent in the Cooperative Election Study reported that their family earned about $52,000 per year. In Figure 14.6 several religious groups are close to that average, including Orthodox Christians, Mormons, Buddhists, and Protestants. There are only two religious groups who make significantly less than that: Muslims and nothing in particulars. In data collected between 2020 and 2022, nothing in particulars reported a total household income of just over $42,000 per year. That's $10,000 a year lower than the overall average.

Obviously, having a lower household income does not preclude one from being a part of a religious congregation, but there are ample reasons to believe that it could have a measurable impact on religious attendance. Every

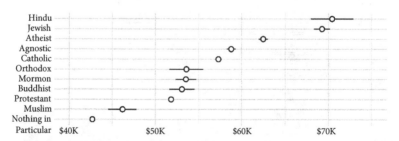

Figure 14.6 Median income by religious group
Data: Cooperative Election Study

major religion encourages its membership to give to their local house of worship or to the needs they see in the community. This is not compulsory, but it stands to reason that when the offering plate is passed during worship gatherings, some may feel embarrassed for not being able to drop in a few dollars. Additionally, those with lower household incomes may be more likely to work jobs with inconsistent hours and weekend shifts. Both those factors make it more difficult for people at the lower end of the income spectrum to be part of a religious congregation.

Another factor that sets nothing in particulars apart is their lower marriage rates, overall. The Cooperative Election Study asks respondents about their marital status with these options: married, separated, divorced, widowed, and never been married. When looked at by age in Figure 14.7, it's clear that nothing in particulars are less likely to marry as well. A majority of nothing in particulars remain unmarried until their thirty-third birthday, whereas in the general population that happens right around thirty years old. There's a consistent gap in the data between the marriage rates of the entire sample and nothing in particulars. That gap is never large—usually running between two and four percentage points. But it points to the conclusion that nothing in particulars are opting out of more parts of American society than religion alone.

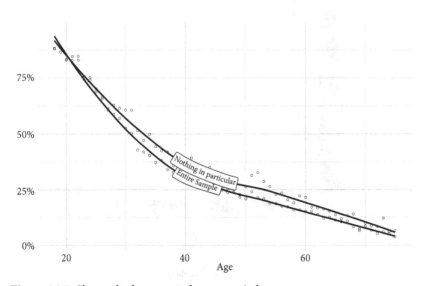

Figure 14.7 Share who have never been married
Data: Cooperative Election Study

One interesting result when considering nothing in particulars is their overall racial composition, as in Figure 14.8. Given that this group tends to skew younger, and knowing that racial diversity is quite a bit more prominent among younger Americans than older ones, it would logically follow that nothing in particulars would have a lower percentage of white respondents than the overall sample. That's not what the data reveal, though.

In the general sample, 68% of respondents identify as white; among the nothing in particulars, it is much higher at 80%. The only other major disparity is among Black respondents. In the overall sample, they are 13%; however, just 4% of all nothing in particulars are Black. Among Hispanics, Asians, and all other racial groups, there is not a statistically significant difference between the two samples. For comparison, if atheists, agnostics, and nothing in particulars are combined, their racial composition is 68% white, which is the same as the share in the overall sample. Thus, nothing in particulars clearly stand out on this measure.

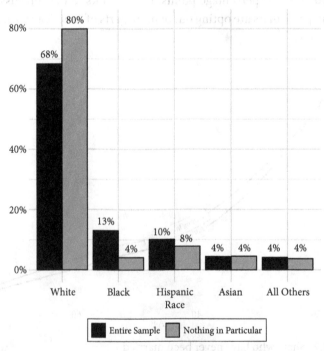

Figure 14.8 The racial composition of nothing in particulars
Data: Cooperative Election Study

The Geography of Nothing in Particulars

Given that the nothing in particulars have grown to nearly a quarter of the adult population in the United States, it logically follows that they would have reached some level of geographic dispersion. Clearly, nothing in particulars are not like Latter-day Saints, who have a unique concentration in one specific part of the country. The nonreligious can now be found in large numbers in every state. However, that's not to say that they are not a bit more prevalent in certain regions of the United States, as can be seen in Figure 14.9.

The variation in the concentration of nothing in particulars from state to state is worth considering. The states with the lowest concentration are New Jersey and North Dakota at 18%. The state with the highest concentration is Hawaii at 32%, with Maine coming in second at 30%. Again, there's nothing that geographically ties those four states together, and this speaks to the pervasive nature of this religious group. That's not to say there aren't patterns in the spatial data, however. Clearly, there are more nothing in particulars on the West Coast. In California, Oregon, and Washington, 26% of the population is nothing in particular. But there are also high numbers just inland with Nevada, Idaho, and Montana at 28% each. It's also interesting to note that

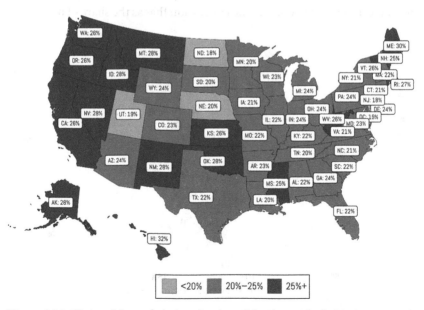

Figure 14.9 Share of the population that is nothing in particular
Data: Cooperative Election Study

there's a pocket in the middle of the country of relatively high numbers as well in Oklahoma, Kansas, and New Mexico.

But most states across the Midwest, the South, and even New England report an average between 20% and 25%. What's interesting is how difficult it is to ascertain a clear conclusion from this data. Part of that is driven by just how little variation there is between states—most report nothing in particulars in the low 20% range. But when Mississippi has essentially the same share as Washington, it's hard to find the commonalities between the two.

One possible avenue for exploration is a relationship between the share of atheists/agnostics and nothing in particulars at the state level. For instance, maybe as the percentage of atheists/agnostics rises, it creates a more hospitable climate for formerly religious people to identify as nothing in particular. Or the opposite could be happening: atheists/agnostics are cannibalizing the ranks of nothing in particulars.

A scatterplot of those two variables, in Figure 14.10, clearly points to the first theory—as the share of nothing in particulars rises, so does the percentage of a state that identifies as atheist or agnostic. This is clearly not a situation where atheists/agnostics are swelling at the expense of nothing in particulars. Just the opposite—the percentages rise in tandem. Obviously, it's not possible to know which factor is the independent versus dependent variable here, but the data point to the conclusion that as the share of nothing in

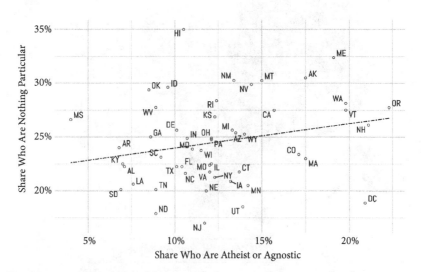

Figure 14.10 The relationship between the types of none, state level
Data: Cooperative Election Study

particulars rises, so does the percentage who identify as atheist/agnostic and vice versa.

The outliers are interesting to ponder. For instance, Hawaii has a very high level of nothing in particulars compared to its percentage of those who are atheist/agnostic. The same is true in other states, as well: Alaska, Maine, Montana, and New Mexico. However, New Jersey proves to be an outlier in the other direction. Its share of nothing in particulars is very similar to the percentage who are atheist/agnostic; that's not the case in other states.

Nothing and Particulars and Religion

As previously noted, scholars contend that nothing in particulars represent a different manifestation of the nones than atheists or agnostics. Atheists and agnostics have replaced a religious worldview with a secular one. They believe that answers to life's questions can be found through science, logic, and reason. Nothing in particulars are in a different spot entirely. They have set aside a religious worldview, but they haven't adopted a different way of looking at the world. One practical implication of this divergence is that atheists/agnostics should exhibit a lower likelihood of religious behavior or belief compared to nothing in particulars. The data confirm that assumption.

In 2021, the General Social Survey asked how the different types of nones thought about the concept of God, which Figure 14.11 displays. Seventy percent of self-identified atheists said that they did not believe that God exists, and another 21% said that they couldn't know if God existed or not. In comparison, just 8% of nothing in particulars definitively said that God doesn't exist, and another 22% said that there was no way to find out if God existed or not. This means that 70% of nothing in particulars express at least some level of belief in the Divine.

The differences between atheists, agnostics, and nothing in particulars come into sharper focus when looking at just the share of each who says that they believe in God without any doubt. Zero atheists in the sample expressed a certain belief in God, and it was only 2% of agnostics. In comparison, nearly one in five nothing in particulars expressed a certain belief in God. If one sums the bottom two categories in Figure 14.11 (believe no doubts and believe but doubts), that encompasses no atheists, 9% of agnostics, and 39% of nothing in particulars. Clearly, nothing in particulars have a different conception of the Divine than the other types of nones.

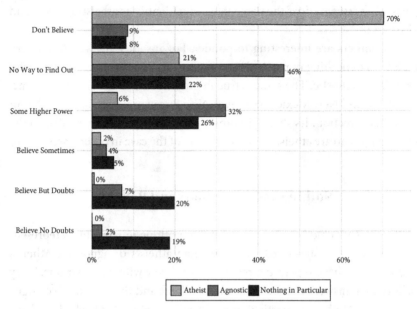

Figure 14.11 View of God among the nonreligious
Data: Cooperative Election Study

There is also a noticeable divergence in religious attendance among atheists/agnostics and nothing in particulars, as well. In Figure 14.12, 96% of atheists report that they attend religious services less than once a year, which is statistically the same as agnostics. In both cases, less than 1% report weekly attendance at religious services. Nothing in particulars are slightly more likely to engage in corporate worship. Only 84% describe their attendance as seldom or never. Another 12% say that they attend services yearly or monthly, and 4% are attending religious services weekly.

It's important to note that even though nothing in particulars are more likely to attend religious services compared to atheists and agnostics, their attendance patterns are still much lower than other religious groups. For instance, just 38% of Protestants and 44% of Catholics say that they attend church services less than once a year. At the same time, 34% of Protestants and 26% of Catholics are attending weekly, compared to just 4% of nothing in particulars. From this angle, it's clear that the attendance pattern of nothing in particulars looks more similar to atheists/agnostics than it does to any religious group.

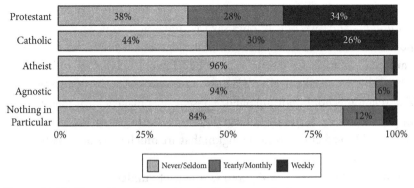

Figure 14.12 How often do you attend religious service?
Data: Cooperative Election Study

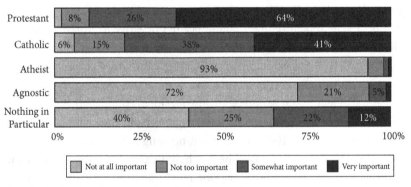

Figure 14.13 How important is religion to you?
Data: Cooperative Election Study

When it comes to attendance, nothing in particulars behave more like atheists/agnostics than Protestants or Catholics. However, when looking at a question about the importance of religion, as in Figure 14.13, things get a bit murkier. It should come as no surprise that 93% of atheists say that religion is not important at all. That same view is shared by just 72% of agnostics. However, it's important to point out that the share of atheists and agnostics who say that religion is very important is essentially the same—around 1%. For nothing in particulars, just 40% say religion is not important at all, and another quarter describe religion as not too important. That means that a third say that religion is somewhat or very important. That's twenty-eight points higher than agnostics and thirty-two points higher than atheists.

Again, it's important to put these percentages in a larger context: 90% of Protestants and 79% of Catholics say that religion is somewhat or very important. But it's also clearly the case that a significant portion of nothing in particulars seem to have some type of belief about religion. Recall that just 30% of this group take an atheist/agnostic view of God, and only 40% indicate that religion is not important at all. These results make it clear that nothing in particulars are certainly not as religious as Catholics or Protestants, but they do exhibit feelings toward religion that are much more positive than the other types of nones.

One final look at this in Figure 14.14 helps to understand where to place nothing in particulars in relation to other nones. The Public Religion Research Institute asked respondents if "religion causes more problems in society than it solves" in 2019. Of course, very few Protestants and Catholics agree with that statement—less than a quarter of each. Atheists are easily the most likely to believe that religion is a net negative in American society at 88%. There is a sizable gap between atheists and agnostics on this question. Only 72% of agnostics think that religion causes more problems than it solves. But nothing in particulars are even lower at just 60%.

Again, it's clear that it would be inappropriate to conclude that nothing in particulars are just like atheists in their religious belief, behavior, and overall perception of religion. If one were to put nothing in particulars in religious space, atheists/agnostics would be to their left, and religious Americans would be to their right. They are not nearly as religious as a group like Muslims or Latter-day Saints, but they also tend to feel a bit warmer toward religion than atheists and agnostics. Thus, they are a group that is not easy to pin down and easily characterize.

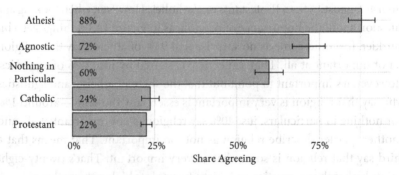

Figure 14.14 Religion causes more problems in society than it solves
Data: PRRI 2019

Conclusion

Obviously, nothing in particulars are an incredibly diverse group. That would naturally be the case for any segment of American society that compromises tens of millions of people. However, that isn't to say that they don't have some things that unite them. The biggest one is that they seem to reject any type of label or institution. As has been visualized in this chapter, nothing in particulars are more likely to end their formal education at the high school level and get married at rates that are lower than the overall average. This also comes through when looking at survey questions about political partisanship and ideology. Surveys typically give people some predetermined response options like liberal or conservative for ideology and Republican or Democrat for partisanship. But surveys also allow people to choose the "other" option.

As can be seen in Figure 14.15, nothing in particulars are much more likely to eschew the typical partisan or ideological labels compared to other religious groups. One in five nothing in particulars describes their political

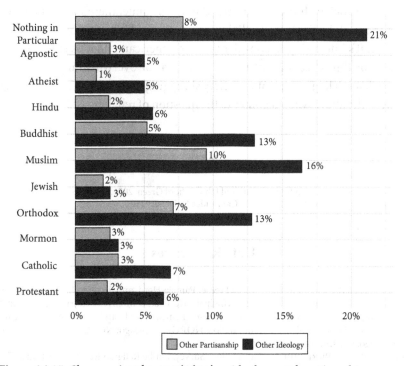

Figure 14.15 Share saying they are 'other' on ideology and partisanship
Data: Cooperative Election Study

248   THE AMERICAN RELIGIOUS LANDSCAPE

partisanship as "other." That's easily the highest of any religious group. At the same time, 8% of nothing in particulars do not identify as conservative, moderate, or liberal. That is the second highest of any other religious group. For comparison, just 2% of Protestants say that their partisanship is "other" and only 6% identify as an "other" ideology. In short, nothing in particulars seem to reject labels in every facet of their social lives—not just religion.

There's an important concept among social scientists called social capital. These are the invisible bonds that make individuals care about each other outside a typical family structure. It's what makes people want to see the school system improve even after their children graduate, or want to fund a new playground even though it will be located on the other side of town. These bonds are typically formed in social institutions like churches, schools, or social clubs. Unfortunately, it looks like nothing in particulars are rejecting many of those opportunities to build ties with others in their community and thus suppressing social capital. This could have long-term implications for American religion and American democracy.

Without a doubt, nothing in particulars represent a growing segment of American society. If the current trend lines continue, there's a good chance that they will be the largest religious group in the United States in the next decade. It's interesting to consider that the American religious landscape in twenty or thirty years is not primarily secular or overwhelming Christian. Instead, it is a large segment of society shrugging its shoulders and choosing none of the above when it comes to the question of religious affiliation.

Note

1. David E. Campbell, Geoffrey Layman, and John Clifford Green. 2021. *Secular Surge: A New Fault Line in American Politics.* Cambridge: Cambridge University Press.

Data References

Davern, Michael, Rene Bautista, Jeremy Freese, Pamela Herd, and Stephen L. Morgan. 2023. General Social Survey 1972–2022. Principal investigator, Michael Davern; Co-principal investigators, Rene Bautista, Jeremy Freese, Pamela Herd, and Stephen L. Morgan. Sponsored by National Science Foundation. NORC ed. Chicago: NORC at the University of Chicago. https://gssdataexplorer.norc.org.

Jones, R. P. 2021. PRRI 2019 American Values Survey. Public Religion Research Institute. The Association of Religion Data Archives. doi:10.17605/OSF.IO/PH68V.

Schaffner, Brian, Stephen Ansolabehere, Sam Luks, Shiro Kuriwaki, and Marissa Shih. 2006-2023. Cooperative Election Study Common Content, 2006–2022. Harvard Dataverse. https://cces.gov.harvard.edu/.

15

The Future of American Religion

In February 2002, Secretary of Defense Donald Rumsfeld was giving a press briefing regarding several topics, including the likelihood of Iraq possessing weapons of mass destruction. During an answer to one reporter's question, Rumsfeld stated, "There are known knowns; there are things we know we know. We also know there are unknown unknowns; that is to say, we know there are some things we do not know. But there are also unknown unknowns—the ones we don't know we don't know."[1] Perhaps inadvertently, Rumsfeld managed to describe the fundamental problem with prediction: it's always going to be a fool's errand.

In this case, scholars of American religious demography are fully aware of some larger patterns going on in society, but there may be things out there that even the keenest observer of the religious landscape would not be able to predict. What would some of those unknowns be in the case of American religion? The most likely culprit would be some type of spiritual revival that would be similar to what the United States experienced during the First and Second Great Awakenings. In each of these events, the religious landscape of the United States was radically altered by charismatic preachers and peer pressure.

Millions of Americans, from all walks of life, responded to the Christian message of transformation. The pews of Protestant churches swelled with new members in all regions of the inhabited United States. These revivals led to the ascendance of denominations like the Methodists and Baptists. Mass revivals are totally unpredictable and defy any attempts at modeling them using standard statistical techniques. Thus, they must be excluded by default when endeavoring to provide a statistically grounded projection of American religion. Religious demographers know that the more precisely specified could be thrown out the window when a story of revival makes the national news.

There are other significant factors that could shape the American religious landscape that may not be so random as a religious revival but are still hard to conceptualize when thinking about the future. A good example is

The American Religious Landscape. Ryan P. Burge, Oxford University Press. © Oxford University Press 2025.
DOI: 10.1093/oso/9780197762837.003.0016

immigration. As this volume has laid out, there are many smaller religious groups in the United States (Muslims, Hindus, Buddhists) that are highly dependent on immigrants coming to American shores. While it may be possible to have a decent grasp on immigration patterns in the next few years, projections that rely on immigration become more untenable when looking at the United States in twenty or thirty years.

It's impossible to know with any degree of certainty whether the United States will open up its borders to new immigrants or whether the opposite will occur and immigration will be significantly curtailed. The issue of immigration plays a central role when trying to chart the trajectory of Islam in the United States. For instance, when Donald Trump was the president of the United States, he signed an executive order that banned immigration from several majority-Muslim countries in the Middle East and Africa.[2] It's impossible to know if such an event like this will happen in ten or twenty years from now.

But there are other factors that could have a tremendous impact on the trajectory of religious groups. For instance, there could be some type of pandemic that could kill millions of older Americans, many of whom are Christians, while sparing younger people who tend to be nonreligious. Or there could be a significant medical breakthrough that could extend the lifespan of the average person—thus, ensuring that Christianity will remain dominant in the American religious landscape for several decades into the future.

But then there are always the possibilities of what Rumsfeld called the "unknown unknowns." These are changes in American society that could have never been foreseen. For instance, I don't think that many scholars of technology were talking about the importance of online social networks in 1980. Even in the early days of websites like Myspace, few academics were discussing how they would dominate almost every aspect of American society in the decades to come. One reason was that those early networks were created before the advent of smartphones. Without the proliferation of the iPhone, there's ample reason to believe that companies like Facebook and Twitter would have only taken up a small portion of the American conscience in 2024. It took the introduction of smartphones and social networks—two innovations that were certainly not well understood even twenty years ago—to help us arrive at our current situation.

Thus, what follows is an analysis that assumes that current trends will continue based on observable trajectories that exist in the data. There will be no attempt at trying to model a religious revival or a massive influx of immigrants from a specific part of the world. Instead, this work will be based on a general assumption that what will happen in the future looks very much like what happened in the recent past. The best way to describe these trend lines is conservative in their assumption. This surely means that some of these predictions will be incorrect for reasons that are, to use Rumsfeld's term, "unknown unknowns."

Trend 1: Christianity Will Still Dominate the Religious Landscape for the Immediate Future

A frequent question that is often asked of religious demographers is a simple one, "Is the United States a Christian nation?" While there are a variety of ways to answer that question that range from the theoretical to the political, from a pure empirical point of view the answer is: yes. The majority of American adults in 2023 still identify as some type of Christian. However, that share is clearly and noticeably declining, as can be seen in Figure 15.1. When the General Social Survey was launched in 1972, the share of Americans who identified as Catholic, Protestant, or Orthodox

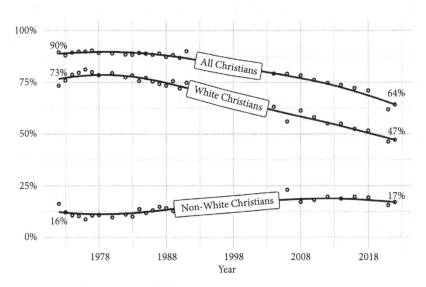

Figure 15.1 The trajectory of Christianity, 1972–2002
Data: General Social Survey

Christians was 90%. In those days it would be statistically accurate to say that the United States was dominated by Christians. Additionally, the majority of those Christians were white. In fact, in the early 1970s, about 80% of all Christians were white in the United States, but that has slowly changed over time.

In the 2022 General Social Survey, the share of Christians had declined precipitously to just 64%. If one traces the trend line, it becomes clear that this drop began in earnest around 1990 and has continued to accelerate in the last two decades. However, the composition of that decline is worth considering. The share of Americans who were white and Christian was 73% in 1972. The most recent figure puts that percentage at just 47%. Now, white Christianity is not the majority in American religion. However, at the same time, the share of the United States who are non-white Christians has held remarkably steady. In 1972, it was 16% of the population, and the most recent estimate is statistically the same at 17%.

What this means is that the overall racial composition of American Christianity is changing. In the 1970s, just 15% of all Christians were non-white. In the United States in 2022, nearly 27% of Christians were people of color. This shift is happening for primarily two reasons—one is that the United States is becoming a more racially diverse country, and second is that a significant number of white Americans are moving into the category of nonreligious. This will have several significant impacts on the future of the United States and American religious demography.

In the near term, there's ample reason to believe that Christianity will still be the dominant type of religion in the United States. Even as the trend line for the share of Americans who are Christians continues to point downward, it will likely remain above 50% for the next several decades (when exactly this will happen will be explored in further detail below). From a cultural standpoint, it seems likely that Christianity will still monopolize the conversation about religion in the United States. Even if it drops below majority status, Christianity will still be the plurality religion for the foreseeable future. However, given the changing racial composition of American Christianity, we should expect to see new voices emerge in the Christian world that look, think, and preach differently than those who have come before.

Trend 2: Religious Switching Will Accelerate and Significantly Impact the Landscape

The strongest predictor of one's current religious affiliation is the religion in which they were raised. That's been the case in American religion for decades. Yes, some people do leave their childhood faith for a different religious tradition, but, again, that has always represented the minority outcome. However, if one grew up going to a house of worship on a regular basis, it's commonplace to hear compelling and often dramatic testimonies of individuals experiencing a spiritual epiphany that leads them to embrace a new faith or leave their previous tradition behind. A story where someone recounts how they were born to two Catholic parents—baptized and confirmed—and remained a faithful Mass attender for the rest of their life does not have nearly the same emotional impact. However, the data show that the story of someone maintaining the same religion for the entire course of their life is becoming less frequent with each successive generation.

For decades, evangelicals have enjoyed a significant conversion bonus, as can be seen in Figure 15.2. While about 20% of people born over the last

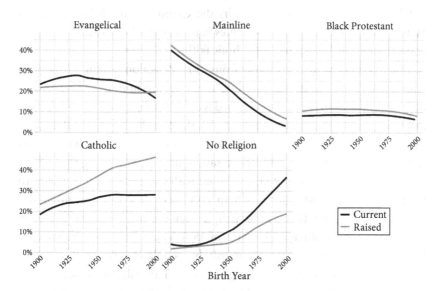

Figure 15.2 In what religion were you raised versus current religion?
Data: General Social Survey

254   THE AMERICAN RELIGIOUS LANDSCAPE

hundred years indicated that they were raised in an evangelical household, the share of the entire population that identified as evangelical as an adult was noticeably higher than that. For people born in the 1940s through the early 1970s, 5%–7% were currently evangelical when they had been raised in another faith tradition. However, among people born in 1990 or later, things have begun to change. While the share who were raised evangelical has stayed relatively steady, the percentage who align with the evangelical tradition has dipped. This means that the conversion bonus has completely disappeared and now evangelicalism is facing more outflows than inflows. This portends a difficult future for American evangelicalism and is an early indicator of future declines in the decades to come.

The other tradition that has struggled in this regard is the American Catholic Church; however, the gap between the two lines has always been fairly large. Among people born around 1950, about 37% indicated that they were raised Catholic, but the share who currently identify as Catholic was much lower at just 27%. But that gap has only widened among the youngest adult Americans. Among those born around 2000, the share who were raised Catholic has never been higher, just above 45%. Yet the share of people who were born around 2000 who currently identify as Catholic is just below 30%. This means that the defection problem with American Catholicism is only accelerated. The primary reason why the Catholic Church in the United States is not seeing significant declines is because an increasing number of young people are born into the Catholic faith.

Who is benefiting the most from this defection among American Christianity? It's clearly the swelling ranks of the nones. Among people born around 1925, very few were raised without a religious tradition. In fact, just one in twenty adults born prior to World War II reports that they were raised in a nonreligious household. However, over time that share began to move upward, beginning with those raised after 1950. Among those born around 1970, about one in ten was raised with no religion. For those born around the year 2000, a bit less than 20% were raised in a nonreligious household. However, the share of people born around 2000 who currently claim no religious affiliation is north of 35%. This means that the ranks of the nonreligious are growing primarily by people leaving other religious traditions behind and now affiliating as a none. This will undoubtedly result in a rise in nonreligious households over time, further fueling the expansion of nonreligious populations.

Trend 3: Mainline Protestant Christianity Will Largely Disappear

One of the most unmistakable trends in the American religious landscape over the last several decades is the collapse of mainline Protestant Christianity. Recall from the earlier chapter that these are the types of churches that tend to be less conservative in their theology. Many members do not take the Bible to be literally true, they allow women to have full access to all leadership roles, and many of these religious denominations are open and affirming to couples in same-sex relationships. These are well-known denominations with long histories in the United States, such as the Episcopal Church, the Presbyterian Church (USA), and the United Methodist Church (UMC). It's hard to convey how dominant these churches were in every aspect of American life in the post–World War II period. Scholar of religious history James Hudnut-Beumler contends that in the late 1950s, over half of all Americans were aligned with a mainline church.[3]

However, in the decades to come, the mainline would begin to shed members by the millions. When the General Social Survey began in 1972, about 28% of adults aligned with a mainline tradition. In just the period between 1958 and 1972, the mainline had lost close to half its membership. But things would only decline from there. By the early 1990s, the share of Americans who were mainline dropped below 20% for the first time. In the last few years of the General Social Survey, the share who are mainline has hovered right around 10% of the sample. It's staggering to consider that a tradition that counted half of Americans as members seventy-five years ago is now just a small fraction of the population.

In Figure 15.3, a linear projection is estimated for the future of mainline Protestant Christianity based on the previously described data from the General Social Survey. This model estimates that by 2030, just 5% of all Americans will be mainline Protestant, and this number will reach zero somewhere around 2040. Obviously, mainline Protestants will not entirely disappear in the next two decades. Any cursory study of organizational decline finds that as membership moves closer to zero, the trajectory of the decline begins to level off. Almost every organization has "die-hard" members who will hold on to the bitter end. This means that many of these denominations will be faced with a remnant of several hundred thousand that will continue to support their local churches for as long as they are physically and financially able to do so.

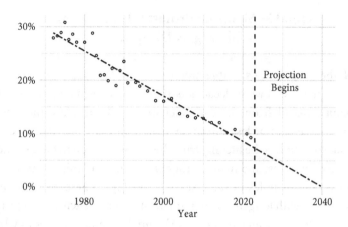

Figure 15.3 The past and future of mainline Christianity
Data: General Social Survey

However, there are ample data points available that point toward the demise of the mainline. For instance, in the 2022 General Social Survey, the share of the sample that were mainline Protestants between the ages of eighteen and thirty-five years old was just 1.6%. It's hard to see a future for the tradition when there are almost no young adults to take over the responsibilities of leading these denominations. The Episcopal Church's 2022 annual report indicates that just 8% of their membership are children under the age of twelve and another 5% are youth between the ages of thirteen and seventeen years old.[4] At the same time, half of the members have celebrated their sixty-fifth birthday.[5]

What also will accelerate this decline for the mainline is that their largest denomination—the UMC is facing the largest and most consequential schism in the history of American Protestant Christianity. The root of the divide is over the issue of same-sex marriage. Some clergy and members would like the UMC to welcome same-sex couples into full fellowship, while others believe that the Bible teaches that marriage is between one man and one woman. The UMC agreed to a plan that would allow local churches to decide whether they would like to remain in the UMC or leave the denomination. The deadline for exit was December 31, 2023. The most recent figures indicate that nearly 7,700 churches chose to leave—which represents at least a quarter of all churches in the denomination.[6]

While the dust is still settling among the United Methodists, there's reason to believe that while a quarter of churches have left, this may end up

THE FUTURE OF AMERICAN RELIGION   257

in a significantly larger share of members falling off the rolls of the UMC. It's highly likely that a denomination that reported 7 million members in 2015 could be half that size a decade later. The other six major mainline denominations reported a total membership of about 8 million in 2021; the UMC had 5.7 million members. The schism in the UMC could lead to the overall share of the mainline dropping by 25% in just a two-year window of time.

Trend 4: The Rise of the Nones Will Slow

Undoubtedly, the most important story in American religious demography over the last several decades is the meteoric rise of the share of Americans who claim no religious affiliation on surveys. It was just 5% throughout the 1970s and 1980s, but it then began to rise consistently from the early 1990s onward. As was laid out in detail in Chapter 13 and 14, the percentage of Americans who could be classified as religious "nones" today is likely at least 30%, and among the younger generations, it's at least 40%. It's almost inevitable that the next wave of any survey that assesses American religion will report that the nones are a larger share this year than they were last year. However, there are some indications in a variety of data sources that this era may be coming to an end.

When looking at data from the Cooperative Election Study, General Social Survey, and Pew Research Center's National Public Opinion Reference Survey, over the last several years the data paints a much more mixed picture about the rise of the nones, as can be seen in Figure 15.4.[7] For instance, the share of Americans who were nonreligious in the Cooperative Election Study was 34% in 2020, then rose to 36% in 2021 but stayed at that same level during the 2022 collection period. Data from the General Social Survey were not reported in 2020, but in 2021 the share of the nones was 28% and that estimate dropped just slightly to 27% in the data from 2022. In the Pew data, the nones were 28% in 2020, 29% in 2021, and 31% in 2022.

Obviously, these estimates diverge quite a bit—putting the share of the nones as low as 27% or as high as 36%; however, the trend lines in each individual survey are more pertinent to this discussion. In one data source, there was no rise in the nones between 2021 and 2022; in another there was a small, but statistically insignificant decline. And, in the Pew data, there was an increase, but it was not statistically significant between 2021 and

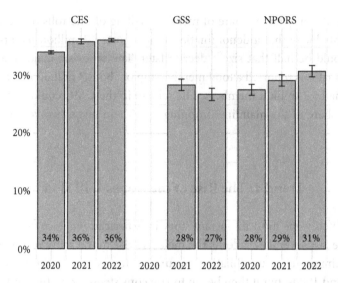

Figure 15.4 The share of the sample who are nonreligious in three surveys. CES, Cooperative Election Study; GSS, General Election Survey; NPORS, National Public Opinion Reference Survey

2022, either. Taken in totality, it's hard to say that there's been a clear increase in the number of nones over the last few years. That certainly has not been the case in the previous two decades. This could just be a statistical blip—a possible plateau in the data—or it could portend a change in the trajectory of the nones. There is some evidence to suggest the latter explanation is possible.

Figure 15.5 is a trend line of the share of the sample that identifies as atheist, agnostic, or nothing in particular by birth year. Among those born around 1940, about 15% identify as nonreligious. This share continues to rise with each successive decade. For instance, nearly 30% of those who were born in the early 1960s claim no religious affiliation. For those born in the 1980s, the nones share rises above 40%. But notice that the trend line begins to flatten out among the youngest adults in the sample. For those born around 1990, the share who are nones is slightly above 45%. It's just 47% of those who were born around the year 2000. For older Americans, the jump in the nones percentage is seven to eight percentage points every ten years.

This could just be an aberration in the data. It's possible that the youngest adults who took the survey tend to be a bit more religious than expected. Or it could be evidence that there's a bit of a ceiling on the rise of the nones. For

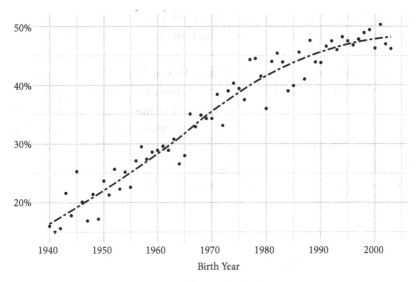

Figure 15.5 Share who were nonreligious by birth year
Data: Cooperative Election Study

decades, the ones who were the most marginally attached to religion were the ones who became nonreligious. Once those folks left religion behind, the remainder consisted of people who were more deeply committed to their faith tradition and thus were less likely to become nones. From this angle, it appears unlikely that the nones will move past half of the American population in the next few decades.

Trend 5: It Will Become Even More Difficult to Project the Future of American Religion

In September 2022, the Pew Research Center released a report in which they tried to predict what the American religious landscape would look like around the year 2070.[8] Using an extensive amount of data, including surveys of fifteen-to-nineteen-year-olds, the best available information on patterns related to fertility, mortality, migration, and religious transmission/switching—the team at Pew tried to understand how all these factors would impact the share of Americans who are Christians, nonreligious, and those who align with a non-Christian faith tradition. Instead of arriving at one estimate of these percentages in 2070, the Pew team decided to project four different scenarios based on a varying set of assumptions about religious switching. The end results of these models are visualized in Figure 15.6.

Scenario 1 is described by the team at Pew as "steady switching." In this approach, the model holds constant the current rate of switching that they estimate in which about 31% of Christians become religiously unaffiliated and 21% of those who were raised without religion become Christians later in life. Using this assumption as the baseline, the share of Christians remains relatively robust for the next five decades, and even into 2070, the number of Christians in the United States will be larger than the unaffiliated (46% compared to 41%).

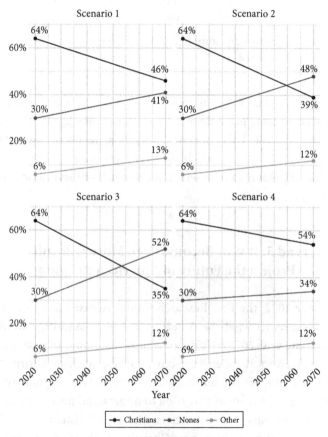

Figure 15.6 Four projections about the future of American religion
Data: Pew

THE FUTURE OF AMERICAN RELIGION   261

The only other scenario in which Christianity is larger than the nones according to Pew's modeling is Scenario 4. This one is much more straightforward—they describe it as "no switching." The assumptions here are simply that everyone in the United States who was born into a religious tradition, whether that be Christian, none, or some other faith, will maintain that religious affiliation for the rest of their lives. Of course, this would lead to a much slower decline in American Christianity as a majority of people who are born today are raised in Christian households. In this projection, the nones rise to 34% by 2070 and those of other faith groups double in size from 6% to 12%, while Christianity declines from 64% to 54%.

The middle two scenarios offer a set of assumptions that lie between the two models previously described. Instead of switching at current rates, as seen in Scenario 1, or no switching at all, as seen in Scenario 4—the Pew team created a different set of parameters. For instance, in Scenario 2, the share of young people who were raised Christian but leave the faith by their thirtieth birthday increases with each successive generation, while fewer Americans move from being a none to being a Christian. However, this projection assumes that the defection rate from Christianity will not exceed 50% in the next five decades.

Using this set of parameters, the model predicts that the share of Christians and nones will be statistically similar somewhere around 2050 when both are around 45%. By 2070, the lines will have clearly crossed and nearly half of all American adults will be nonreligious compared to just 39% who will identify as Christians. Those from other faith groups will make up the rest of the American population.

Scenario 3 is similar to Scenario 2 in that it assumes that each successive generation will be more likely to switch away from Christianity than the prior one and the share of Americans who grow up without religion but switch to Christianity will also be smaller as each year passes. However, Scenario 3 does not put a cap on the defection rate that was present in Scenario 2. If this cap is removed, then the numeric decline in Christianity is pushed forward by a few years and the lines would then cross around 2045. The end result of this projection is that by 2070 just 35% of the population would identify as Christian, while the unaffiliated would be significantly larger at 52%.

Which one of these scenarios is the most likely to occur is impossible to predict. The team at Pew did what good analysis does: it provides multiple possible assumptions for how things will unfold. In one, switching continues as it does now. In another, switching stops entirely. Then, in the middle two, several "best guesses" are employed about how switching will accelerate in the decades to come. However, in all four scenarios, the following things are true: Christianity will shrink, and the nones and other religious traditions will continue to rise.

What is looming in the background of all this work is a foundational concept among demographers: generational replacement. Put simply, younger generations look, think, and worship differently than their parents or grandparents. The reason that the United States is becoming more racially diverse is simply because of generational replacement. Older generations have a larger percentage of white individuals, and younger generations are made up of more African American, Hispanic, and Asian Americans. Each day, thousands of Americans from the Silent Generation and the Baby Boomers die. At the same time, thousands of members of Generation Z celebrate their eighteenth birthday and move into adulthood. Aggregated over a decade, this can lead to some pretty big changes in every facet of American society.

Figure 15.7 makes this generational replacement argument clear. Among Baby Boomers who were born between 1945 and 1965, Christianity dominates. Over two-thirds of individuals in this generation identify as Protestant or Catholic. At the same time, the share who are nonreligious is much smaller at just 27%. But as one moves down the graph into each successive generation, the Protestant and Catholic shares get smaller and the nones continue to get larger. Among Generation Z, just 22% identify as Protestant compared to 46% of Baby Boomers. A member of Generation Z is twice as likely to be an atheist, agnostic, or have no religion in particular, compared to someone born in the 1950s. Every day in the United States, a

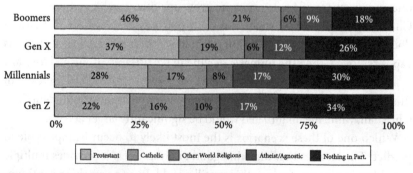

Figure 15.7 Religious composition by generation
Data: Cooperative Election Study

person from the top row of bars is replaced by someone from the bottom row—thus, American religion changes in an almost imperceptible way in the short term. However, over a five- or ten-year time horizon, the changes come into full view.

Conclusion

If there's one thing that scholars of American religion can all agree on it's simply this: religion is not going away in the United States at any point in the near future. For reasons that are complicated and nuanced, the United States is a vastly more religious country today than any of its closest cultural neighbors in Western Europe and continues to have an enduring strain of religiosity that will endure for decades. Even if churches, synagogues, and mosques close by the hundreds (and they likely will in the years to come), politicians, athletes, and celebrities will still thank God when they win an election, score a touchdown, or have a box office smash. That cultural acceptance of a belief in the Divine and a general sense of cultural religiosity will still be commonplace in the cultural discourse.

However, what will change is that the actual impact of American religion will continue to recede. Houses of worship have been doing charitable work in their communities for centuries. They provide food for the hungry, clothes for those living in poverty, after-school tutoring programs for the local school district, and counseling for prisoners who seek to rehabilitate themselves. These ministries have been organized, funded, and implemented by people of faith with very little government oversight or support. In the future, these programs will begin to close, and there's little evidence that points toward the growing number of nonreligious Americans being able to organize in a meaningful way to replace these types of social services for the local community. In this absence, there are only two real possible outcomes. One is that the government expands its services in ways that have not been seen since Lyndon Johnson's Great Society programs, which seems unlikely given the disdain that the average American has for any type of "welfare" program. The other outcome is that millions of Americans fall through the cracks of the social safety net as the holes become larger. These will be people who suffer from food insecurity, mental illness, and addiction.

When religion recedes in a society, it is more than just a theoretical exercise about how secularization plays out in a highly industrialized democratic

264 THE AMERICAN RELIGIOUS LANDSCAPE

society. While the trends in American religion provide plenty of fodder for social scientists, it is also a lived reality for hundreds of millions of people living in the United States. There is no doubt that houses of worship have impacts (both big and small) on the lives of nearly every American. The lives of millions of Americans will be changed by the shifting religious landscape—there is little doubt of that. How these shifts will ripple into every facet of American society is only now being explored.

Notes

1. Donald Rumsfeld. 2002. "Defense.Gov Transcript: DoD News Briefing—Secretary Rumsfeld and Gen. Myers." *U.S. Department of Defense.* February 12. Archived on *Internet Archive Wayback Machine.* May 6, 2016. https://web.archive.org/web/20160406235718/http://archive.defense.gov/Transcripts/Transcript.aspx?TranscriptID=2636.
2. Donald Trump. 2017. Executive Order 13769 of January 27, 2017, Protecting the Nation from Foreign Terrorist Entry into the United States. *Federal Register.* 82 FR 8977. https://www.federalregister.gov/documents/2017/02/01/2017-02281/protecting-the-nation-from-foreign-terrorist-entry-into-the-united-states.
3. James David Hudnut-Beumler and Mark Silk, eds. 2018. *The Future of Mainline Protestantism in America.* New York: Columbia University Press, 1, 18.
4. Charissa Mikoski. 2023. *The Episcopal Church: Analysis of the 2022 Parochial Report Data,* 13. https://generalconvention.org/parochial-report-results/.
5. Mikoski, *The Episcopal Church,* 13..
6. "Disaffiliations Approved by Annual Conferences." 2022. *United Methodist News Service.* https://www.umnews.org/en/news/disaffiliations-approved-by-annual-conferences.
7. Pew Research Center. 2023. "National Public Opinion Reference Survey (NPORS)." *Pew Research Center Methods.* https://www.pewresearch.org/methods/fact-sheet/national-public-opinion-reference-survey-npors/.
8. Pew Research Center. 2022. *Modeling the Future of Religion in America.* https://www.pewresearch.org/religion/2022/09/13/modeling-the-future-of-religion-in-america/.

Data References

Davern, Michael, Rene Bautista, Jeremy Freese, Pamela Herd, and Stephen L. Morgan. 2023. General Social Survey 1972–2022. Principal investigator, Michael Davern; Co-principal investigators, Rene Bautista, Jeremy Freese, Pamela Herd, and Stephen L. Morgan. Sponsored by National Science Foundation. NORC ed. Chicago: NORC at the University of Chicago. https://gssdataexplorer.norc.org.
National Public Opinion Reference Survey (NPORS), 2020–2022. 2020–2022. Pew Research Center. https://www.pewresearch.org/methods/fact-sheet/national-public-opinion-reference-survey-npors/.
Schaffner, Brian, Stephen Ansolabehere, Sam Luks, Shiro Kuriwaki, and Marissa Shih. 2006–2023. Cooperative Election Study Common Content, 2006–2022. Harvard Dataverse. https://cces.gov.harvard.edu/.

Bibliography

Ansolabehere, Stephen, Brian F. Schaffner, and Sam Luks. Cooperative Congressional Election Study. Cambridge, MA: Harvard University. http://cces.gov.harvard.edu.

"Answers to Frequently Asked Questions about Blaine Amendments." 2022. *Institute for Justice.* https://ij.org/issues/school-choice/blaine-amendments/answers-frequently-asked-questions-blaine-amendments/.

Anti-Defamation League. 2020. "Anti-Semitic Stereotypes Persist in America, Survey Shows." *ADL.* https://www.adl.org/resources/press-release/anti-semitic-stereotypes-persist-america-survey-shows.

Armstrong, Karen. 2009. *The Case for God.* 1st ed. New York: Alfred A. Knopf.

Arthur, Charles. 2013. "Tech Giants May Be Huge, but Nothing Matches Big Data." *The Guardian.* https://www.theguardian.com/technology/2013/aug/23/tech-giants-data.

"Association of Statisticians of American Religious Bodies." 2023. *Association of Statisticians of American Religious Bodies.* http://www.asarb.org/.

Bagby, Ihsan. 2023. "Appendix K: Muslim Estimate." In *2020 U.S. Religion Census: Religious Congregations & Membership Study.* Association of Statisticians of American Religious Bodies. https://www.usreligioncensus.org/sites/default/files/2023-03/Appendix_K--Muslim_Estimate.pdf.

Bailey, Sarah Pulliam. 2015. "A Startling Number of Americans Still Believe President Obama Is a Muslim." *The Washington Post.* https://www.washingtonpost.com/news/acts-of-faith/wp/2015/09/14/a-startling-number-of-americans-still-believe-president-obama-is-a-muslim/.

Barney, Kevin. 2006. "A Peculiar People?" *By Common Consent* [blog]. https://bycommonconsent.com/2006/07/17/a-peculiar-people/.

Bebbington, D. W. 1989. *Evangelicalism in Modern Britain: A History from the 1730s to the 1980s.* London: Unwin Hyman.

Benagiano, Giuseppe, Sabina Carrara, Valentina Filippi, and Ivo Brosens. 2011. "Condoms, HIV and the Roman Catholic Church." *Reproductive BioMedicine Online* 22, no. 7: 701–709.

Bharath, Deepa. 2023. "Vivek Ramaswamy's Hindu Faith Is Front and Center in His GOP Presidential Campaign." *AP News.* https://apnews.com/article/vivek-ramaswamy-hindu-republican-presidential-campaign-68a09925f38fb23d69fa31a2271c0ca8.

Bowman, Matthew Burton. 2012. *The Mormon People: The Making of an American Faith.* New York: Random House.

"Breckinridge Long (1881–1958)." 2019. *PBS American Experience.* https://www.pbs.org/wgbh/americanexperience/features/holocaust-long/.

Burge, Ryan. 2017. "Who's Afraid of Female Clergy." *Religion in Public.* https://religioninpublic.blog/2017/10/25/whos-afraid-of-female-clergy/.

Burge, Ryan. 2023a. "Approval for Same-Sex Marriage Has Stopped Increasing." *Graphs about Religion.* https://www.graphsaboutreligion.com/p/approval-for-same-sex-marriage-has.

Burge, Ryan. 2023b. "Let's Have a Talk about Education and Religious Attendance." *Graphs about Religion.* https://www.graphsaboutreligion.com/p/lets-have-a-talk-about-education.

Burge, Ryan. 2023c. "Religion Has Become a Luxury Good." *Graphs about Religion.* https://www.graphsaboutreligion.com/p/religion-has-become-a-luxury-good.

"Call for Teams for the 2022 CES." *Harvard University.* https://cces.gov.harvard.edu/news/call-teams-2022-ces.

266 BIBLIOGRAPHY

Campbell, David E., Geoffrey Layman, and John Clifford Green. 2021. *Secular Surge: A New Fault Line in American Politics*. Cambridge: Cambridge University Press.

Campbell, James T. 1995. *Songs of Zion: The African Methodist Episcopal Church in the United States and South Africa*. New York: Oxford University Press.

Carroll, Matt, Sacha Pfeiffer, Michael Rezendes, and Walter V. Robinson. 2002. "Spotlight: Clergy Sex Abuse Crisis." *The Boston Globe*. https://www3.bostonglobe.com/metro/speci als/clergy/.

CBS Detroit. 2021. "Dearborn's First Arab-American Mayor Has a Message for Its Youth: 'Be Proud of Your Name.'" https://www.cbsnews.com/detroit/news/dearborns-first-arab-ameri can-mayor-has-a-message-for-its-youth-be-proud-of-your-name/.

Central Intelligence Agency. "Real GDP per Capita." *The World Factbook*. https://www.cia. gov/the-world-factbook/field/real-gdp-per-capita/country-comparison/.

Chadwick, Henry. 2003. *East and West: The Making of a Rift in the Church: From Apostolic Times until the Council of Florence*. Oxford: Oxford University Press.

Chernow, Ron. 2010. *Titan: The Life of John D. Rockefeller, Sr*. New York: Vintage Books.

Chishti, Muzaffar, Faye Hipsman, and Isabel Ball. 2015. "Fifty Years on, the 1965 Immigration and Nationality Act Continues to Reshape the United States." *Migration Policy Institute*. https://www.migrationpolicy.org/article/fifty-years-1965-immigration-and-nationality-act-continues-reshape-united-states.

The Church of Jesus Christ of Latter-Day Saints Newsroom. 2014. "2013 Statistical Report for 2014 April General Conference." *The Church of Jesus Christ of Latter-Day Saints Newsroom*. https://newsroom.churchofjesuschrist.org/article/2013-statistical-report-2014-april-gene ral-conference.

The Church of Jesus Christ of Latter-Day Saints Newsroom. 2015. "2014 Statistical Report for 2015 April General Conference." *The Church of Jesus Christ of Latter-Day Saints Newsroom*. https://newsroom.churchofjesuschrist.org/article/2014-statistical-report-for-2015-april-general-conference.

The Church of Jesus Christ of Latter-Day Saints Newsroom. 2016. "2015 Statistical Report for April 2016 General Conference." *The Church of Jesus Christ of Latter-Day Saints Newsroom*. https://newsroom.churchofjesuschrist.org/article/2015-statistical-report-april-2016-gene ral-conference.

The Church of Jesus Christ of Latter-Day Saints Newsroom. 2017. "2016 Statistical Report for 2017 April General Conference." *The Church of Jesus Christ of Latter-Day Saints Newsroom*. https://newsroom.churchofjesuschrist.org/article/2016-statistical-report-2017-april-con ference.

The Church of Jesus Christ of Latter-Day Saints Newsroom. 2018. "2017 Statistical Report for 2018 April Conference." *The Church of Jesus Christ of Latter-Day Saints Newsroom*. https:// newsroom.churchofjesuschrist.org/article/2017-statistical-report-april-2018-general-con ference.

The Church of Jesus Christ of Latter-Day Saints Newsroom. 2019. "2018 Statistical Report for 2019 April Conference." *The Church of Jesus Christ of Latter-Day Saints Newsroom*. https:// newsroom.churchofjesuschrist.org/article/2018-statistical-report.

The Church of Jesus Christ of Latter-Day Saints Newsroom. 2020. "2019 Statistical Report for 2020 April Conference." *The Church of Jesus Christ of Latter-Day Saints Newsroom*. https:// newsroom.churchofjesuschrist.org/article/2019-statistical-report.

The Church of Jesus Christ of Latter-Day Saints Newsroom. 2021. "2020 Statistical Report for the April 2021 Conference." *The Church of Jesus Christ of Latter-Day Saints Newsroom*. https://newsroom.churchofjesuschrist.org/article/april-2021-general-conference-statisti cal-report.

The Church of Jesus Christ of Latter-Day Saints Newsroom. 2022. "2021 Statistical Report for the April 2022 Conference." *The Church of Jesus Christ of Latter-Day Saints Newsroom*. https://newsroom.churchofjesuschrist.org/article/2021-statistical-report-april-2022-con ference.

BIBLIOGRAPHY 267

The Church of Jesus Christ of Latter-Day Saints Newsroom. 2023. "Facts and Statistics." Salt Lake City, UT: The Church of Jesus Christ of Latter-day Saints. https://newsroom.churchof jesuschrist.org/facts-and-statistics.

The Church of Jesus Christ of Latter-Day Saints Newsroom. 2023. "On Juneteenth, How the NAACP and the Church Are Carrying Out a Prophet's Vision." *The Church of Jesus Christ of Latter-Day Saints Newsroom.* http://newsroom.churchofjesuschrist.org/article/junetee nth-naacp-church-of-jesus-christ-2023.

Coffman, Keith. 2011. "Latter-day Saints Launch 'I'm a Mormon' Ad Campaign." *Reuters.* October 2. https://www.reuters.com/article/us-mormons-media/latter-day-saints-launch-im-a-mormon-ad-campaign-idUKTRE7911CM20111002.

Curtis, Edward E. IV. 2009. *Muslims in America: A Short History.* New York: Oxford University Press.

Davern, Michael, Rene Bautista, Jeremy Freese, Stephen L. Morgan, and Tom W. Smith. General Social Survey 2021 Cross-section. 2021. [Machine-readable data file]. Principal investigator, Michael Davern; Co-principal investigators, Rene Bautista, Jeremy Freese, Stephen L. Morgan, and Tom W. Smith. NORC ed. Chicago. 1 datafile (68,846 cases) and 1 codebook (506 pages). https://www.google.com/url?q=https://gss.norc.org/Docume nts/codebook/GSS%25202021%2520Codebook%2520R1.pdf&sa=D&source=docs&nst= 1705792597898904&usg=AOvVaw3Ba_EG74avzjI_GqrNCJsI.

Davern, Michael, Rene Bautista, Jeremy Freese, Pamela Herd, and Stephen L. Morgan. 2023. General Social Survey 1972–2022. Principal investigator, Michael Davern; Co-principal investigators, Rene Bautista, Jeremy Freese, Pamela Herd, and Stephen L. Morgan. Sponsored by National Science Foundation. NORC ed. Chicago: NORC at the University of Chicago. https://gss.norc.org/us/en/gss/faq.html.

Davidson, Lee. 2021. "Salt Lake County Keeps Losing Latter-Day Saints, and There Are Multiple Theories as to Why." *The Salt Lake Tribune.* https://www.sltrib.com/religion/ 2021/01/14/salt-lake-county-keeps/.

DellaPosta, Daniel. 2018. "Gay Acquaintanceship and Attitudes toward Homosexuality: A Conservative Test." *Socius* 4: 1–12.

DeRose, Jason. 2023. "Southern Baptists Say No to Women Pastors, Uphold Expulsion of Saddleback Megachurch." *NPR.* https://www.npr.org/2023/06/14/1182141691/southern-baptist-convention-sbc-women-pastors-saddleback-megachurch.

Deseret News. 2013. *Deseret News Church Almanac 2012.* Salt Lake City, UT: Deseret News.

Diner, Hasia R. 2004. *The Jews of the United States, 1654 to 2000.* Berkeley: University of California Press.

"Disaffiliations Approved by Annual Conferences." 2022. *United Methodist News Service.* https://www.umnews.org/en/news/disaffiliations-approved-by-annual-conferences.

The Doctrine and Covenants of The Church of Jesus Christ of Latter-day Saints. 2013. *Official Declaration 2.* Salt Lake City, UT: The Church of Jesus Christ of Latter-day Saints. https:// www.churchofjesuschrist.org/study/scriptures/dc-testament/od/2?lang=eng.

Dubov, Mendel. 2019. "Why Do Observant Jews Have So Many Kids?" *Chabad.org.* https:// www.chabad.org/library/article_cdo/aid/4372320/jewish/Why-Do-Observant-Jews-Have-So-Many-Kids.htm.

Duncan, Jason K. 2005. *Citizens or Papists?: The Politics of Anti-Catholicism in New York, 1685–1821.* 1st ed. New York: Fordham University Press.

Earls, Aaron. 2023. "Southern Baptists Decline in Membership, Grow in Attendance, Baptisms." *Lifeway Research.* https://research.lifeway.com/2023/05/09/southern-baptists-decline-in-membership-grow-in-attendance-baptisms/

Elliott, Andrea. 2006. "Muslim Immigration Has Bounced Back." *The Seattle Times.*

Evangelical Lutheran Church in America. "Resources for the LGBTQIA+ Community." *ELCA. org.* https://www.elca.org:443/LGBTQ.

Fahmy, Dalia. 2019. "7 Facts about Southern Baptists." *Pew Research Center.* https://www.pewr esearch.org/short-reads/2019/06/07/7-facts-about-southern-baptists/.

268 BIBLIOGRAPHY

Ferrari, Lisa L. 2011. "Catholic and Non-Catholic NGOs Fighting HIV/AIDS in Sub-Saharan Africa: Issue Framing and Collaboration." *International Relations* 25, no. 1: 85–107.

Finke, Roger, and Rodney Stark. 2005. *The Churching of America, 1776–2005: Winners and Losers in Our Religious Economy.* 2nd ed. New Brunswick, NJ: Rutgers University Press.

"The First American Muslims." *The Pluralism Project.* Harvard University. https://pluralism.org/the-first-american-muslims.

Frascella, Tom. 2014. "Early U.S. Catholics and Catholic Immigrants, 1790–1850." *San Felese Society of New Jersey.* http://www.sanfelesesocietynj.org/History%20Articles/Early_US_Catholics_and_immigrants_1790-1850.htm.

Frey, William H. 2020. "The Nation Is Diversifying Even Faster Than Predicted, According to New Census Data." *Brookings.* https://www.brookings.edu/articles/new-census-data-shows-the-nation-is-diversifying-even-faster-than-predicted/.

Froese, Paul. 2017. *Baylor Religion Survey, Wave V (2017).* Waco, TX: Baylor Institute for Studies of Religion. https://www.thearda.com/data-archive?fid=BRS5.

Gibson, Dawn-Marie. 2012. *A History of the Nation of Islam: Race, Islam, and the Quest for Freedom.* Santa Barbara, CA: Praeger.

Grammich, Clifford, Kirk Hadaway, Richard Houseal, Dale E. Jones, Alexei Krindatch, Richie Stanley, and Richard H. Taylor. 2023. "2020 U.S. Religion Census: Religious Congregations & Membership Study." *Association of Statisticians of American Religious Bodies.* https://www.usreligioncensus.org/node/1639.

Greek Orthodox Archdiocese of America. 2023. "About the Greek Orthodox Archdiocese of America." *Greek Orthodox Archdiocese of America.* https://www.goarch.org/about.

Green, Donald P., and Janelle S. Wong. 2009. "Tolerance and the Contact Hypothesis: A Field Experiment." In *The Political Psychology of Democratic Citizenship,* edited by Eugene Borgida, Christopher M. Federico, and John L. Sullivan, 228–246. Oxford: Oxford University Press.

"GSS General Social Survey FAQ." *The General Social Survey.* https://gss.norc.org/faq.

Holliday, Derek, Tyler Reny, Alex Rossell, Aaron Rudkin, Chris Tausanotich, and Lynn Vavreck. 2021. "Democracy Fund + UCLA Nationscape Methodology and Representativeness Assessment." *Democracy Fund Voter Study Group.* https://www.voterstudygroup.org/data/nationscape.

Horsmanden, Daniel. 1899. *The Trial of John Ury: "for Being an Ecclesiastical Person, Made by Authority Pretended from the See of Rome, and Coming into and Abiding in the Province of New York," and with Being One of the Conspirators in the Negro Plot to Burn the City of New York, 1741.* Philadelphia: M.I.J. Griffin.

Hudnut-Beumler, James David, and Mark Silk, eds. 2018. *The Future of Mainline Protestantism in America.* New York: Columbia University Press.

Johnson, Jenna, and Abigail Hauslohner. 2017. "'I Think Islam Hates Us': A Timeline of Trump's Comments about Islam and Muslims." *The Washington Post,* May 20, 2017.

Johnson, Paul. 2001. *History of the Jews.* London: Phoenix.

Johnson, Todd M., and Brian J. Grim. 2013. *The World's Religions in Figures: An Introduction to International Religious Demography.* 1st ed. Hoboken, NJ: John Wiley & Sons, Incorporated.

Jones, R. P. 2021. *PRRI 2019 American Values Survey.* Public Religion Research Institute. The Association of Religion Data Archives. doi:10.17605/OSF.IO/PH68V.

Kaminker, Mendy. 2011. "Why Do We Not Count Jews?" *Chabad.org.* https://www.chabad.org/library/article_cdo/aid/1635539/jewish/Why-Do-We-Not-Count-Jews.htm.

Klostermaier, Klaus K. 2000. *Hinduism: A Short History.* Oxford: Oneworld Publications.

Krindatch, Alexei. N.d. "The Greek Orthodox Archdiocese of America (GOA) from 2010 to 2020: Changes in Parishes, Membership, and Worship Attendance." *Orthodox Reality.* https://orthodoxreality.org/wp-content/uploads/2021/09/Report-GOA-From2010To2020Reduced1-1.pdf.

Lee, Martha F. 1988. *The Nation of Islam, an American Millenarian Movement.* Lewiston, NY: The Edwin Mellen Press.

Leonard, Lewis Alexander. 1918. *Life of Charles Carroll of Carrollton.* New York: Moffat, Yard and Company.

BIBLIOGRAPHY 269

Li, David K., and Corky Siemaszko. 2023. "Baltimore's Catholic Church Sexually Abused at Least 600 Children over 60 Years, Maryland AG Says." *NBC News.* https://www.nbcnews.com/news/us-news/maryland-ag-documents-widespread-sexual-abuse-least-600-victims-baltim-rcna78378.

Linder, Douglas. n.d. "H.L. Mencken (1880–1956)." *UMKC School of Law—Famous Trials.* https://famous-trials.com/scopesmonkey/2094-mencken.

Linder, Douglas. 2008. "Day 7." *Scopes Trial—Day 7—UMKC School of Law.* http://law2.umkc.edu/faculty/projects/ftrials/scopes/day7.htm.

Lipka, Michael, and Jessica Martínez. 2014. "So, You Married an Atheist . . ." *Pew Research Center.* https://www.pewresearch.org/short-reads/2014/06/16/so-you-married-an-atheist/.

Lipka, Michael, and Gregory A. Smith. 2020. "Among Democrats, Christians Lean toward Biden, While 'Nones' Prefer Sanders." *Pew Research Center.* https://www.pewresearch.org/short-reads/2020/01/31/among-democrats-christians-lean-toward-biden-while-nones-prefer-sanders/.

Manitoba Education. 2021. *Buddhism: A Supplemental Resource for Grade 12 World of Religions: A Canadian Perspective.* Winnipeg, Manitoba: Manitoba Education. https://www.edu.gov.mb.ca/k12/docs/support/world_religions/buddhism/index.html.

Margolies, Jane. 2019. "The Church with the $6 Billion Portfolio." *The New York Times.* https://www.nytimes.com/2019/02/08/nyregion/trinity-church-manhattan-real-estate.html.

Marsden, George M. 2014. *The Twilight of the American Enlightenment: The 1950s and the Crisis of Liberal Belief.* New York: Basic Books.

Marsh, Clifton E. 2000. *The Lost-Found Nation of Islam in America.* Lanham, MD: Scarecrow Press.

Martinich, Matthew. 2018. "Percent LDS by Country—2017." Growth of The Church of Jesus Christ of Latter-day Saints (LDS Church). *Blogger* [blog]. http://ldschurchgrowth.blogspot.com/2018/04/percent-lds-by-country-2017.html.

Masci, David. 2019. "In U.S., Familiarity with Religious Groups Is Associated with Warmer Feelings toward Them." *Pew Research Center.* https://www.pewresearch.org/short-reads/2019/10/31/in-u-s-familiarity-with-religious-groups-is-associated-with-warmer-feelings-toward-them/

Mikoski, Charissa. 2023. *The Episcopal Church: Analysis of the 2022 Parochial Report Data.* The Episcopal Church. https://generalconvention.org/parochial-report-results/.

Miller, Patricia. 2001. "The Lesser Evil: The Catholic Church and the AIDS Epidemic." *Conscience* 22, no. 3: 6.

Mohamed, Besheer. 2018. "New Estimates Show U.S. Muslim Population Continues to Grow." *Pew Research Center.* https://www.pewresearch.org/short-reads/2018/01/03/new-estimates-show-u-s-muslim-population-continues-to-grow/.

National Public Opinion Reference Survey (NPORS), 2020–2022. 2020–2022. Pew Research Center. https://www.pewresearch.org/methods/fact-sheet/national-public-opinion-reference-survey-npors/.

Obama, Barack. 2009. "President Barack Obama's Inaugural Address." Washington, DC. Transcript. *National Archives.* https://obamawhitehouse.archives.gov/blog/2009/01/21/president-Barack-obamas-inaugural-address#.

O'Brien, Brendan. 2023. "Southern Baptists Finalize Expulsion of Two Churches with Female Pastors." *Reuters.* https://www.reuters.com/world/us/southern-baptists-finalize-expulsion-two-churches-with-female-pastors-2023-06-14/.

Oppel, Richard A. Jr., and Erik Eckholm. 2011. "Prominent Pastor Calls Romney's Church a Cult." *The New York Times.* https://www.nytimes.com/2011/10/08/us/politics/prominent-pastor-calls-romneys-church-a-cult.html.

Orth, Taylor. 2022. "Americans' Views on 35 Religious Groups, Organizations, and Belief Systems." *YouGov.* https://today.yougov.com/society/articles/44850-americans-views-religious-groups-yougov-pol.

"Our History." 2019. *American Baptist Churches USA.* https://www.abc-usa.org/what-we-believe/our-history/.

270 BIBLIOGRAPHY

Palmer, Michael. 2006. "Data Is the New Oil." *ANA Marketing Maestros* [blog]. https://ana.blogs.com/maestros/2006/11/data_is_the_new.html.

Paullin, Charles Oscar, and John Kirtland Wright. 1932. *Atlas of the Historical Geography of the United States*. Washington, DC: published jointly by Carnegie Institution of Washington and the American Geographical Society of New York. Cited in Finke, Roger, and Rodney Stark. 2005. *The Churching of America, 1776–2005: Winners and Losers in Our Religious Economy*. 2nd ed. New Brunswick, NJ: Rutgers University Press.

"A People at Risk." *Library of Congress*. https://www.loc.gov/classroom-materials/immigration/polish-russian/a-people-at-risk/.

Perlstein, Rick. 2012. "Exclusive: Lee Atwater's Infamous 1981 Interview on the Southern Strategy." *The Nation*. https://www.thenation.com/article/archive/exclusive-lee-atwaters-infamous-1981-interview-southern-strategy/.

Peterson, Elder Mark E. 1954. *Race Problems–As They Affect the Church*. August 27. In Jerald Tanner and Sandra Tanner, *Curse of Cain?: Racism in the Mormon Church*. Sandy, UT: Utah Lighthouse Ministry. http://www.utlm.org/onlinebooks/curseofcain_appendix_b.htm.

Pew Research Center. 2011. *The Future of the Global Muslim Population: Projections for 2010–2023*.https://www.pewresearch.org/religion/2011/01/27/the-future-of-the-global-muslim-population/.

Pew Research Center. 2012. "Hindus." https://www.pewresearch.org/religion/2012/12/18/global-religious-landscape-hindu/.

Pew Research Center. 2012. "Buddhists." https://www.pewresearch.org/religion/2012/12/18/global-religious-landscape-buddhist.

Pew Research Center. 2017. "Orthodox Christianity in the 21st Century." https://www.pewresearch.org/religion/2017/11/08/orthodox-christianity-in-the-21st-century/.

Pew Research Center. 2021. "Jewish Americans in 2020." https://www.pewresearch.org/religion/2021/05/11/jewish-americans-in-2020/#:~:text=In%20absolute%20numbers%2C%20the%202020,adults%20and%201.3%20million%20children.

Pew Research Center. 2022. *Modeling the Future of Religion in America*. https://www.pewresearch.org/religion/2022/09/13/modeling-the-future-of-religion-in-america/.

Pew Research Center. 2023. "Measuring Religion in China." https://www.pewresearch.org/religion/wp-content/uploads/sites/7/2023/08/PF_2023.08.30_religion-china_REPORT.pdf.

Pew Research Center. 2023. "National Public Opinion Reference Survey (NPORS)." *Pew Research Center Methods*. https://www.pewresearch.org/methods/fact-sheet/national-public-opinion-reference-survey-npors/.

Pontificium Consilium pro Familia. 1997. *Vademecum for Confessors Concerning Some Aspects of the Morality of Conjugal Life*. Città del Vaticano: Libreria Editrice Vaticana. https://www.vatican.va/roman_curia/pontifical_councils/family/documents/rc_pc_family_doc_12021997_vademecum_en.html.

Popkin, Samuel. 2012. "Nate Silver: Poll Prophet." *Salon*. https://www.salon.com/2012/10/29/nate_silver_poll_prophet/.

"Religious Statistics & Demographics." *US Religion Census*. https://usreligioncensus.org/.

Rumsfeld, Donald. 2002. "Defense.Gov Transcript: DoD News Briefing—Secretary Rumsfeld and Gen. Myers." *U.S. Department of Defense*. February 12. Archived on *Internet Archive Wayback Machine*. https://web.archive.org/web/20160406235718/http://archive.defense.gov/Transcripts/Transcript.aspx?TranscriptID=2636.

Sandstrom, Aleksandra. 2021. *Faith on the Hill: The Religious Composition of the 117th Congress*. Pew Research Center. https://www.pewresearch.org/religion/wp-content/uploads/sites/7/2021/01/01.04.21_faith_on_the_hill_fullreport.update.pdf.

Schaffner, Brian, and Stephen Ansolabehere. 2022. CES Common Content, 2021. V1. Cambridge, MA: Harvard Dataverse. doi:10.7910/DVN/OPQOCU.

BIBLIOGRAPHY 271

Schaffner, Brian, Stephen Ansolabehere, and Sam Luks. 2021. Cooperative Election Study Common Content, 2020. V4. Cambridge, MA: Harvard Dataverse. doi:10.7910/DVN/ E9N6PH.

Schaffner, Brian, Stephen Ansolabehere, Sam Luks, Shiro Kuriwaki, and Marissa Shih. 2006– 2023. Cooperative Election Study Common Content, 2006–2022. Harvard Dataverse. https://cces.gov.harvard.edu/.

Schaffner, Brian, Stephen Ansolabehere, and Marissa Shih. 2023. Cooperative Election Study Common Content, 2022. V2. Cambridge, MA: Harvard Dataverse. doi:10.7910/DVN/ PR4L8P.

Schnabel, Landon, Sean Bock, and Mike Hout. 2022. "Switch to Web-Based Surveys during Covid-19 Pandemic Left out the Most Religious, Creating a False Impression of Rapid Religious Decline." *SocArXiv.* https://osf.io/g3cnx/download.

Scopes, John Thomas. 1997. *The World's Most Famous Court Trial: Tennessee Evolution Case: A Complete Stenographic Report of the Famous Court Test of the Tennessee Anti-Evolution Act, at Dayton, July 10 to 21, 1925, Including Speeches and Arguments of Attorneys.* Union, NJ: The Lawbook Exchange.

Shane, Scott. 2011. "In Islamic Law, Gingrich Sees a Mortal Threat to U.S." *The New York Times.* https://www.nytimes.com/2011/12/22/us/politics/in-shariah-gingrich-sees-mortal-thr eat-to-us.html.

Shellnutt, Kate, and Daniel Silliman. 2023. "United Methodists Down 7,659 Churches as Exit Window Ends." *News & Reporting.* https://www.christianitytoday.com/news/2023/decem ber/united-methodist-church-split-total-umc-disaffiliation-lgbt.html.

Sklare, Marshall, and Jonathan D. Sarna. 1993. *Observing America's Jews.* Waltham, MA: Brandeis University Press.

Smith, Andrew J. W. 2018. "Report Discloses History of Slavery and Racism at Southern Seminary." *The Southern Baptist Theological Seminary.* https://news.sbts.edu/2018/12/12/ report-discloses-history-slavery-racism-southern-seminary/.

Smith, Christian. 1998. *American Evangelicalism: Embattled and Thriving.* Chicago: University of Chicago Press.

Smith, Jane I. 2010. *Islam in America.* New York: Columbia University Press.

Smith, Daniel Scott. "Child-Naming Practices, Kinship Ties, and Change in Family Attitudes in Hingham, Massachusetts, 1641 to 1880." *Journal of Social History* 18, no. 4 (1985): 541– 566. Cited in Roger Finke and Rodney Stark. 2005. *The Churching of America, 1776– 2005: Winners and Losers in Our Religious Economy.* 2nd ed. New Brunswick, NJ: Rutgers University Press.

Stack, Peggy Fletcher. 2018. "Mormons Rejoice at News of Shorter Sunday Services, but the Move Will Pose Challenges to Some, Especially Single Members." *The Salt Lake Tribune.* https://www.sltrib.com/religion/2018/10/06/mormons-rejoice-news/.

Steensland, Brian, Lynn D. Robinson, W. Bradford Wilcox, Jerry Z. Park, Mark D. Regnerus, and Robert D. Woodberry. 2000. "The Measure of American Religion: Toward Improving the State of the Art." *Social Forces* 79, no. 1: 291–318.

Stewart, David G., Jr. 2007. *The Law of the Harvest: Practical Principles of Effective Missionary Work.* Henderson, NV: Cumorah Foundation.

Tausanovitch, C., and Vavreck, L. 2023. Democracy Fund + UCLA Nationscape Project (version 20211215). *Harvard Dataverse.* https://doi.org/10.7910/DVN/CQFP3Z.

Trump, Donald. 2017. Executive Order 13769 of January 27, 2017, Protecting the Nation from Foreign Terrorist Entry into the United States. *Federal Register.* 82 FR 8977. https://www. federalregister.gov/documents/2017/02/01/2017-02281/protecting-the-nation-from-fore ign-terrorist-entry-into-the-united-states.

United States Census Bureau. 2021. "New Vintage 2021 Population Estimates Available for the Nation, States, and Puerto Rico." *Census.gov.* https://www.census.gov/newsroom/press-releases/2021/2021-population-estimates.html.

272 BIBLIOGRAPHY

U.S. Census Bureau. 2022. *QuickFacts, Pennsylvania.* V2022. Suitland-Silver Hill, MD: U.S. Census Bureau, 2022.

Vernon, Glenn M. 1968. "The Religious 'Nones': A Neglected Category." *Journal for the Scientific Study of Religion* 7, no. 2: 219–229.

The World Bank. 2024. *World Development Indicators.* Washington, DC: The World Bank (Producer and Distributor). https://data.worldbank.org/indicator/NY.GDP.PCAP.CD.

YouGov. 2022. "Daily Survey: Favorability of Religions, November 22–26, 2022—1,000 US Adult Citizens." https://today.yougov.com/society/articles/44850-americans-views-religious-groups-yougov-poll

Index

For the benefit of digital users, indexed terms that span two pages (e.g., 52–53) may, on occasion, appear on only one of those pages.

Figures are indicated by an italic *f* following the page number.

abortion, 30, 121
African Methodist Episcopal, 75–76, 76*f*
age, 40*f*, 66*f*, 86*f*, 101*f*, 108, 138*f*, 149*f*, 170*f*, 189*f*, 205*f*, 218*f*, 235*f*
American Baptist, 23–24, 53, 58, 59*f*, 64*f*, 66*f*, 67, 144*f*
attendance (religious), 43*f*, 56*f*, 60*f*, 83*f*, 96*f*, 110*f*, 130*f*, 144*f*, 152*f*, 171*f*, 193*f*, 209*f*, 227*f*, 245*f*

Bebbington, David, 33–34
belief in god, 34, 44*f*, 130*f*, 214, 215*f*, 217*f*, 244*f*
biblical literalism, 30, 43–44, 53, 54*f*, 80, 83, 255
Blaine Amendment, 105
born-again, 31–32, 34, 68, 69*f*

church membership data, 6*f*, 10*f*, 11*f*, 76*f*, 91*f*, 107*f*, 143*f*, 164*f*
Civil War, 72, 161
Cold War, 218
Communion, 90
Congregationalists, 5–6, 11, 12, 13, 29
contraceptives, 119*f*, 119
Coppins, McKay, 141
cultural religious identity, 111–12, 128

Declaration of Independence, 3, 29, 105
Disciples of Christ, 58, 59*f*, 59, 64, 67

education, 42*f*, 65*f*, 84*f*, 136*f*, 190*f*, 203*f*, 219*f*, 237*f*
Episcopalians, 29, 58, 59*f*, 63, 65, 143*f*, 255, 256
Evangelical Lutheran Church in America, 59*f*

fertility, 48*f*, 67*f*, 119*f*, 120*f*, 150*f*, 151*f*, 206*f*, 207*f*

Gabbard, Tulsi, 197
gender, 53–54, 222, 223*f*, 225*f*
geospatial analysis, 62*f*, 77*f*, 94*f*, 116*f*, 135*f*, 147*f*, 148*f*, 166*f*, 167*f*, 183*f*, 208*f*, 241*f*

Great Schism, 89

historical geospatial analysis, 5*f*, 7*f*, 8*f*, 9*f*
homosexuality, 30, 55*f*, 56, 81*f*, 224*f*, 256

iconography, 90
immigration, 98*f*, 100*f*, 124, 160–61, 172*f*, 187*f*, 201*f*
income, 65*f*, 84*f*, 136*f*, 191*f*, 204*f*, 221*f*, 238*f*
intermarriage, 127–28, 229*f*

karma, 180

marriage, 239*f*
methodists, 6, 11–12, 12*f*, 29, 59*f*, 61*f*, 255, 256
missionaries, 145

National Baptists, 75
National Missionary Baptist, 75
Nation of Islam, 165
non-denominational, 28, 36*f*, 36, 37*f*, 106–7

Obama, Barack, 161–62, 213–14

Pentecostalism, 28, 75
Pew Research Center, 127–28, 155, 163, 164–65, 197, 198, 200, 232, 257, 258*f*, 260*f*
politics, 79*f*, 218, 247*f*
Pope, 89, 117, 121
prayer, 82*f*, 153*f*, 174*f*, 177, 194*f*, 209*f*, 209, 211, 227*f*
Presbyterian Church USA, 59*f*, 255
projection (statistical), 234*f*, 256*f*
Public Religion Research Institute, 246*f*
purgatory, 118*f*

race, 41*f*, 64*f*, 78*f*, 99*f*, 115*f*, 146*f*, 169*f*, 188*f*, 202*f*, 222*f*, 240*f*, 252
Ramaswamy, Vivek, 197

274 INDEX

religion raised in, 14*f*, 15*f*, 47*f*, 113*f*,
    127*f*, 253–54
religious importance, 82*f*, 97*f*, 129*f*, 210*f*,
    227*f*, 245*f*
RELTRAD, 15, 31, 73, 74, 75, 77, 107*f*, 144*f*
Revolutionary War, 3, 7, 12, 29, 124
Romney, Mitt, 157
Rumsfeld, Donald, 249, 250

Scopes Monkey Trial, 30
September 11th, 161
sexual abuse scandal, 106

Smith, Joseph, 141–42
Southern Baptists, 28, 29–30, 34*f*, 53, 75, 143–
    44, 164*f*, 228*f*

transubstantiation, 118*f*
Trump, Donald, 50, 63, 79, 161–62, 250

United Church of Christ, 58, 59*f*, 63, 66*f*,
    91–92
Ury, John, 105

Young, Brigham, 142

The manufacturer's authorised representative in the EU for product safety is Oxford
University Press España S.A. of El Parque Empresarial San Fernando de Henares,
Avenida de Castilla, 2 – 28830 Madrid (www.oup.es/en or product.safety@oup.com).
OUP España S.A. also acts as importer into Spain of products made by the manufacturer.

Printed in the USA/Agawam, MA
June 6, 2025

888621.005